THE COMET

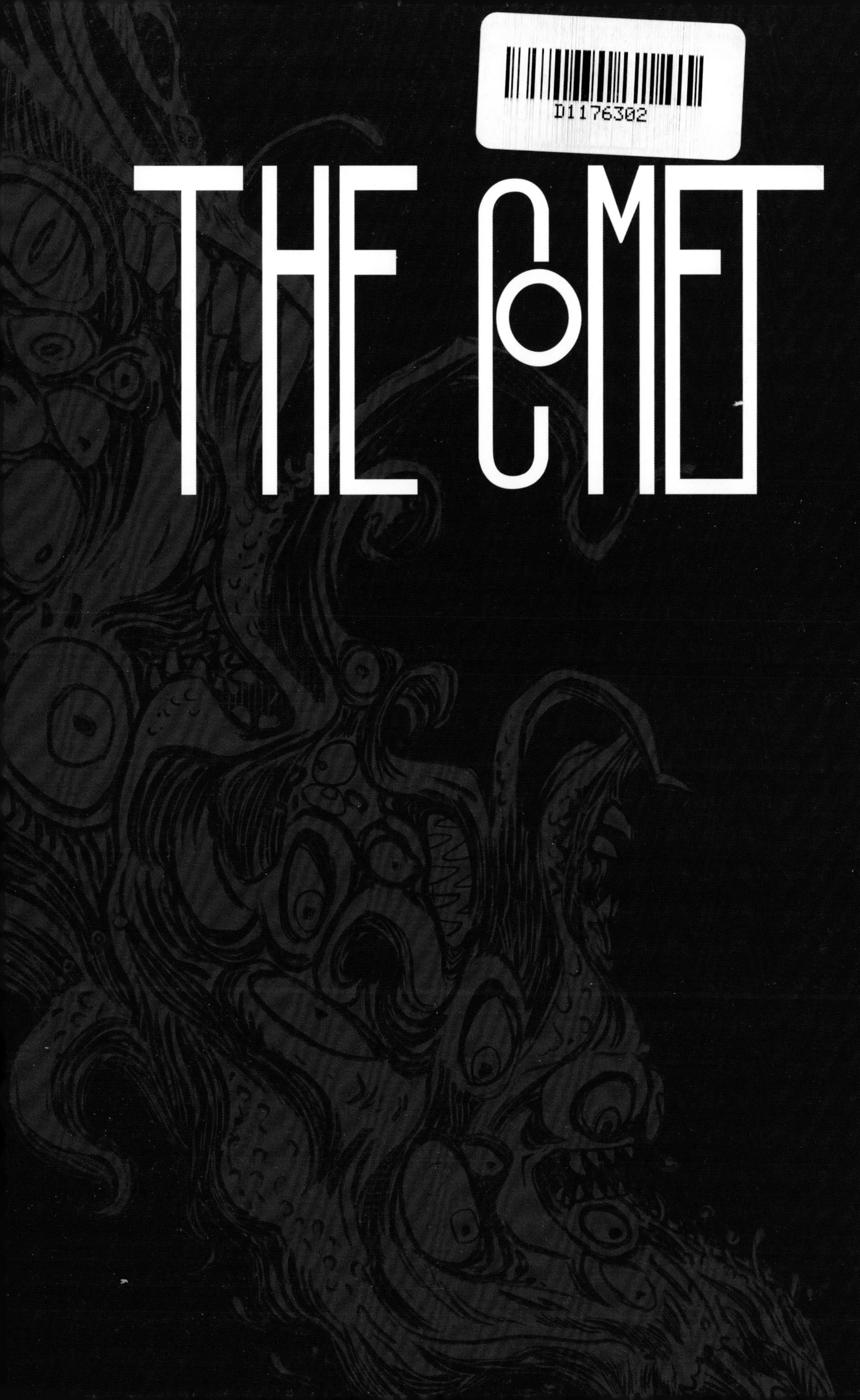

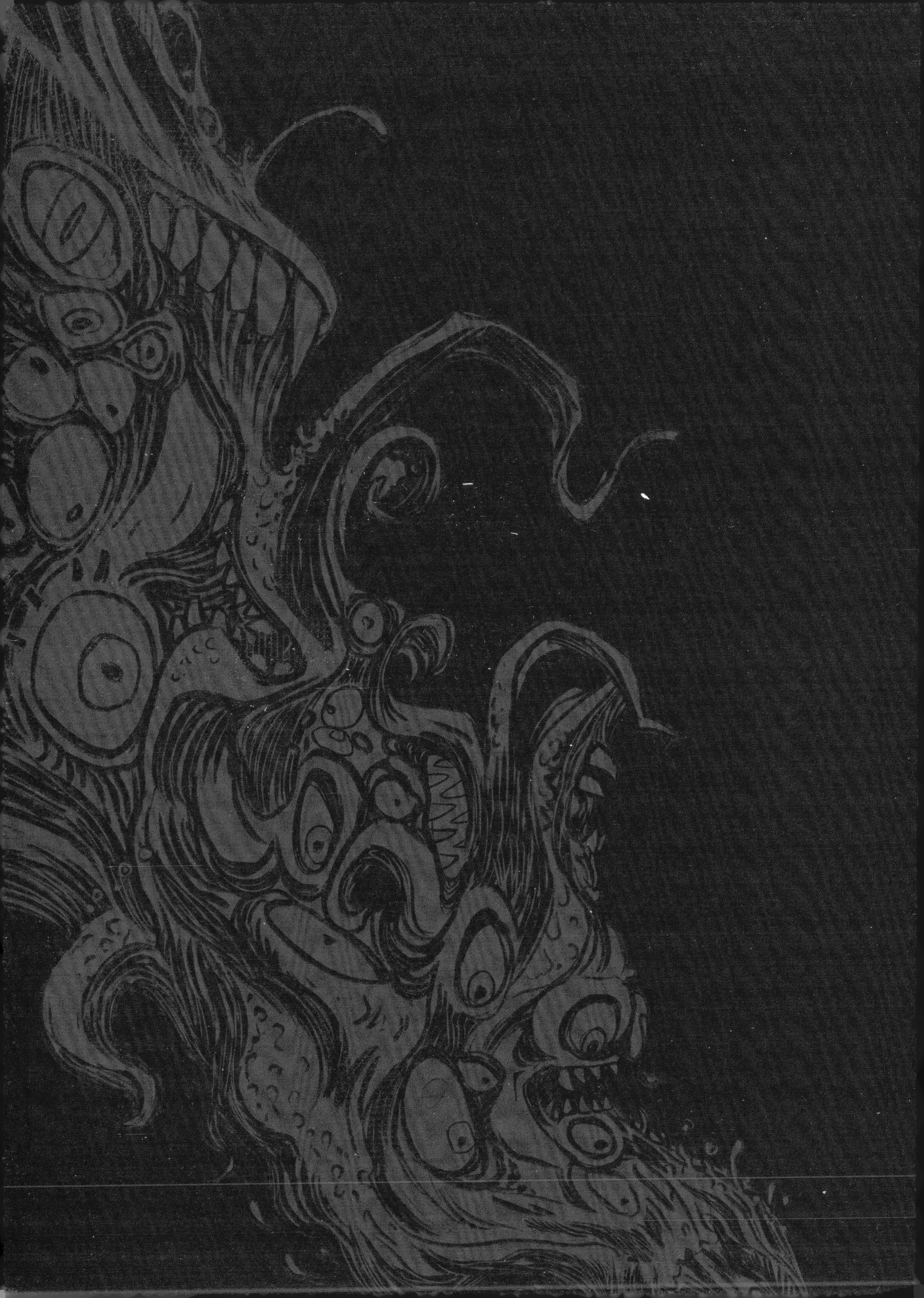

THE COMET

VOL. 1: COMBUSTION

WRITTEN BY
ARIANNA IRWIN

ILLUSTRATED BY
FRANCINE DELGADO

COLORED BY
ALBA CARDONA

LETTERED BY
A LARGER WORLD STUDIOS

INSIGHT
COMICS

San Rafael, California

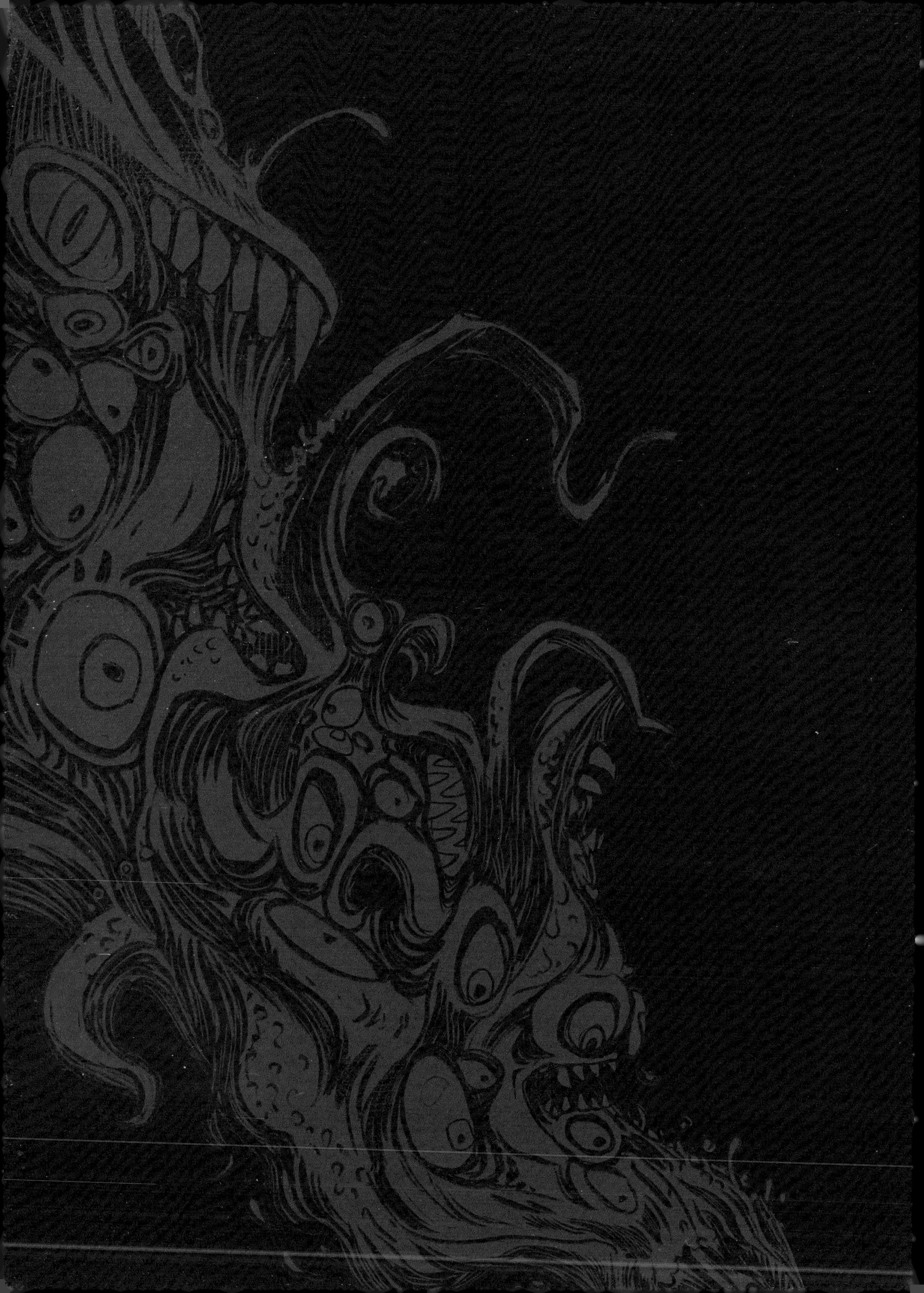

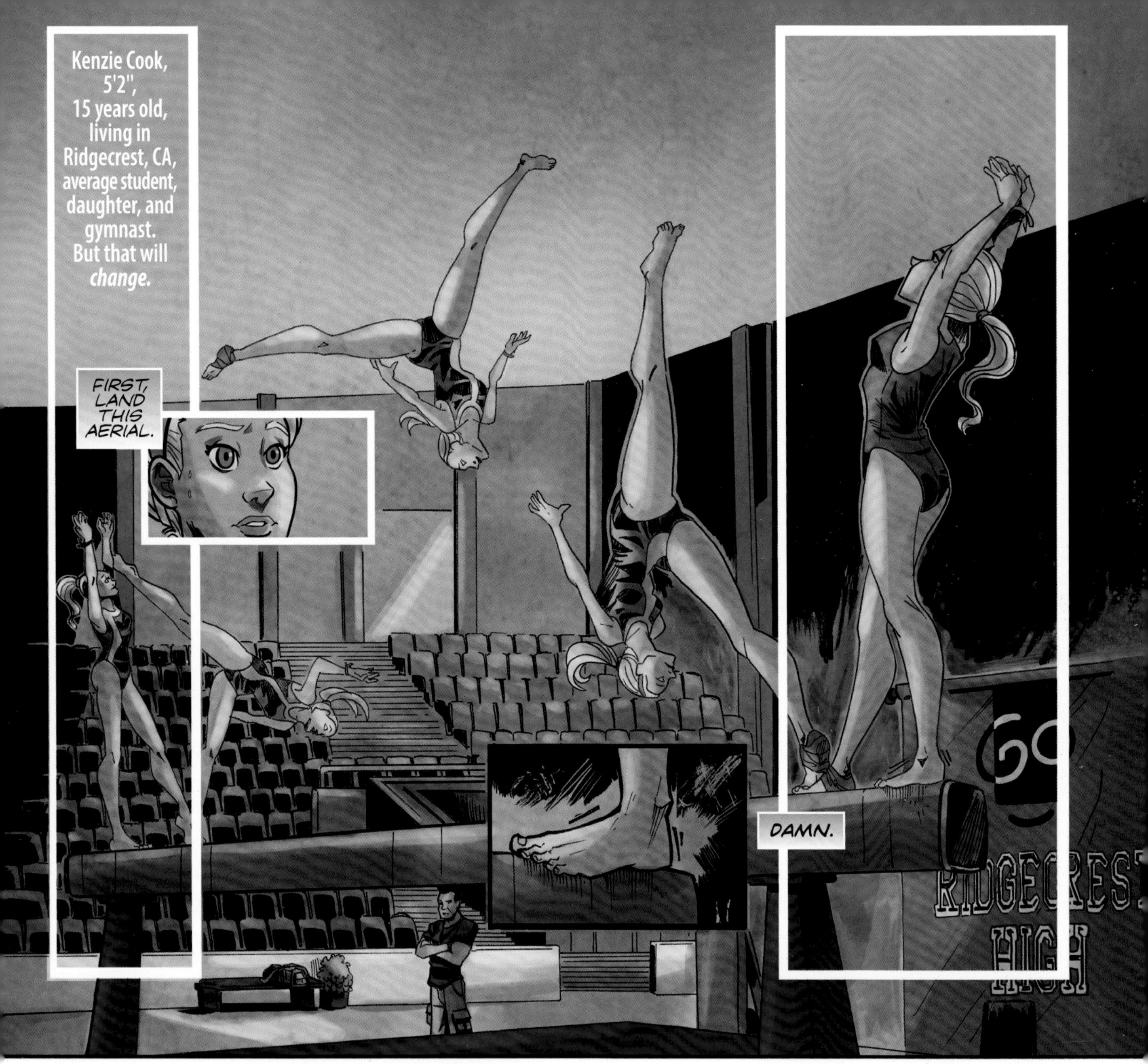
Kenzie Cook, 5'2", 15 years old, living in Ridgecrest, CA, average student, daughter, and gymnast. But that will *change.*
FIRST, LAND THIS AERIAL.
DAMN.
GO
RIDGECREST HIGH

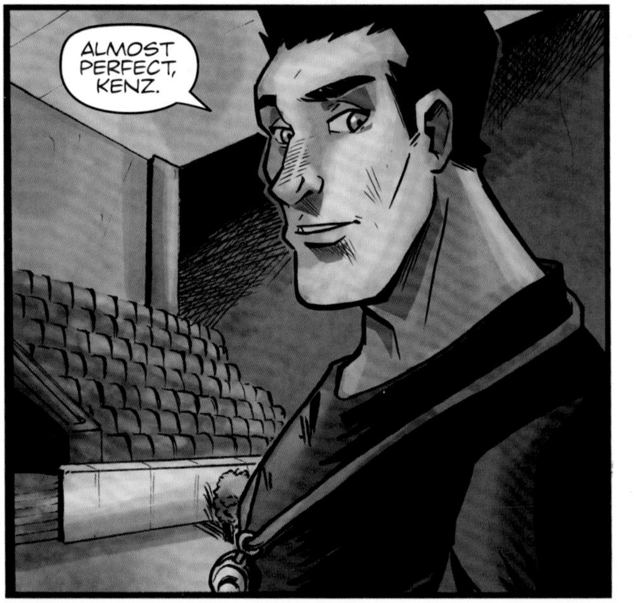
ALMOST PERFECT, KENZ.

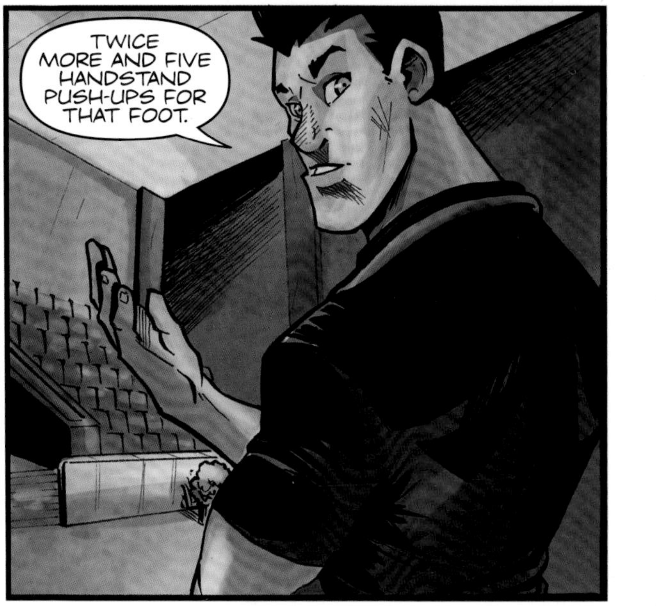
TWICE MORE AND FIVE HANDSTAND PUSH-UPS FOR THAT FOOT.

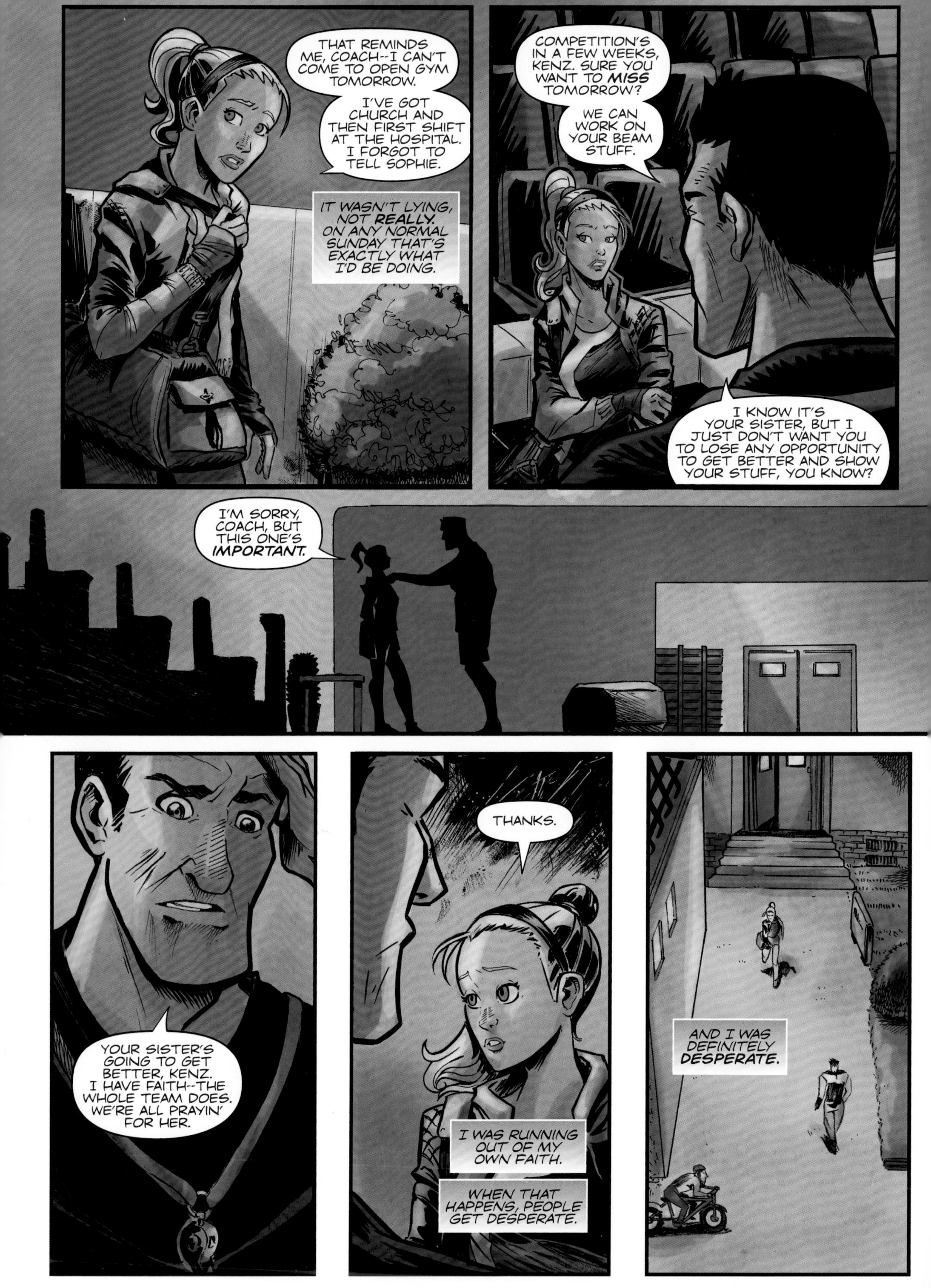
THAT REMINDS ME, COACH--I CAN'T COME TO OPEN GYM TOMORROW.
I'VE GOT CHURCH AND THEN FIRST SHIFT AT THE HOSPITAL. I FORGOT TO TELL SOPHIE.
IT WASN'T LYING, NOT REALLY. ON ANY NORMAL SUNDAY THAT'S EXACTLY WHAT I'D BE DOING.
COMPETITION'S IN A FEW WEEKS, KENZ. SURE YOU WANT TO MISS TOMORROW?
WE CAN WORK ON YOUR BEAM STUFF.
I KNOW IT'S YOUR SISTER, BUT I JUST DON'T WANT YOU TO LOSE ANY OPPORTUNITY TO GET BETTER AND SHOW YOUR STUFF, YOU KNOW?
I'M SORRY, COACH, BUT THIS ONE'S IMPORTANT.
YOUR SISTER'S GOING TO GET BETTER, KENZ. I HAVE FAITH--THE WHOLE TEAM DOES. WE'RE ALL PRAYIN' FOR HER.
THANKS.
I WAS RUNNING OUT OF MY OWN FAITH.
WHEN THAT HAPPENS, PEOPLE GET DESPERATE.
AND I WAS DEFINITELY DESPERATE.

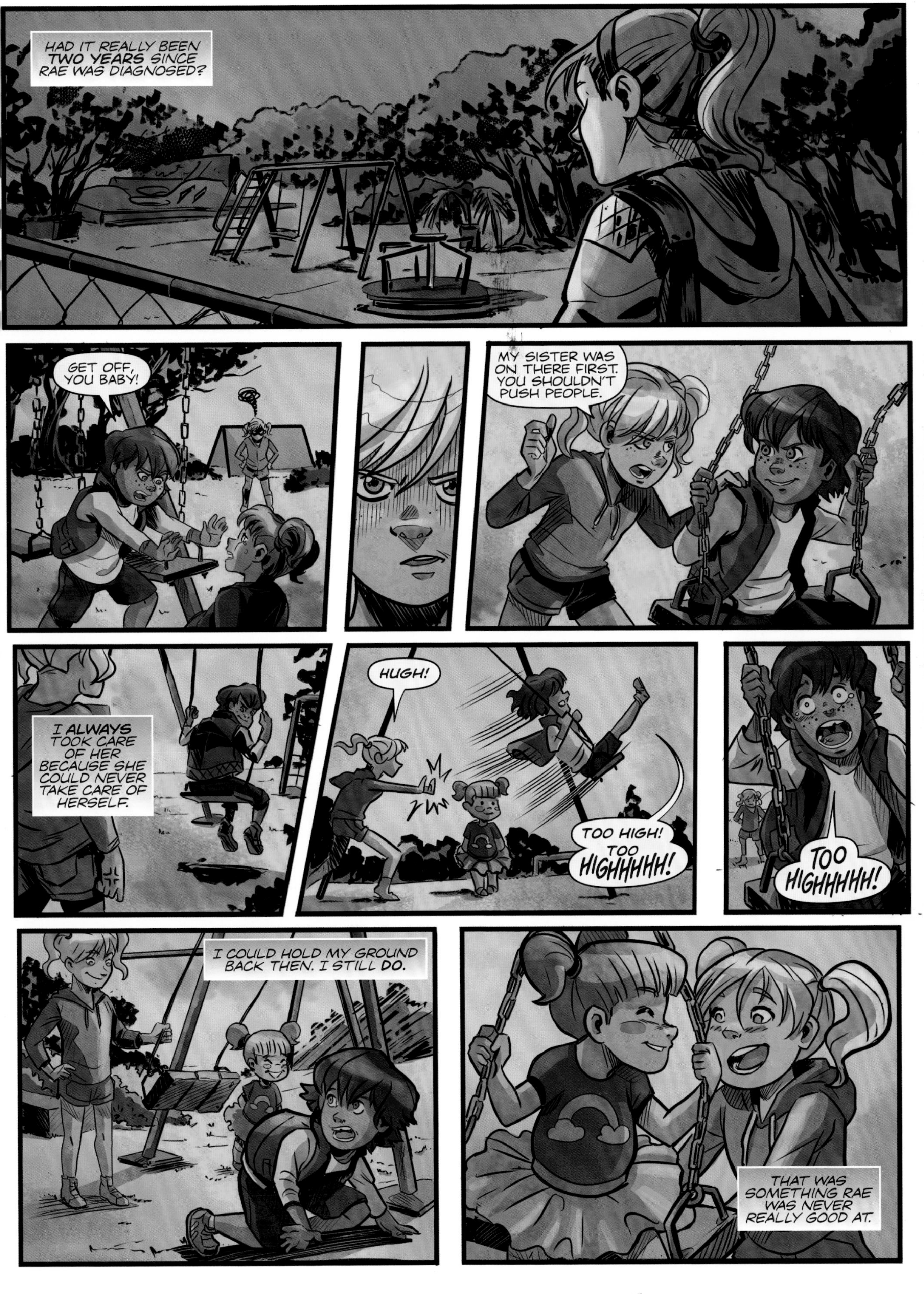
HAD IT REALLY BEEN TWO YEARS SINCE RAE WAS DIAGNOSED?
GET OFF, YOU BABY!
MY SISTER WAS ON THERE FIRST. YOU SHOULDN'T PUSH PEOPLE.
I ALWAYS TOOK CARE OF HER BECAUSE SHE COULD NEVER TAKE CARE OF HERSELF.
HUGH!
TOO HIGH! TOO HIGHHHHH!
TOO HIGHHHHH!
I COULD HOLD MY GROUND BACK THEN. I STILL DO.
THAT WAS SOMETHING RAE WAS NEVER REALLY GOOD AT.

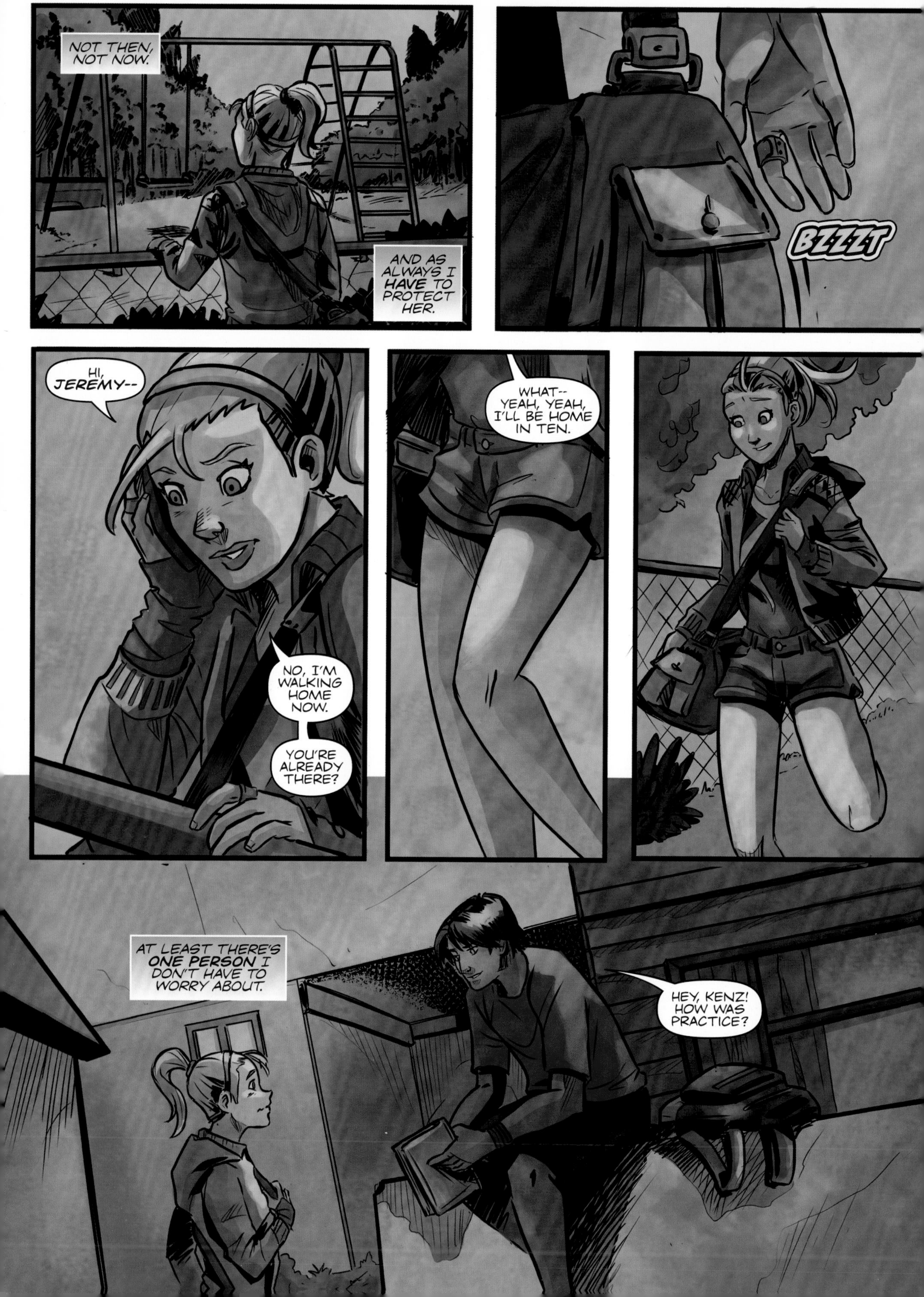
NOT THEN, NOT NOW.
AND AS ALWAYS I HAVE TO PROTECT HER.
BZZZT
HI, JEREMY--
NO, I'M WALKING HOME NOW.
YOU'RE ALREADY THERE?
WHAT-- YEAH, YEAH, I'LL BE HOME IN TEN.
AT LEAST THERE'S ONE PERSON I DON'T HAVE TO WORRY ABOUT.
HEY, KENZ! HOW WAS PRACTICE?

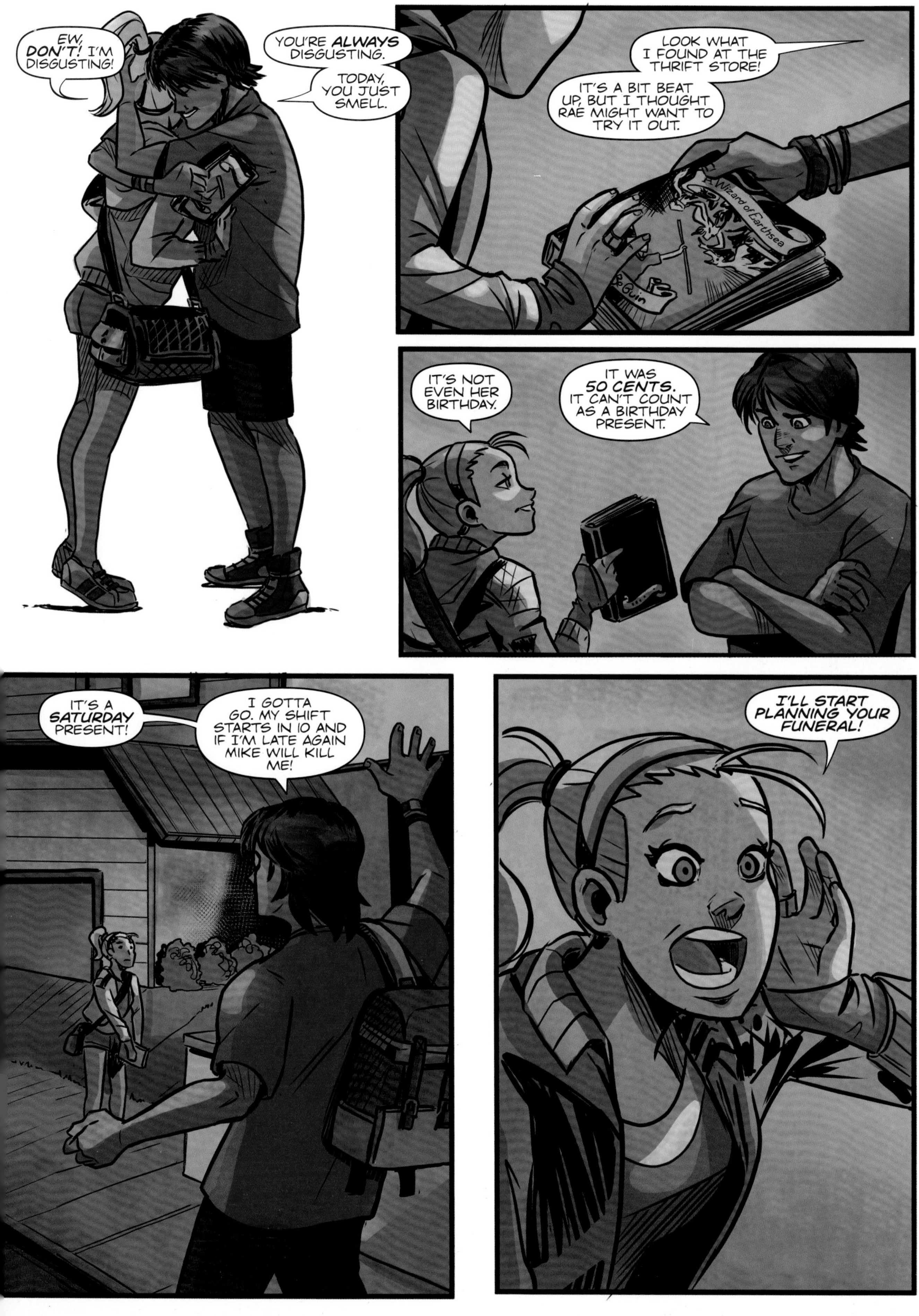
EW, DON'T! I'M DISGUSTING!
YOU'RE ALWAYS DISGUSTING.
TODAY, YOU JUST SMELL.
LOOK WHAT I FOUND AT THE THRIFT STORE!
IT'S A BIT BEAT UP, BUT I THOUGHT RAE MIGHT WANT TO TRY IT OUT.
A Wizard of Earthsea
IT'S NOT EVEN HER BIRTHDAY.
IT WAS 50 CENTS. IT CAN'T COUNT AS A BIRTHDAY PRESENT.
IT'S A SATURDAY PRESENT!
I GOTTA GO. MY SHIFT STARTS IN 10 AND IF I'M LATE AGAIN MIKE WILL KILL ME!
I'LL START PLANNING YOUR FUNERAL!

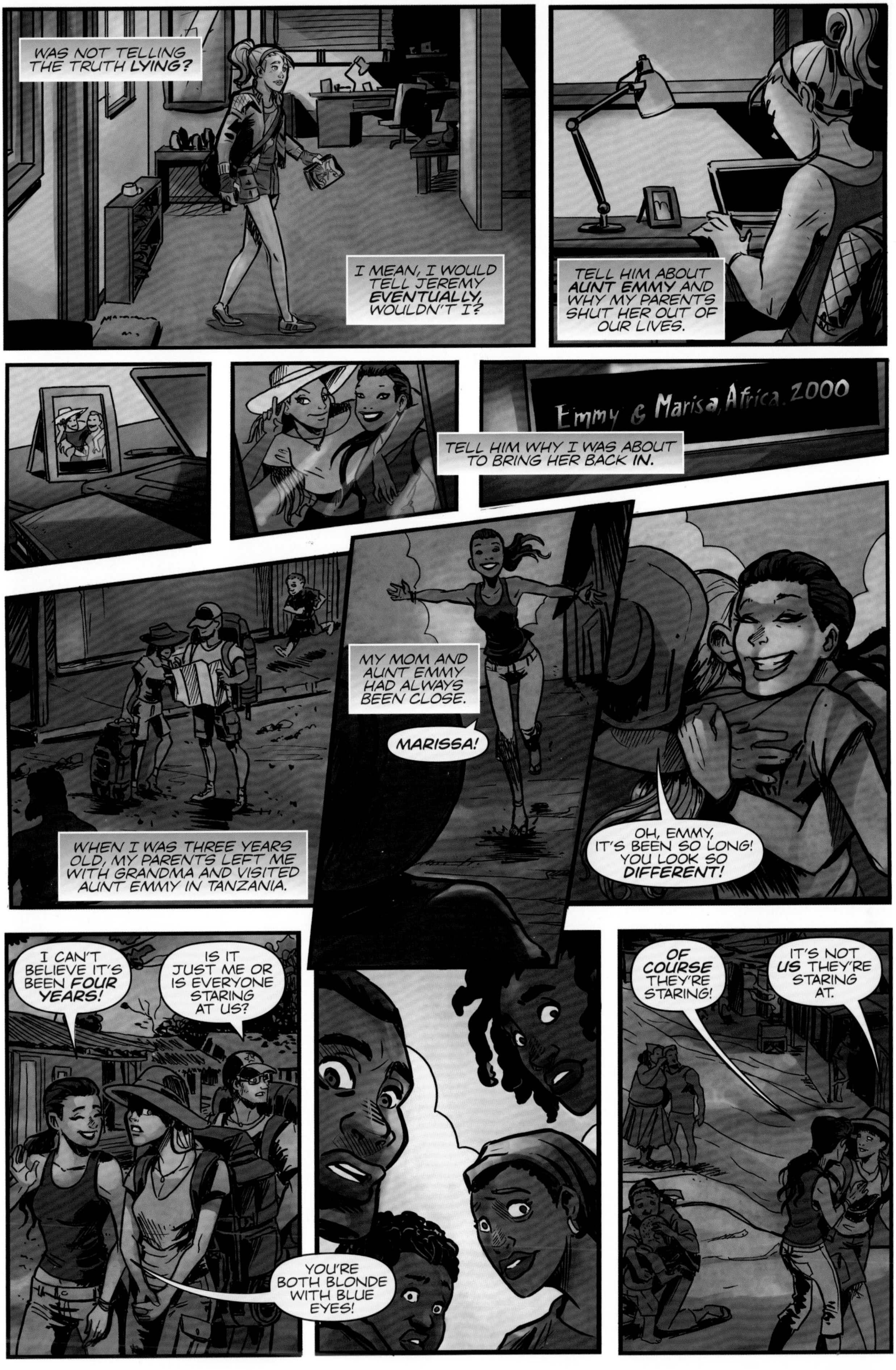
WAS NOT TELLING THE TRUTH LYING?
I MEAN, I WOULD TELL JEREMY EVENTUALLY, WOULDN'T I?
TELL HIM ABOUT AUNT EMMY AND WHY MY PARENTS SHUT HER OUT OF OUR LIVES.
Emmy & Marisa, Africa, 2000
TELL HIM WHY I WAS ABOUT TO BRING HER BACK IN.
WHEN I WAS THREE YEARS OLD, MY PARENTS LEFT ME WITH GRANDMA AND VISITED AUNT EMMY IN TANZANIA.
MY MOM AND AUNT EMMY HAD ALWAYS BEEN CLOSE.
MARISSA!
OH, EMMY, IT'S BEEN SO LONG! YOU LOOK SO DIFFERENT!
I CAN'T BELIEVE IT'S BEEN FOUR YEARS!
IS IT JUST ME OR IS EVERYONE STARING AT US?
YOU'RE BOTH BLONDE WITH BLUE EYES!
OF COURSE THEY'RE STARING!
IT'S NOT US THEY'RE STARING AT.

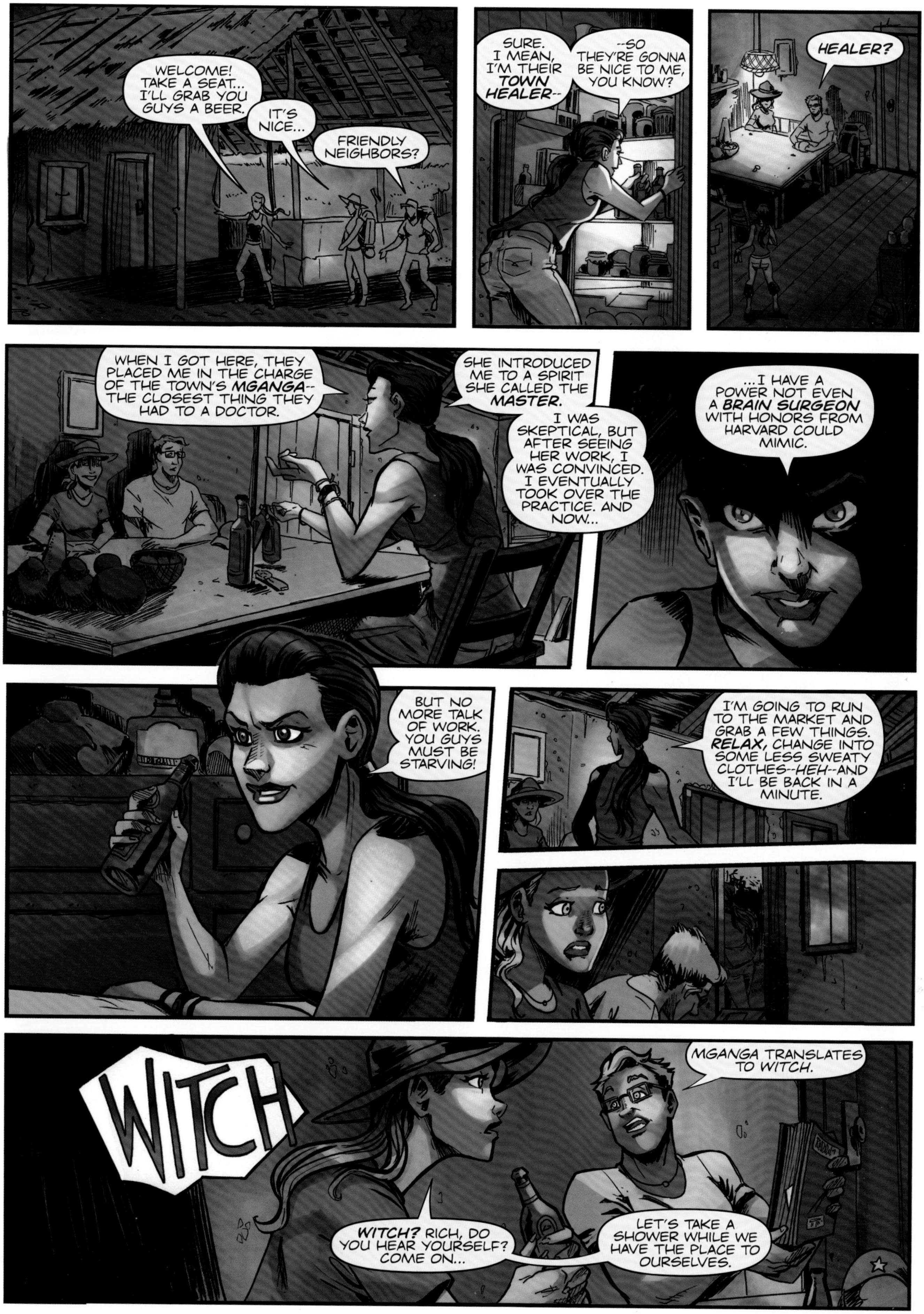
WELCOME! TAKE A SEAT... I'LL GRAB YOU GUYS A BEER.
IT'S NICE...
FRIENDLY NEIGHBORS?
SURE. I MEAN, I'M THEIR TOWN HEALER--
--SO THEY'RE GONNA BE NICE TO ME, YOU KNOW?
HEALER?
WHEN I GOT HERE, THEY PLACED ME IN THE CHARGE OF THE TOWN'S MGANGA-- THE CLOSEST THING THEY HAD TO A DOCTOR.
SHE INTRODUCED ME TO A SPIRIT SHE CALLED THE MASTER.
I WAS SKEPTICAL, BUT AFTER SEEING HER WORK, I WAS CONVINCED. I EVENTUALLY TOOK OVER THE PRACTICE. AND NOW...
...I HAVE A POWER NOT EVEN A BRAIN SURGEON WITH HONORS FROM HARVARD COULD MIMIC.
BUT NO MORE TALK OF WORK. YOU GUYS MUST BE STARVING!
I'M GOING TO RUN TO THE MARKET AND GRAB A FEW THINGS. RELAX, CHANGE INTO SOME LESS SWEATY CLOTHES--HEH--AND I'LL BE BACK IN A MINUTE.
WITCH
MGANGA TRANSLATES TO WITCH.
WITCH? RICH, DO YOU HEAR YOURSELF? COME ON...
LET'S TAKE A SHOWER WHILE WE HAVE THE PLACE TO OURSELVES.

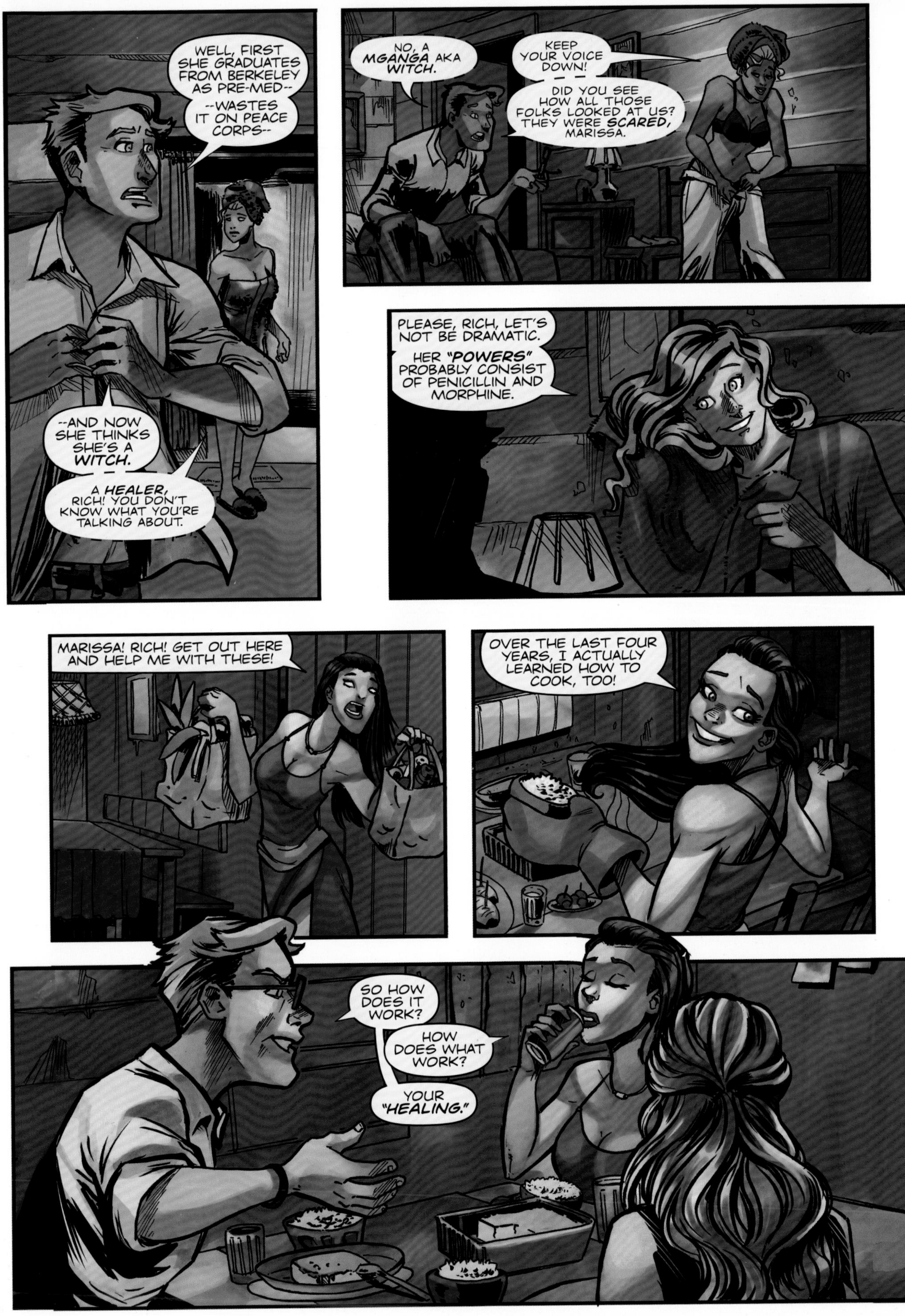
WELL, FIRST SHE GRADUATES FROM BERKELEY AS PRE-MED--
--WASTES IT ON PEACE CORPS--
--AND NOW SHE THINKS SHE'S A **WITCH.**
A **HEALER,** RICH! YOU DON'T KNOW WHAT YOU'RE TALKING ABOUT.
NO, A ***MGANGA*** AKA ***WITCH.***
KEEP YOUR VOICE DOWN!
DID YOU SEE HOW ALL THOSE FOLKS LOOKED AT US? THEY WERE ***SCARED,*** MARISSA.
PLEASE, RICH, LET'S NOT BE DRAMATIC.
HER ***"POWERS"*** PROBABLY CONSIST OF PENICILLIN AND MORPHINE.
MARISSA! RICH! GET OUT HERE AND HELP ME WITH THESE!
OVER THE LAST FOUR YEARS, I ACTUALLY LEARNED HOW TO COOK, TOO!
SO HOW DOES IT WORK?
HOW DOES WHAT WORK?
YOUR ***"HEALING."***

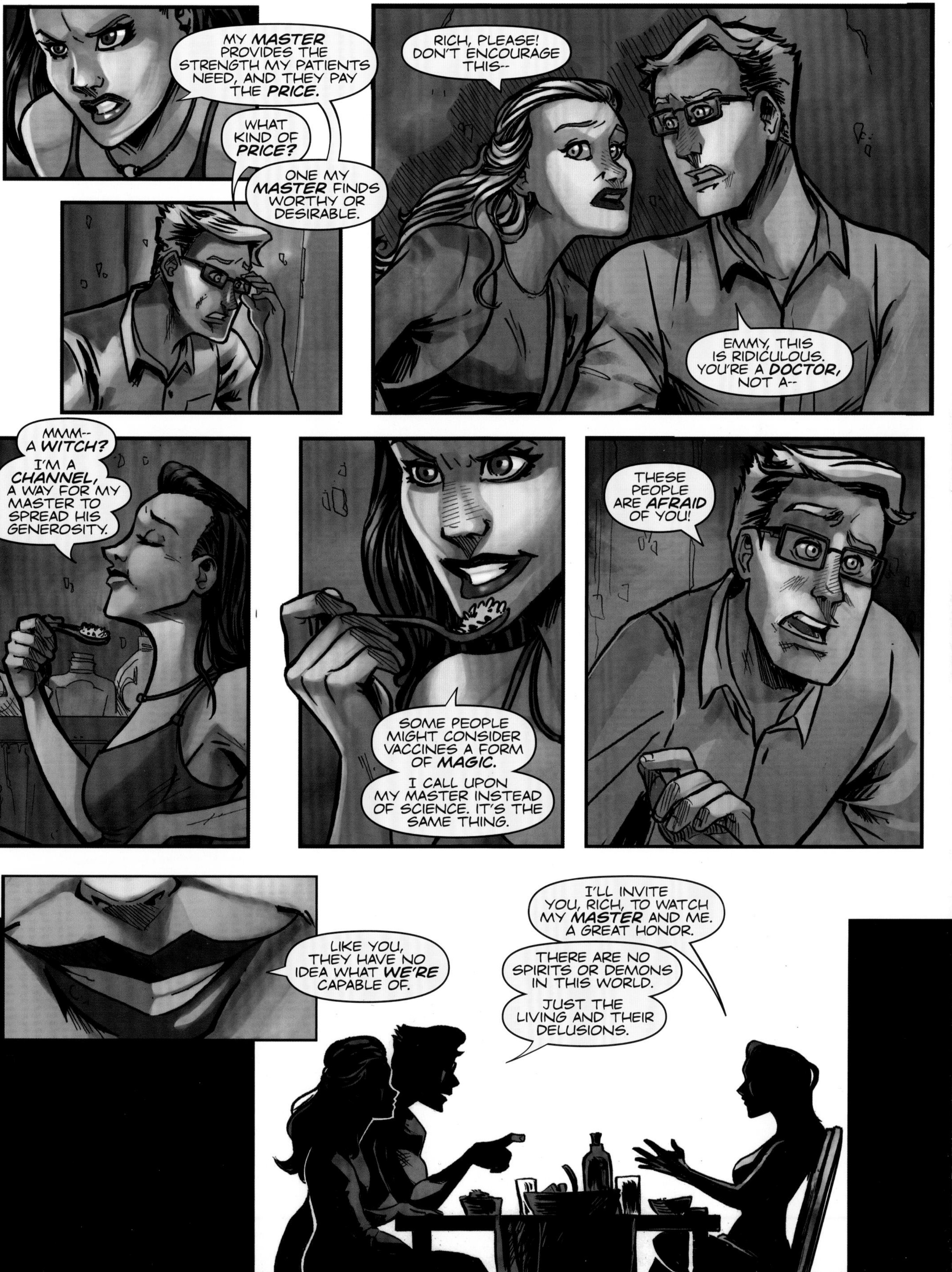
MY MASTER PROVIDES THE STRENGTH MY PATIENTS NEED, AND THEY PAY THE PRICE.
WHAT KIND OF PRICE?
ONE MY MASTER FINDS WORTHY OR DESIRABLE.
RICH, PLEASE! DON'T ENCOURAGE THIS--
EMMY, THIS IS RIDICULOUS. YOU'RE A DOCTOR, NOT A--
MMM-- A WITCH?
I'M A CHANNEL, A WAY FOR MY MASTER TO SPREAD HIS GENEROSITY.
SOME PEOPLE MIGHT CONSIDER VACCINES A FORM OF MAGIC.
I CALL UPON MY MASTER INSTEAD OF SCIENCE. IT'S THE SAME THING.
THESE PEOPLE ARE AFRAID OF YOU!
LIKE YOU, THEY HAVE NO IDEA WHAT WE'RE CAPABLE OF.
I'LL INVITE YOU, RICH, TO WATCH MY MASTER AND ME. A GREAT HONOR.
THERE ARE NO SPIRITS OR DEMONS IN THIS WORLD.
JUST THE LIVING AND THEIR DELUSIONS.

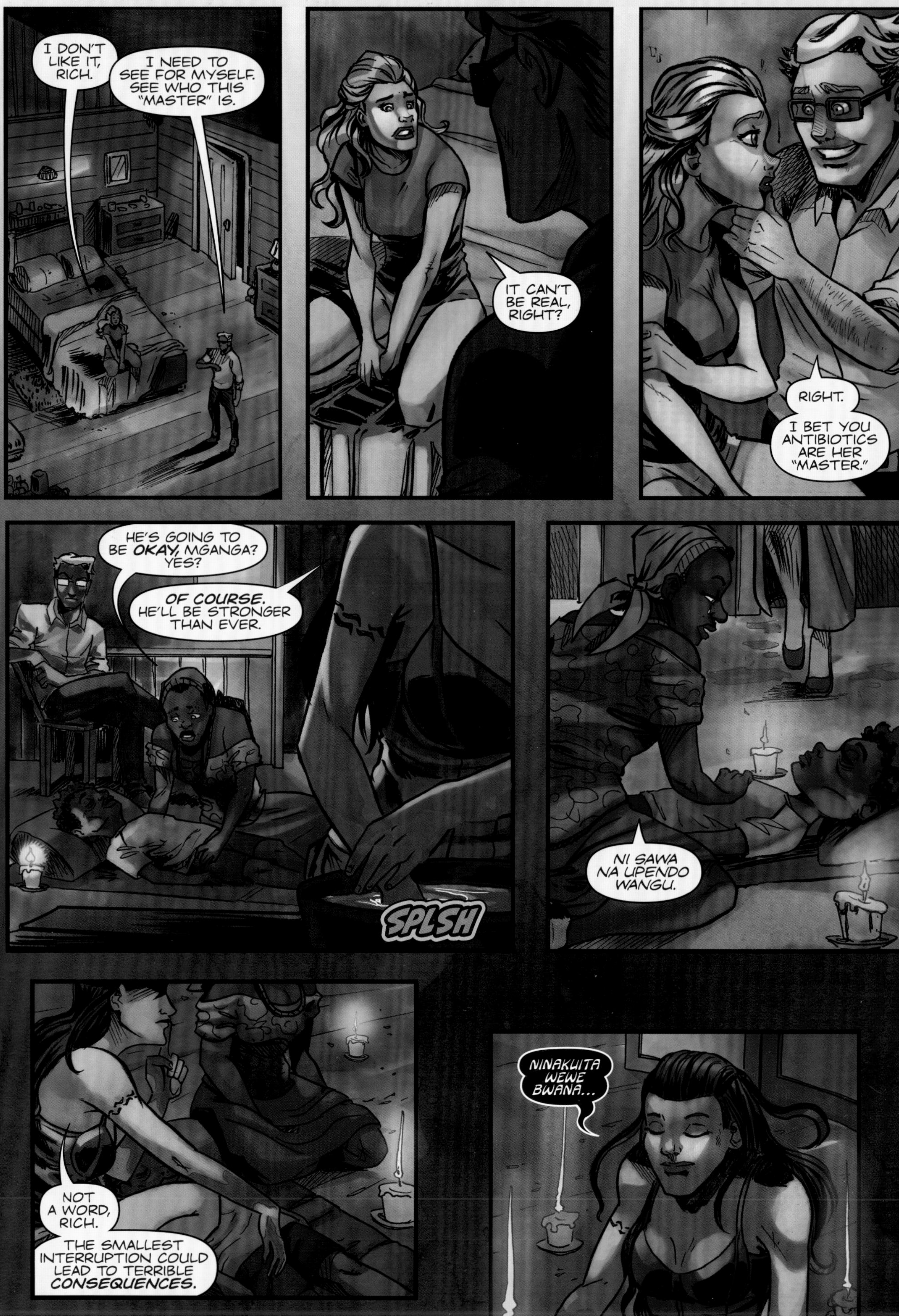
I DON'T LIKE IT, RICH.
I NEED TO SEE FOR MYSELF. SEE WHO THIS "MASTER" IS.
IT CAN'T BE REAL, RIGHT?
RIGHT.
I BET YOU ANTIBIOTICS ARE HER "MASTER."
HE'S GOING TO BE OKAY, MGANGA? YES?
OF COURSE. HE'LL BE STRONGER THAN EVER.
SPLSH
NI SAWA NA UPENDO WANGU.
NOT A WORD, RICH.
THE SMALLEST INTERRUPTION COULD LEAD TO TERRIBLE CONSEQUENCES.
NINAKUITA WEWE BWANA...

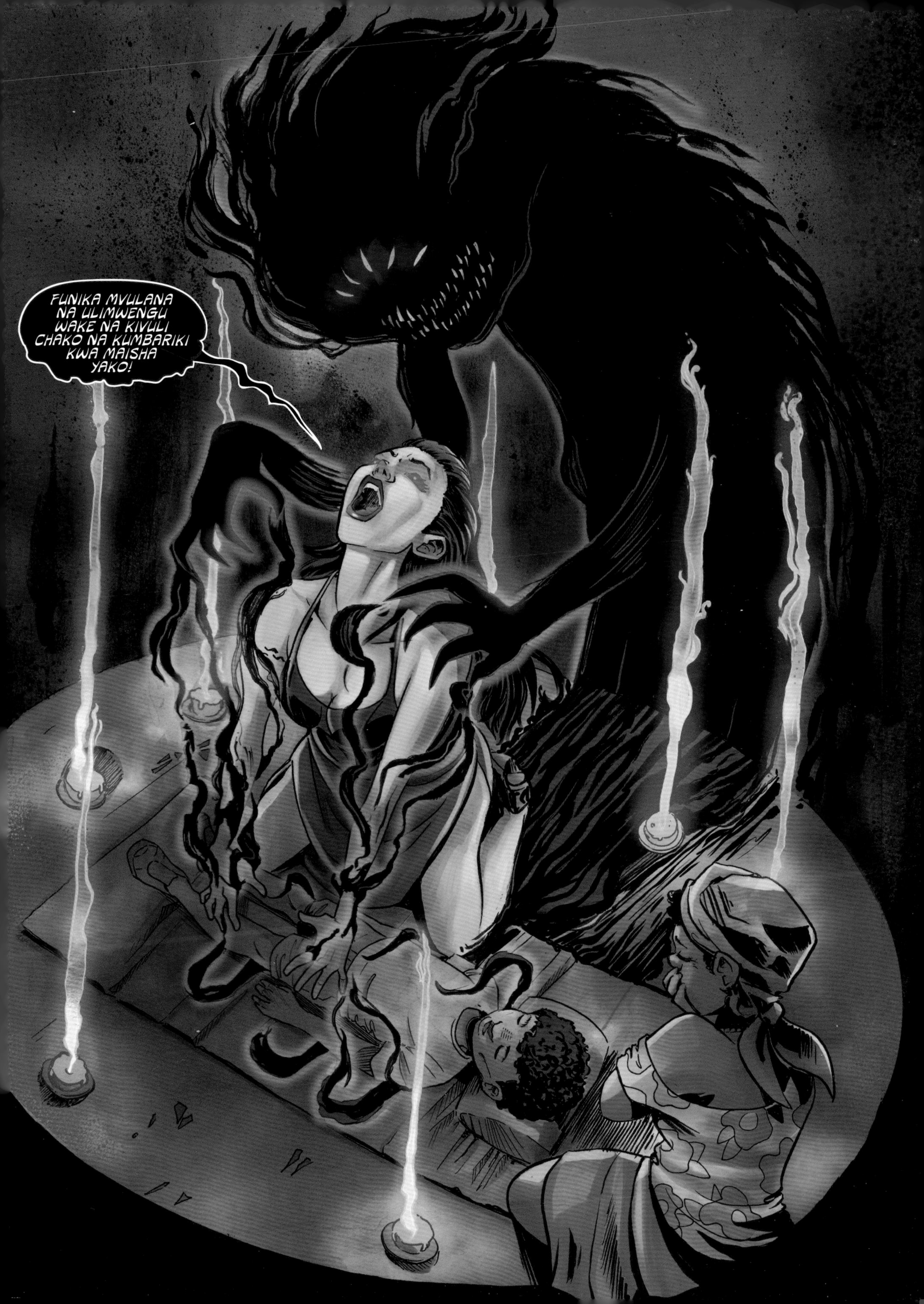
FUNIKA MVULANA NA ULIMWENGU WAKE NA KIVULI CHAKO NA KUMBARIKI KWA MAISHA YAKO!

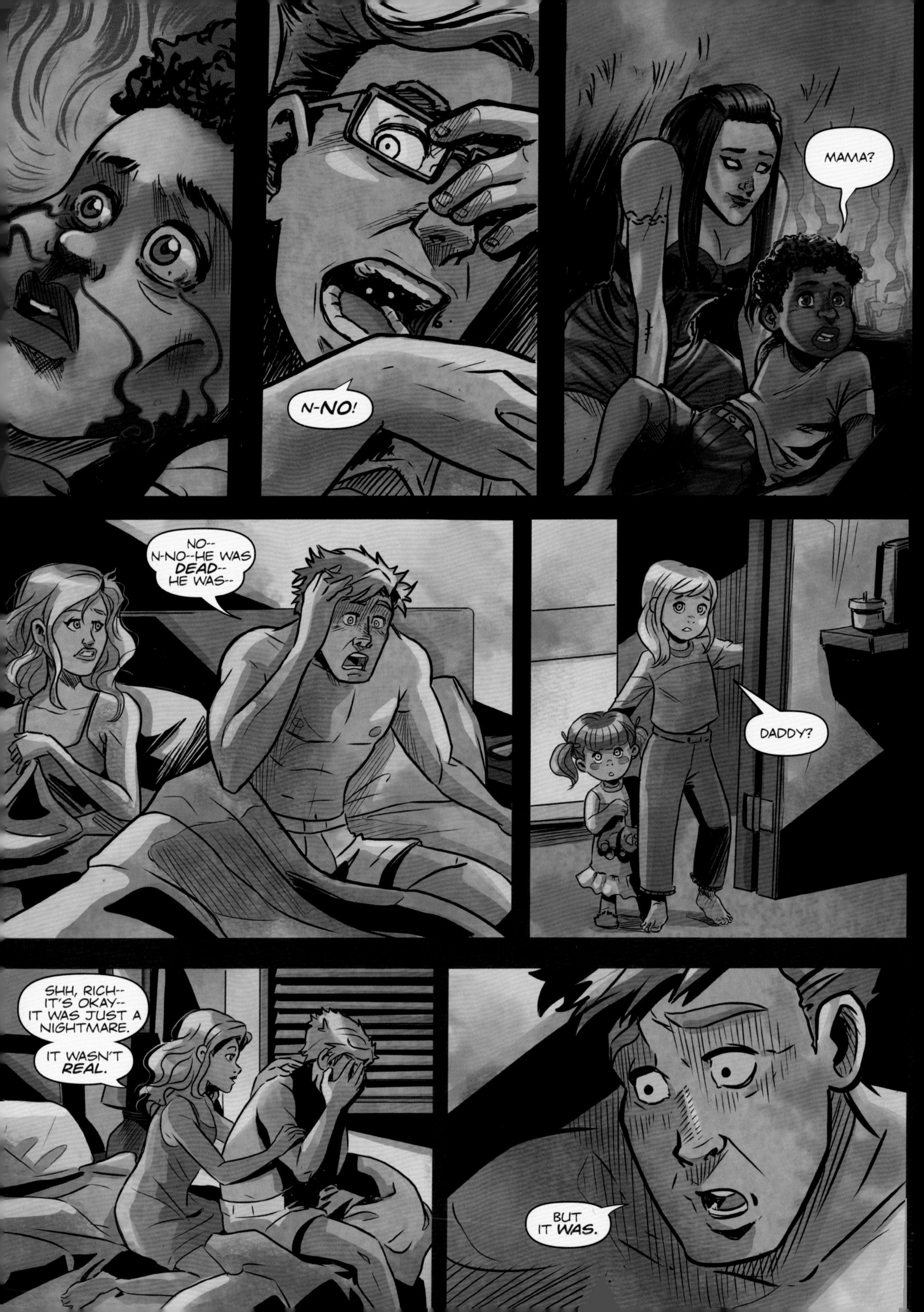
N-NO!
MAMA?
NO--
N-NO--HE WAS
DEAD--
HE WAS--
DADDY?
SHH, RICH--
IT'S OKAY--
IT WAS JUST A
NIGHTMARE.
IT WASN'T
REAL.
BUT
IT WAS.

AFTER THAT TRIP, DAD AND MOM NEVER TALKED ABOUT AUNT EMMY OR HER *POWERS*.

I COULD TELL THEY WERE AFRAID OF HER. SHE LIVED NEARBY, BUT WE NEVER SAW HER.

SSZZZZ

I'M HOME, KENZ! MAN, DOES IT SMELL *GOOD* IN HERE!

IF SHE WAS WHAT I THOUGHT SHE WAS, SHE MIGHT BE ABLE TO HELP RAE.

IF SHE WASN'T, SHE WAS JUST A CRAZY CAT LADY.

KIND OF RANDOM, BUT DO YOU REMEMBER THAT STORY ABOUT AUNT EMMY AND THAT BOY SHE HELPED?

WHAT DID HIS FAMILY HAVE TO PAY FOR AUNT EMMY TO TREAT HIM?

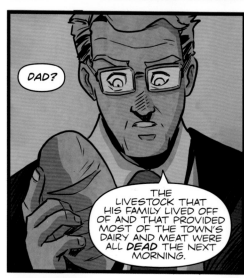

DAD?

THE LIVESTOCK THAT HIS FAMILY LIVED OFF OF AND THAT PROVIDED MOST OF THE TOWN'S DAIRY AND MEAT WERE ALL *DEAD* THE NEXT MORNING.

EVERY *SINGLE* COW, GOAT, AND CHICKEN HAD RED, BLEEDING MARKS ALL OVER IT.

NOT SURE IF IT WAS WORTH IT IN THE END. MOST OF THE TOWN STARVED AFTER THAT.

NOT A VERY PLEASANT STORY OR ONE I LIKE TO REMEMBER.

BEST TO *FORGET* STORIES LIKE THAT IF YOU CAN.

YEAH, I GUESS SO.

WELL, LET'S GET GOING.

VISITING HOURS ARE ALMOST OVER.

IT WAS A *HOPE*.

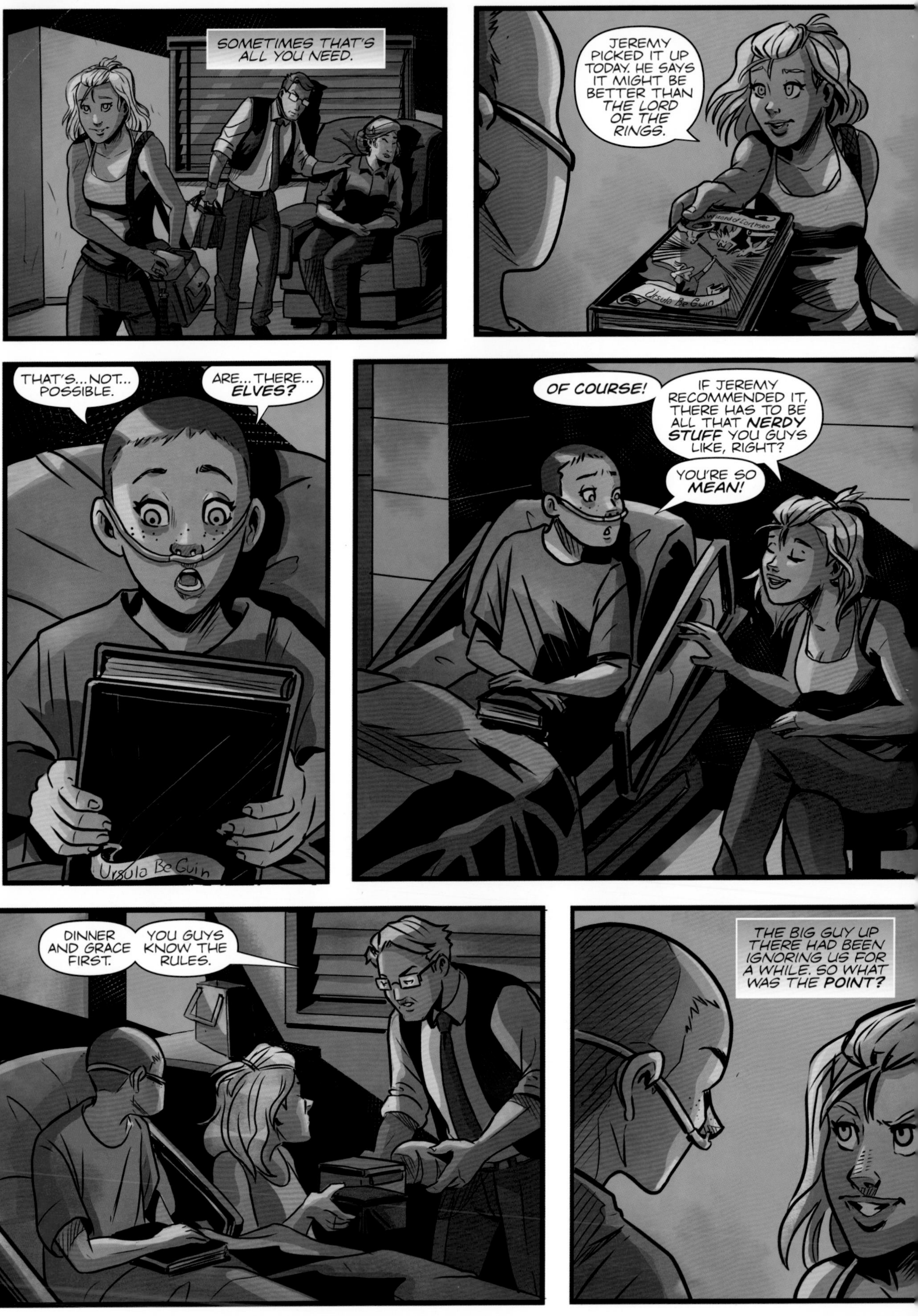
SOMETIMES THAT'S ALL YOU NEED.
JEREMY PICKED IT UP TODAY. HE SAYS IT MIGHT BE BETTER THAN THE LORD OF THE RINGS.
A Wizard of Earthsea
Ursula Be Guin
THAT'S... NOT... POSSIBLE.
ARE... THERE... ELVES?
Ursula Be Guin
OF COURSE!
IF JEREMY RECOMMENDED IT, THERE HAS TO BE ALL THAT NERDY STUFF YOU GUYS LIKE, RIGHT?
YOU'RE SO MEAN!
DINNER AND GRACE FIRST.
YOU GUYS KNOW THE RULES.
THE BIG GUY UP THERE HAD BEEN IGNORING US FOR A WHILE. SO WHAT WAS THE POINT?

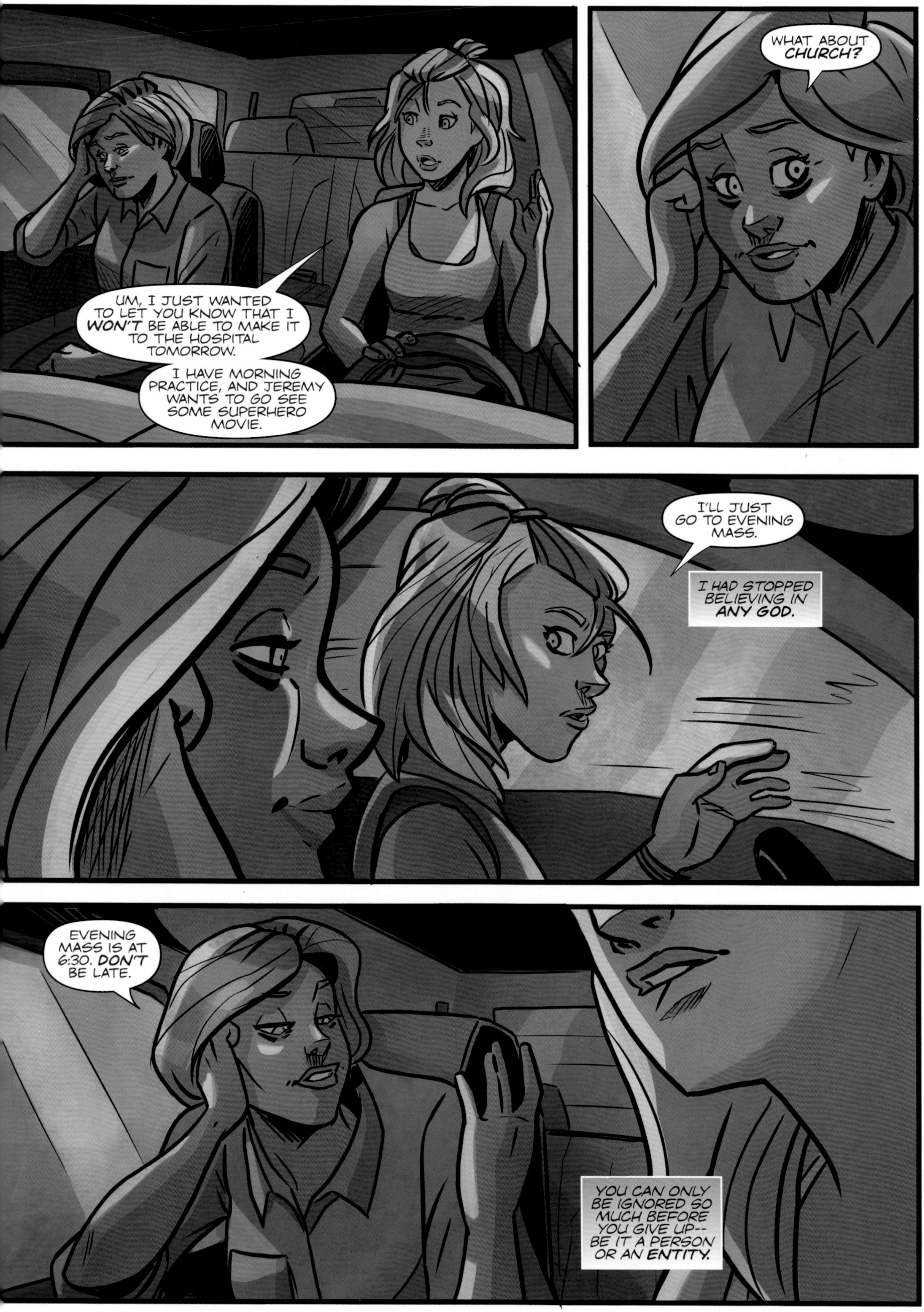
UM, I JUST WANTED TO LET YOU KNOW THAT I WON'T BE ABLE TO MAKE IT TO THE HOSPITAL TOMORROW.
I HAVE MORNING PRACTICE, AND JEREMY WANTS TO GO SEE SOME SUPERHERO MOVIE.
WHAT ABOUT CHURCH?
I'LL JUST GO TO EVENING MASS.
I HAD STOPPED BELIEVING IN ANY GOD.
EVENING MASS IS AT 6:30. DON'T BE LATE.
YOU CAN ONLY BE IGNORED SO MUCH BEFORE YOU GIVE UP-- BE IT A PERSON OR AN ENTITY.

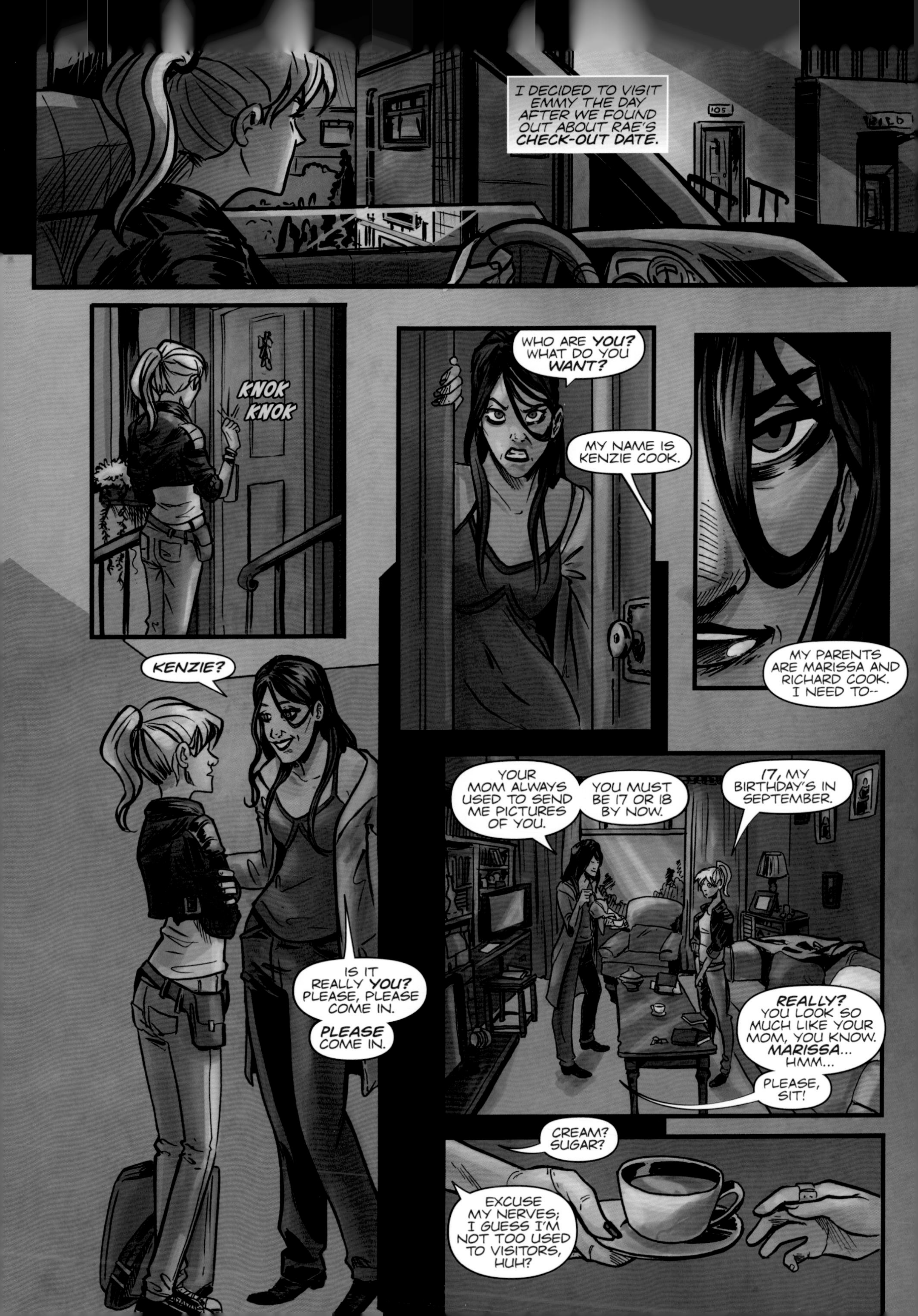

I DECIDED TO VISIT EMMY THE DAY AFTER WE FOUND OUT ABOUT RAE'S CHECK-OUT DATE.
KNOK KNOK
WHO ARE YOU? WHAT DO YOU WANT?
MY NAME IS KENZIE COOK.
MY PARENTS ARE MARISSA AND RICHARD COOK. I NEED TO--
KENZIE?
IS IT REALLY YOU? PLEASE, PLEASE COME IN.
PLEASE COME IN.
YOUR MOM ALWAYS USED TO SEND ME PICTURES OF YOU.
YOU MUST BE 17 OR 18 BY NOW.
17, MY BIRTHDAY'S IN SEPTEMBER.
REALLY? YOU LOOK SO MUCH LIKE YOUR MOM, YOU KNOW. MARISSA... HMM...
PLEASE, SIT!
CREAM? SUGAR?
EXCUSE MY NERVES; I GUESS I'M NOT TOO USED TO VISITORS, HUH?

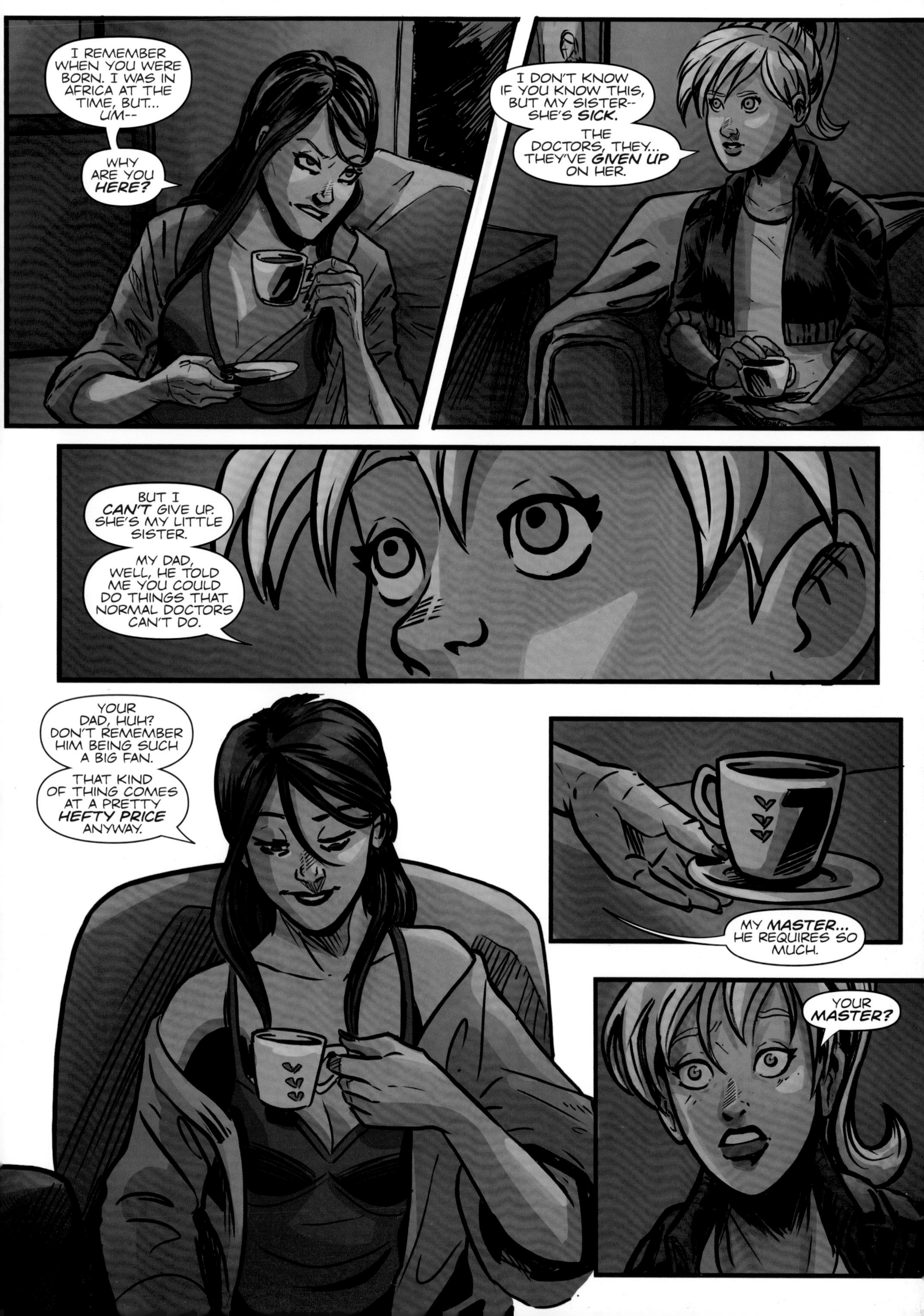

I REMEMBER WHEN YOU WERE BORN. I WAS IN AFRICA AT THE TIME, BUT... UM--
WHY ARE YOU *HERE?*
I DON'T KNOW IF YOU KNOW THIS, BUT MY SISTER-- SHE'S *SICK.*
THE DOCTORS, THEY... THEY'VE *GIVEN UP* ON HER.
BUT I *CAN'T* GIVE UP. SHE'S MY LITTLE SISTER.
MY DAD, WELL, HE TOLD ME YOU COULD DO THINGS THAT NORMAL DOCTORS CAN'T DO.
YOUR DAD, HUH? DON'T REMEMBER HIM BEING SUCH A BIG FAN.
THAT KIND OF THING COMES AT A PRETTY *HEFTY PRICE* ANYWAY.
MY *MASTER...* HE REQUIRES SO MUCH.
YOUR *MASTER?*

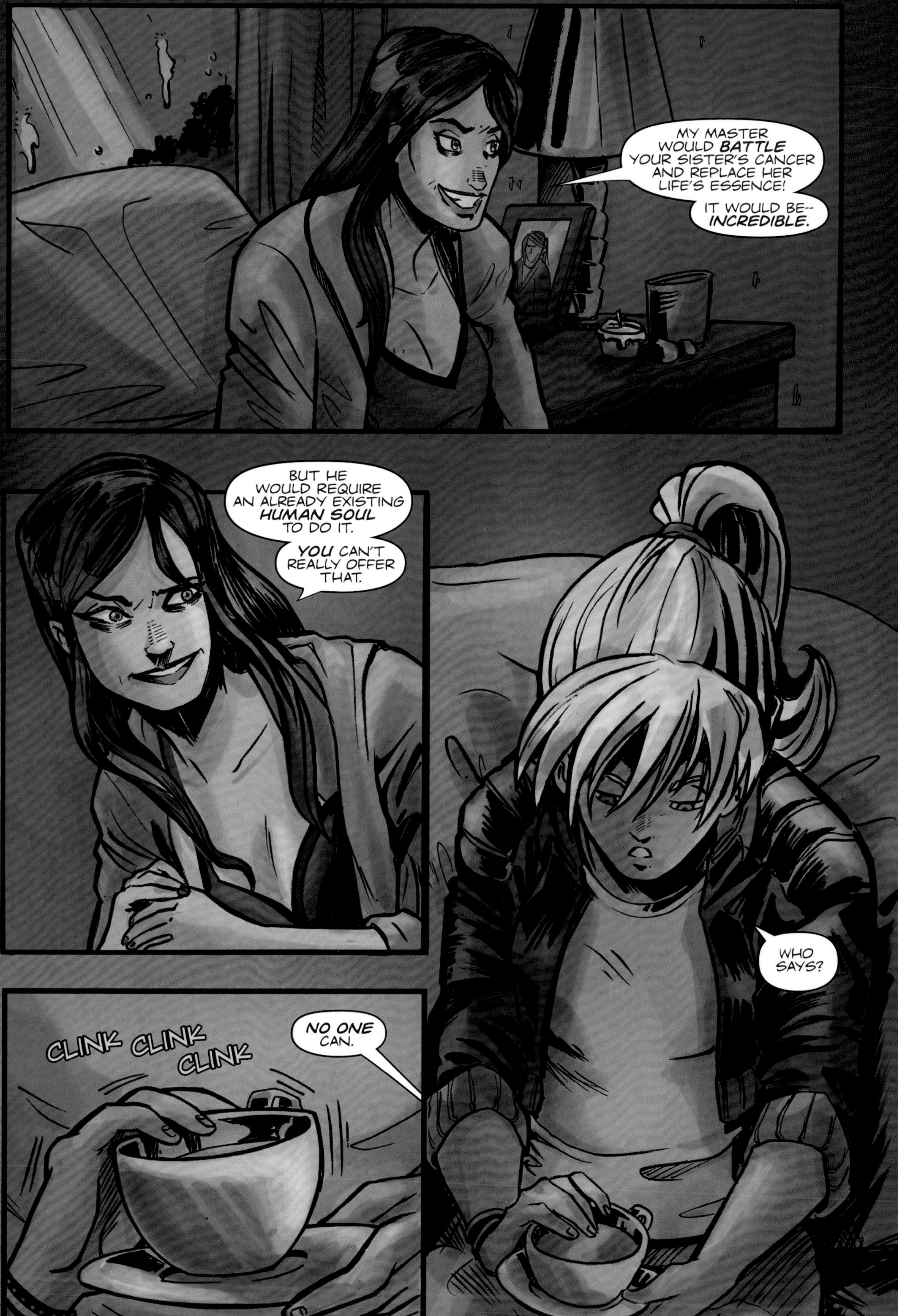

MY MASTER WOULD BATTLE YOUR SISTER'S CANCER AND REPLACE HER LIFE'S ESSENCE!
IT WOULD BE-- INCREDIBLE.
BUT HE WOULD REQUIRE AN ALREADY EXISTING HUMAN SOUL TO DO IT.
YOU CAN'T REALLY OFFER THAT.
WHO SAYS?
NO ONE CAN.
CLINK CLINK CLINK

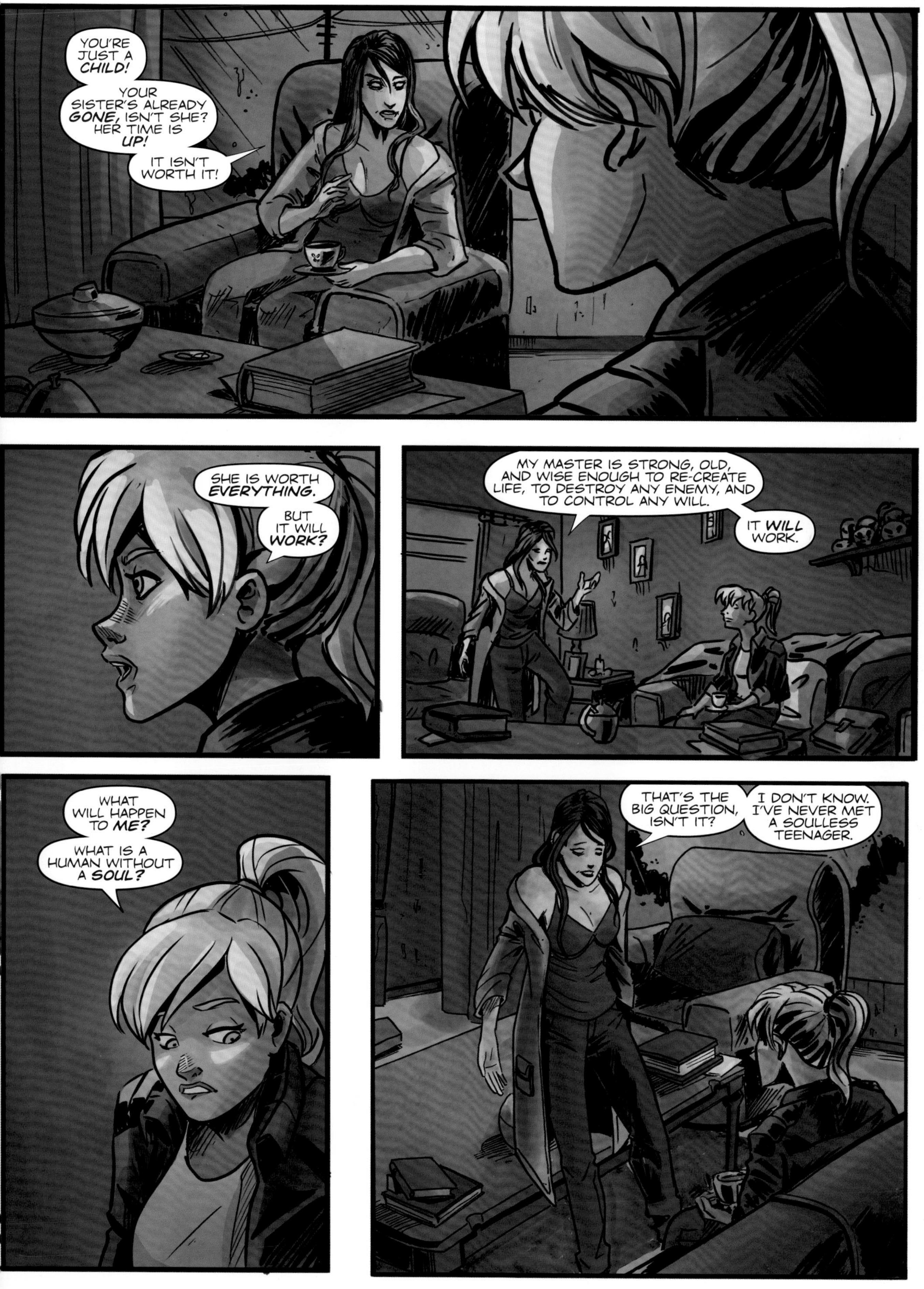
YOU'RE JUST A CHILD!
YOUR SISTER'S ALREADY GONE, ISN'T SHE? HER TIME IS UP!
IT ISN'T WORTH IT!
SHE IS WORTH EVERYTHING.
BUT IT WILL WORK?
MY MASTER IS STRONG, OLD, AND WISE ENOUGH TO RE-CREATE LIFE, TO DESTROY ANY ENEMY, AND TO CONTROL ANY WILL.
IT WILL WORK.
WHAT WILL HAPPEN TO ME?
WHAT IS A HUMAN WITHOUT A SOUL?
THAT'S THE BIG QUESTION, ISN'T IT?
I DON'T KNOW. I'VE NEVER MET A SOULLESS TEENAGER.

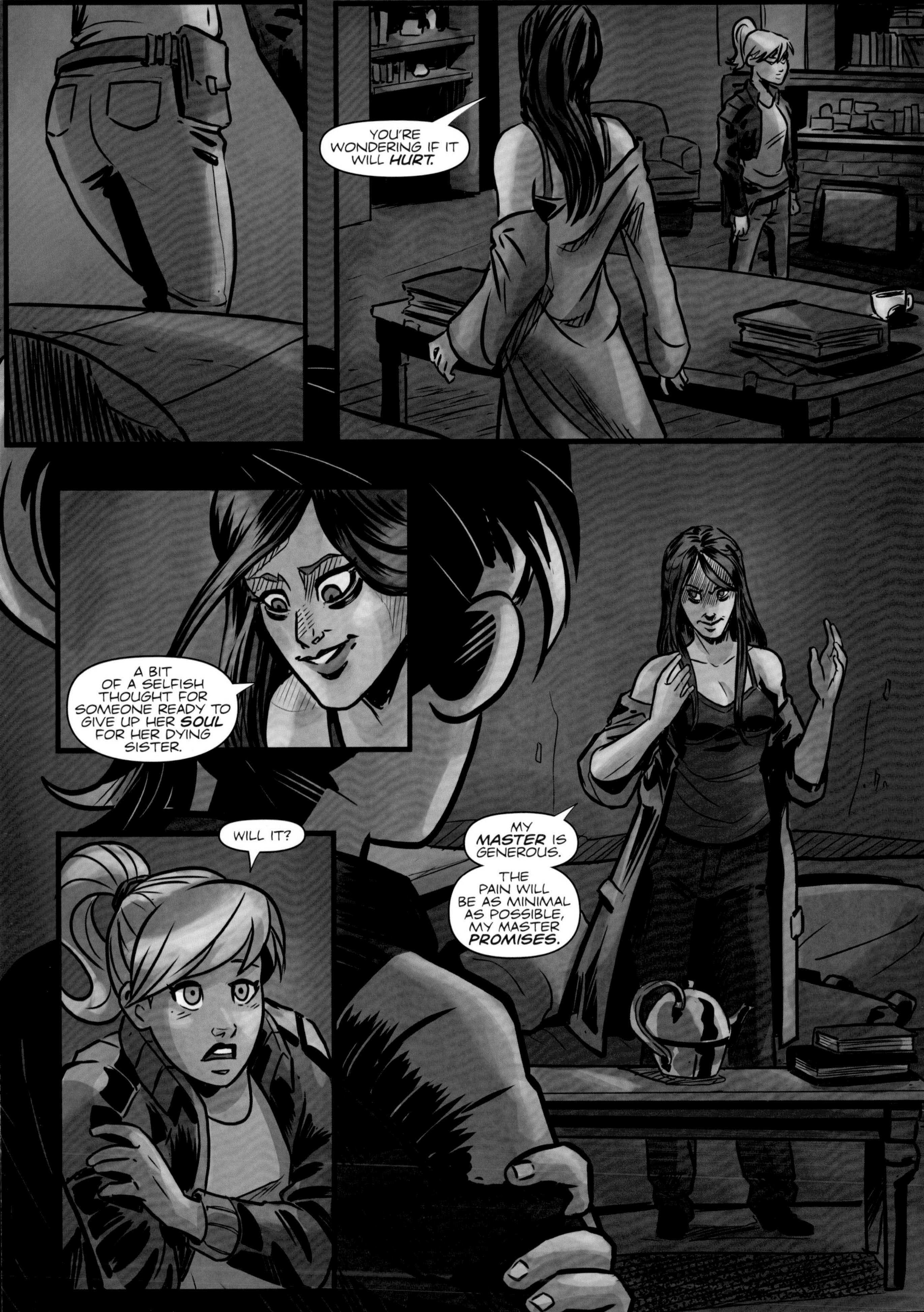
YOU'RE WONDERING IF IT WILL HURT.
A BIT OF A SELFISH THOUGHT FOR SOMEONE READY TO GIVE UP HER SOUL FOR HER DYING SISTER.
WILL IT?
MY MASTER IS GENEROUS.
THE PAIN WILL BE AS MINIMAL AS POSSIBLE, MY MASTER PROMISES.

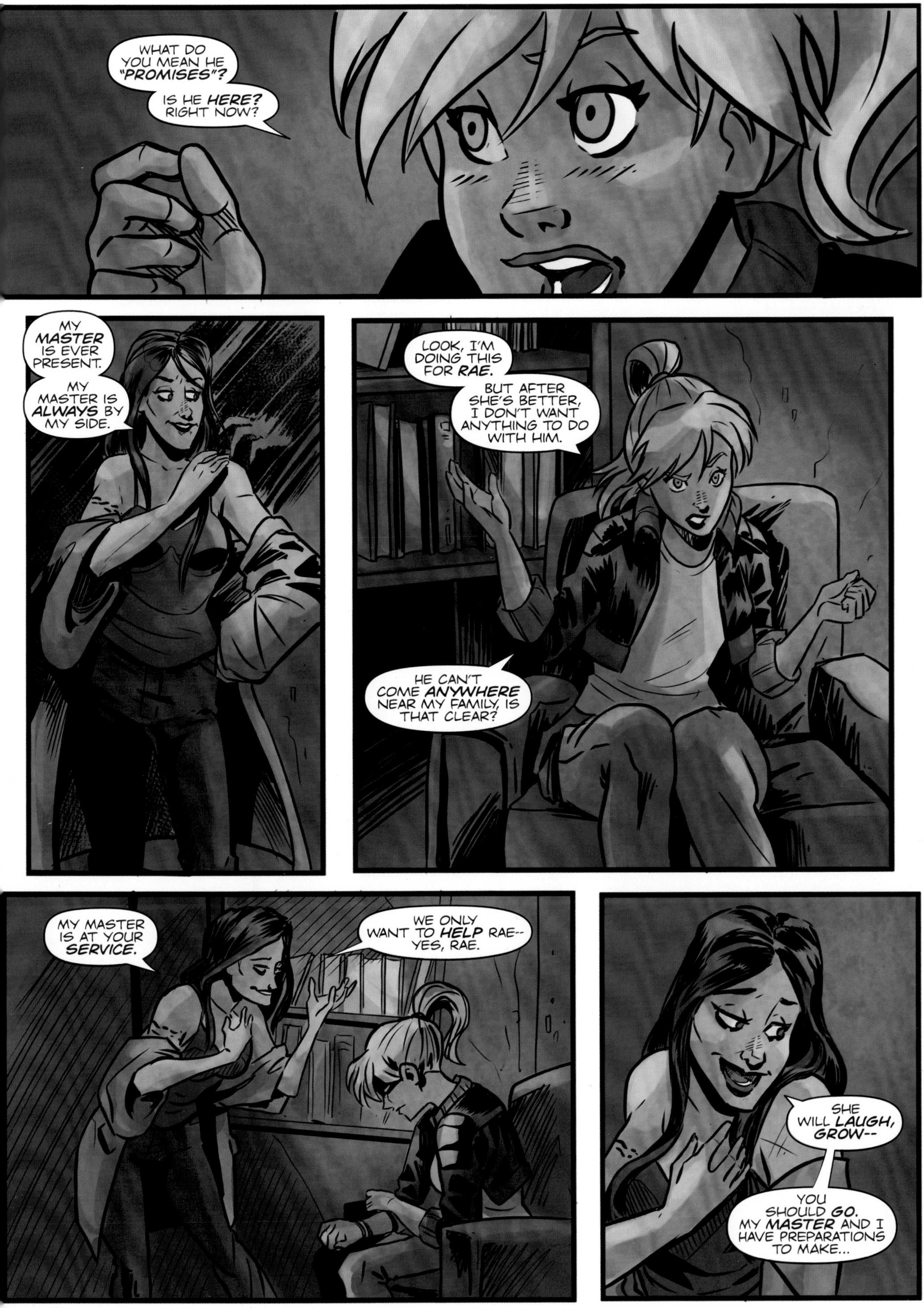
WHAT DO YOU MEAN HE "PROMISES"?
IS HE HERE? RIGHT NOW?
MY MASTER IS EVER PRESENT.
MY MASTER IS ALWAYS BY MY SIDE.
LOOK, I'M DOING THIS FOR RAE.
BUT AFTER SHE'S BETTER, I DON'T WANT ANYTHING TO DO WITH HIM.
HE CAN'T COME ANYWHERE NEAR MY FAMILY, IS THAT CLEAR?
MY MASTER IS AT YOUR SERVICE.
WE ONLY WANT TO HELP RAE-- YES, RAE.
SHE WILL LAUGH, GROW--
YOU SHOULD GO. MY MASTER AND I HAVE PREPARATIONS TO MAKE...

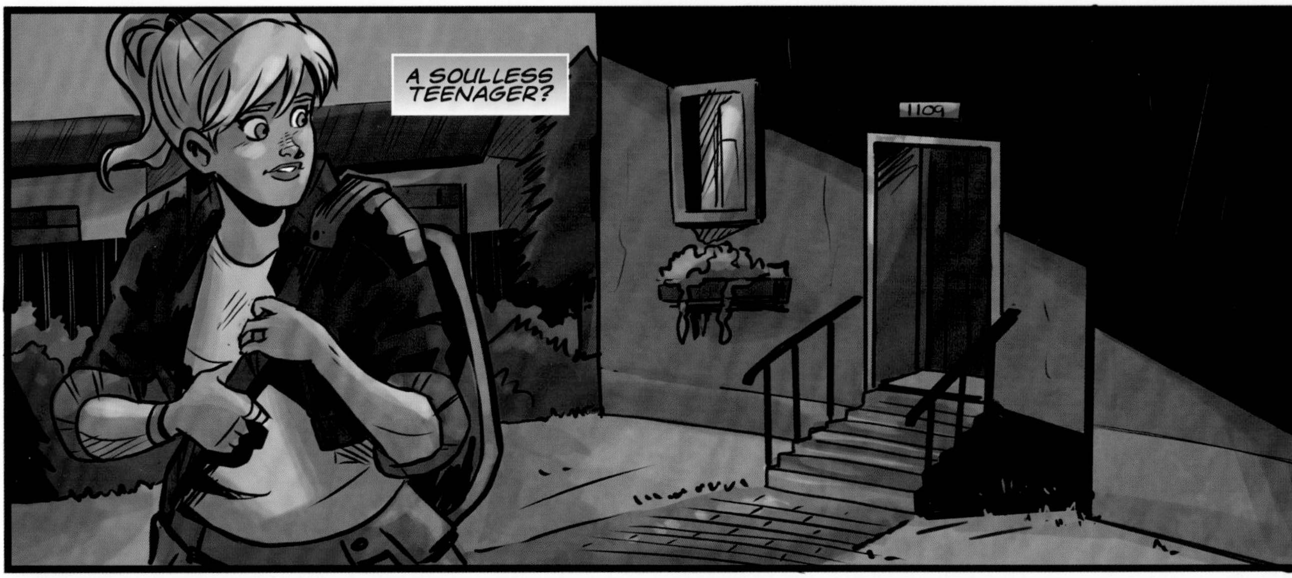
A SOULLESS TEENAGER?
1109

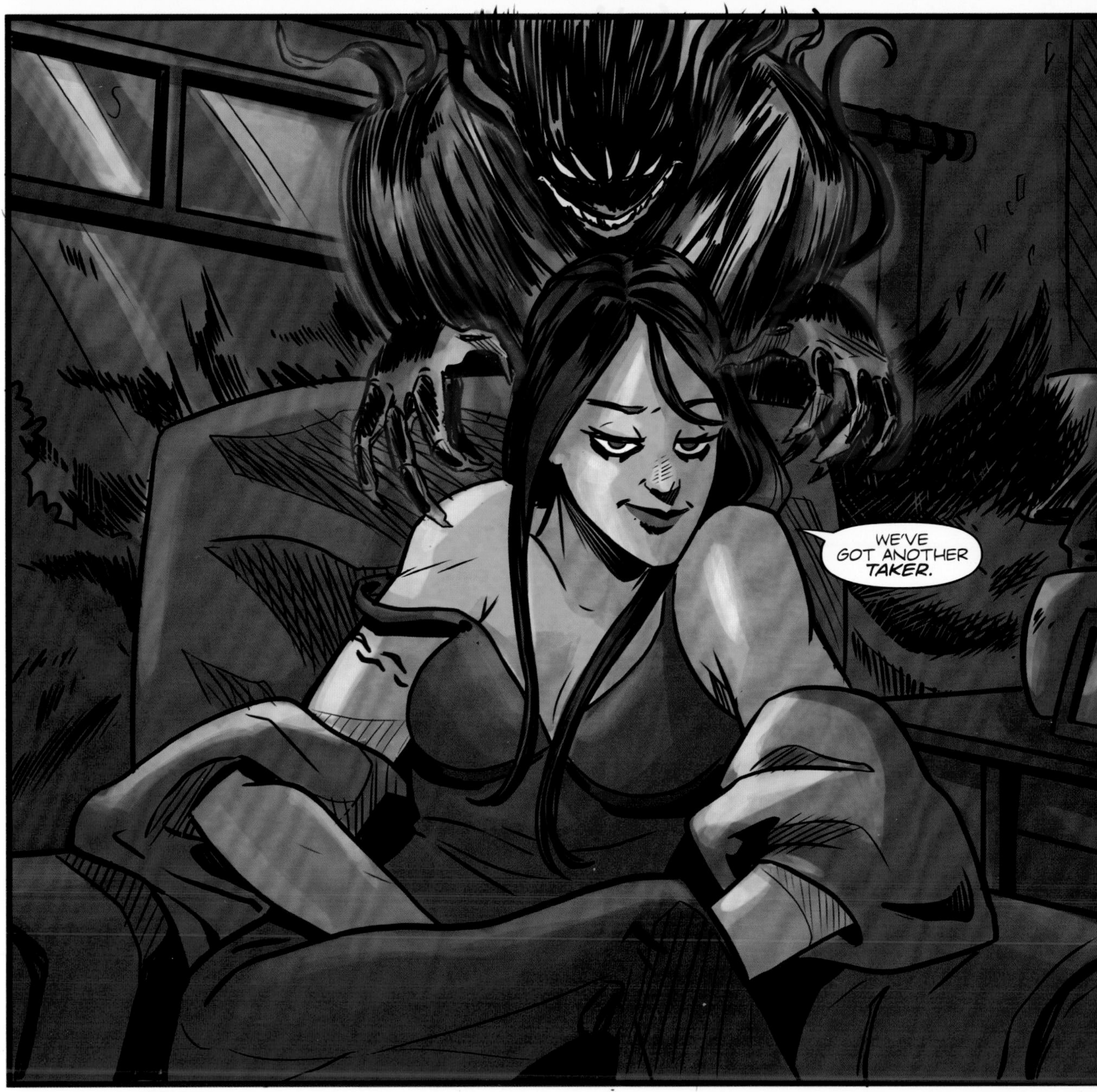
WE'VE GOT ANOTHER TAKER.

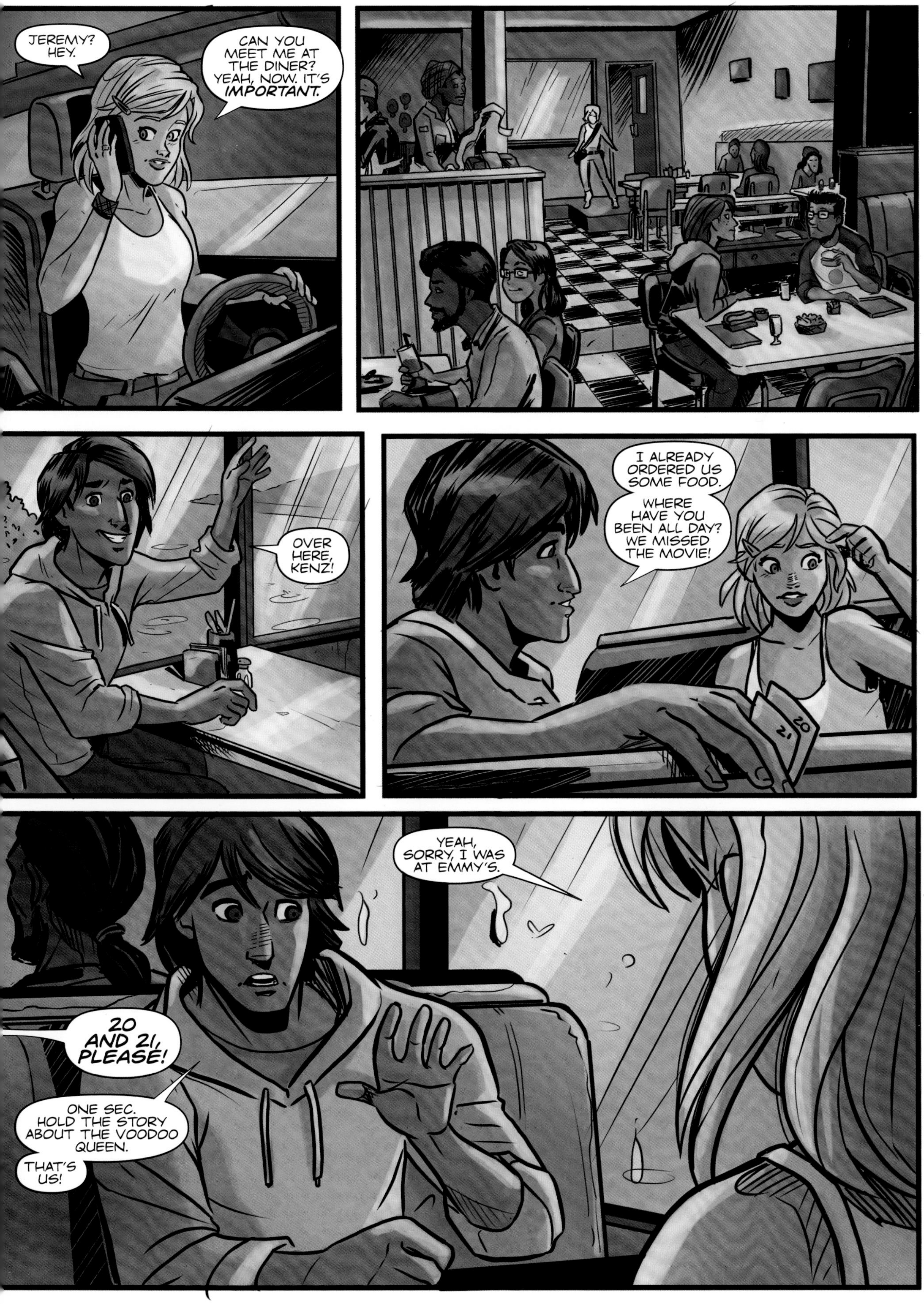
JEREMY? HEY.
CAN YOU MEET ME AT THE DINER? YEAH, NOW. IT'S *IMPORTANT*.
OVER HERE, KENZ!
I ALREADY ORDERED US SOME FOOD.
WHERE HAVE YOU BEEN ALL DAY? WE MISSED THE MOVIE!
20
21
YEAH, SORRY, I WAS AT EMMY'S.
20 AND 21, PLEASE!
ONE SEC. HOLD THE STORY ABOUT THE VOODOO QUEEN.
THAT'S US!

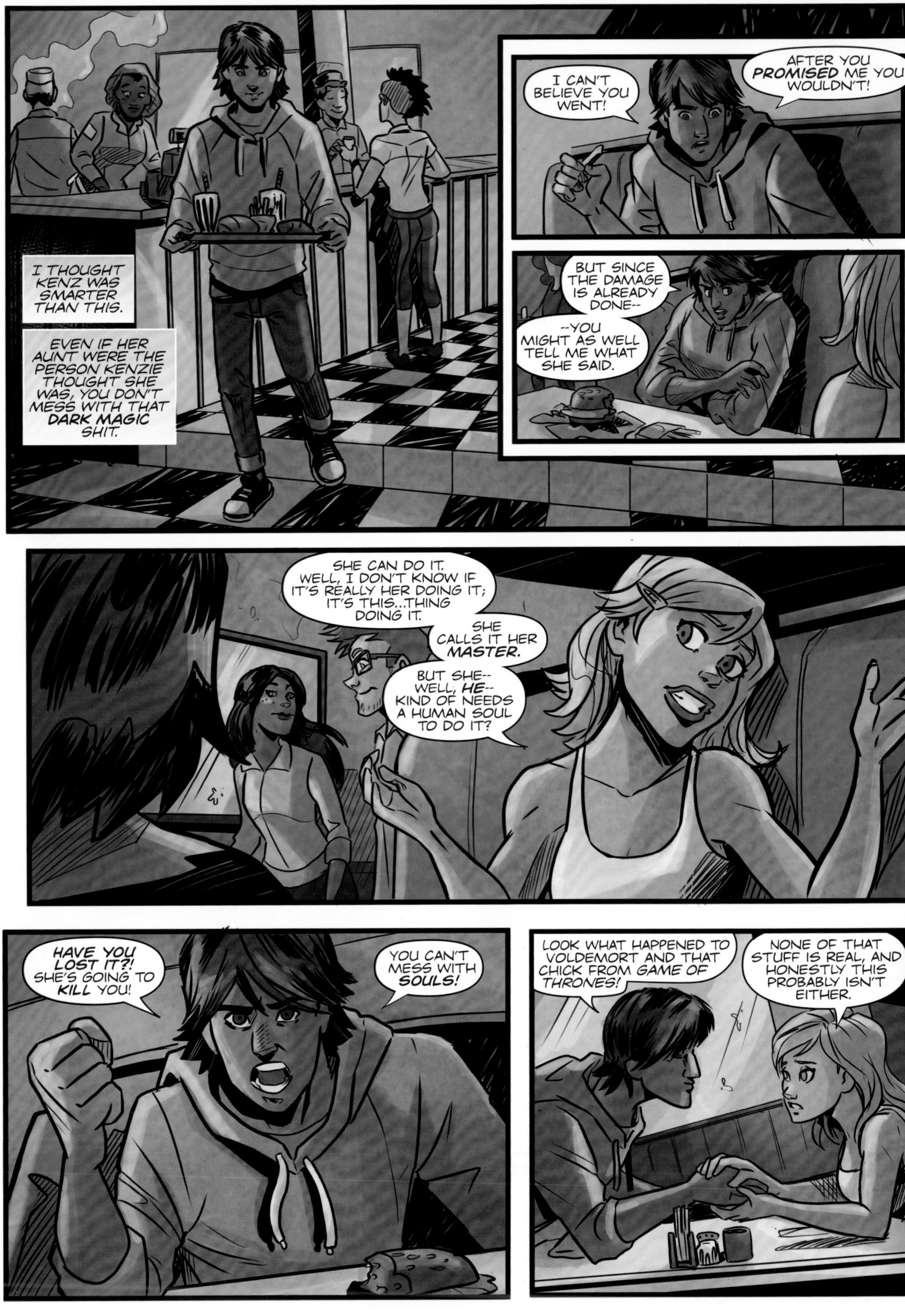
I THOUGHT KENZ WAS SMARTER THAN THIS.
EVEN IF HER AUNT WERE THE PERSON KENZIE THOUGHT SHE WAS, YOU DON'T MESS WITH THAT DARK MAGIC SHIT.
I CAN'T BELIEVE YOU WENT!
AFTER YOU PROMISED ME YOU WOULDN'T!
BUT SINCE THE DAMAGE IS ALREADY DONE--
--YOU MIGHT AS WELL TELL ME WHAT SHE SAID.
SHE CAN DO IT. WELL, I DON'T KNOW IF IT'S REALLY HER DOING IT; IT'S THIS...THING DOING IT.
SHE CALLS IT HER MASTER.
BUT SHE-- WELL, HE-- KIND OF NEEDS A HUMAN SOUL TO DO IT?
HAVE YOU LOST IT?! SHE'S GOING TO KILL YOU!
YOU CAN'T MESS WITH SOULS!
LOOK WHAT HAPPENED TO VOLDEMORT AND THAT CHICK FROM GAME OF THRONES!
NONE OF THAT STUFF IS REAL, AND HONESTLY THIS PROBABLY ISN'T EITHER.

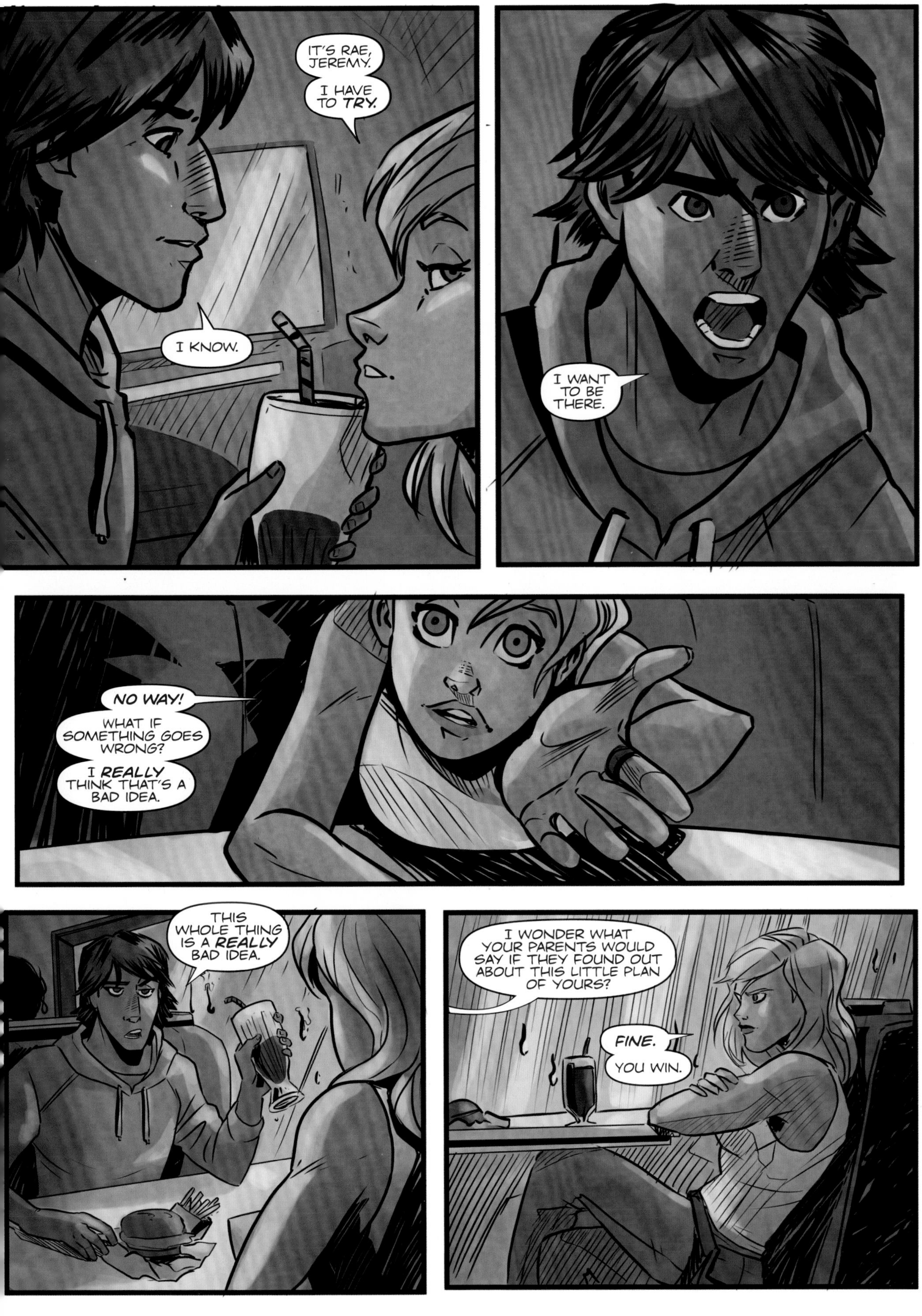
IT'S RAE, JEREMY.
I HAVE TO TRY.
I KNOW.
I WANT TO BE THERE.
NO WAY!
WHAT IF SOMETHING GOES WRONG?
I REALLY THINK THAT'S A BAD IDEA.
THIS WHOLE THING IS A REALLY BAD IDEA.
I WONDER WHAT YOUR PARENTS WOULD SAY IF THEY FOUND OUT ABOUT THIS LITTLE PLAN OF YOURS?
FINE.
YOU WIN.

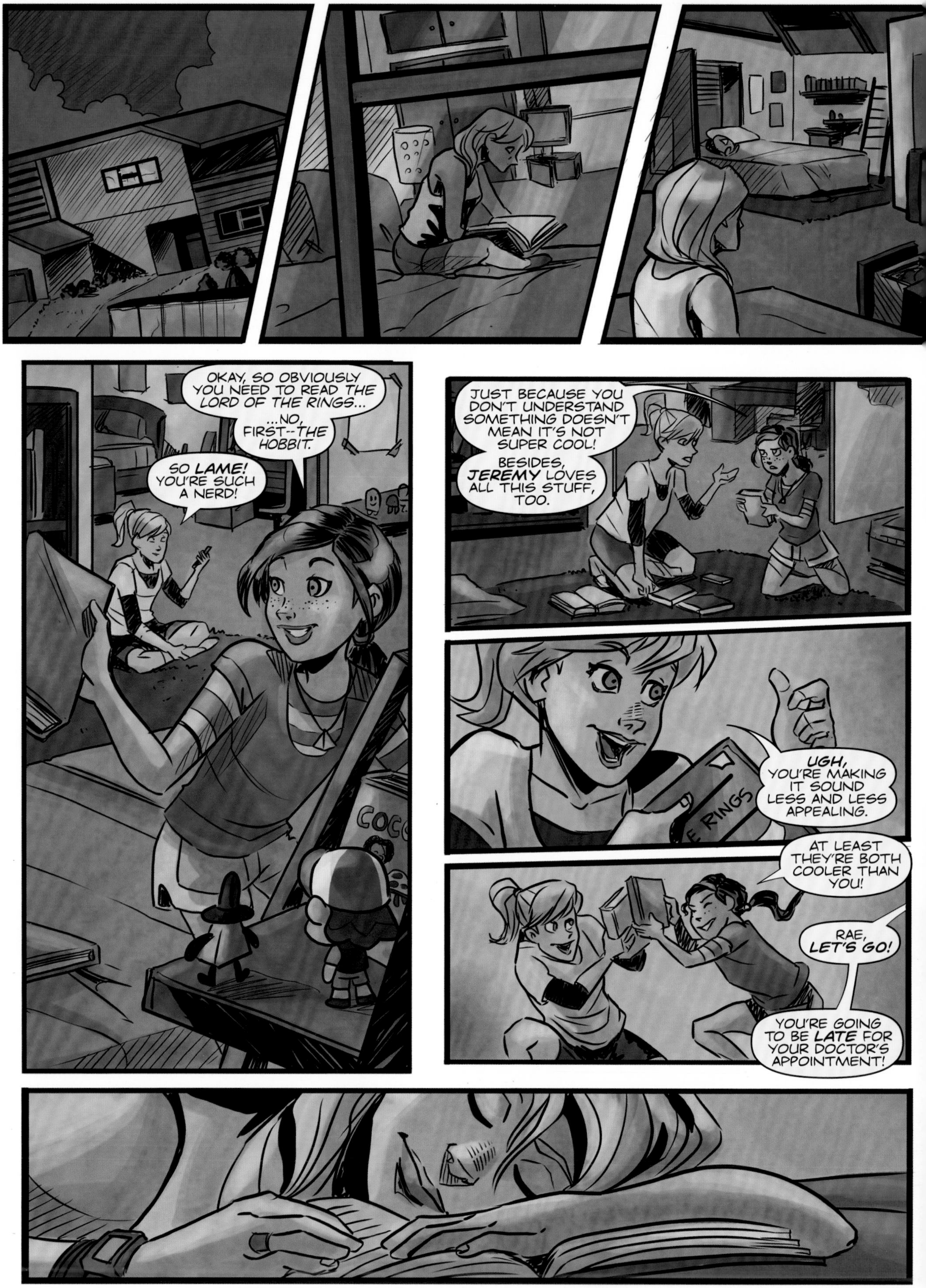

OKAY, SO OBVIOUSLY YOU NEED TO READ THE LORD OF THE RINGS...
...NO, FIRST--THE HOBBIT.
SO LAME! YOU'RE SUCH A NERD!
JUST BECAUSE YOU DON'T UNDERSTAND SOMETHING DOESN'T MEAN IT'S NOT SUPER COOL!
BESIDES, JEREMY LOVES ALL THIS STUFF, TOO.
UGH, YOU'RE MAKING IT SOUND LESS AND LESS APPEALING.
AT LEAST THEY'RE BOTH COOLER THAN YOU!
RAE, LET'S GO!
YOU'RE GOING TO BE LATE FOR YOUR DOCTOR'S APPOINTMENT!

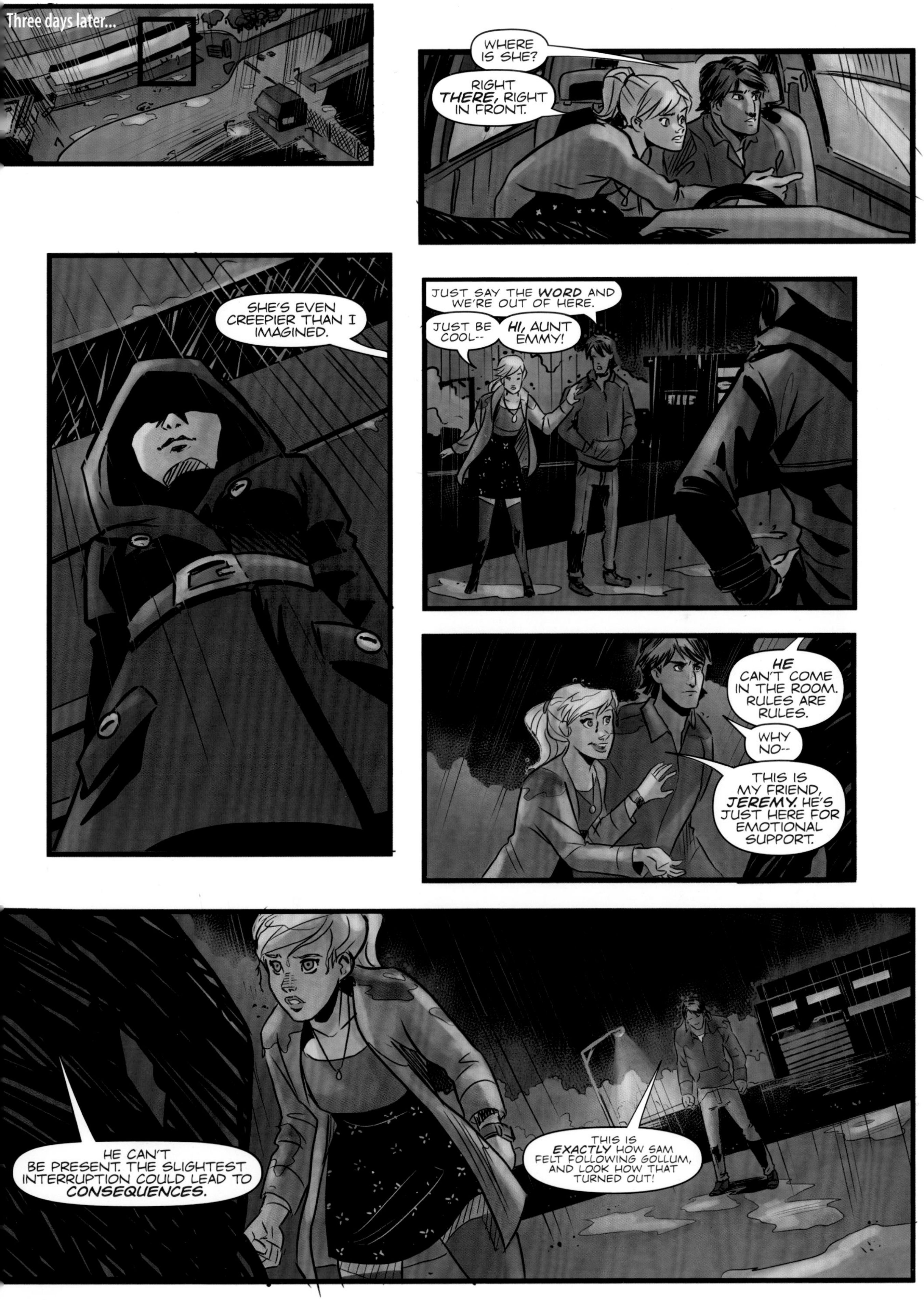
Three days later...
WHERE IS SHE?
RIGHT THERE, RIGHT IN FRONT.
SHE'S EVEN CREEPIER THAN I IMAGINED.
JUST SAY THE WORD AND WE'RE OUT OF HERE.
JUST BE COOL--
HI, AUNT EMMY!
HE CAN'T COME IN THE ROOM. RULES ARE RULES.
WHY NO--
THIS IS MY FRIEND, JEREMY. HE'S JUST HERE FOR EMOTIONAL SUPPORT.
HE CAN'T BE PRESENT. THE SLIGHTEST INTERRUPTION COULD LEAD TO CONSEQUENCES.
THIS IS EXACTLY HOW SAM FELT FOLLOWING GOLLUM, AND LOOK HOW THAT TURNED OUT!

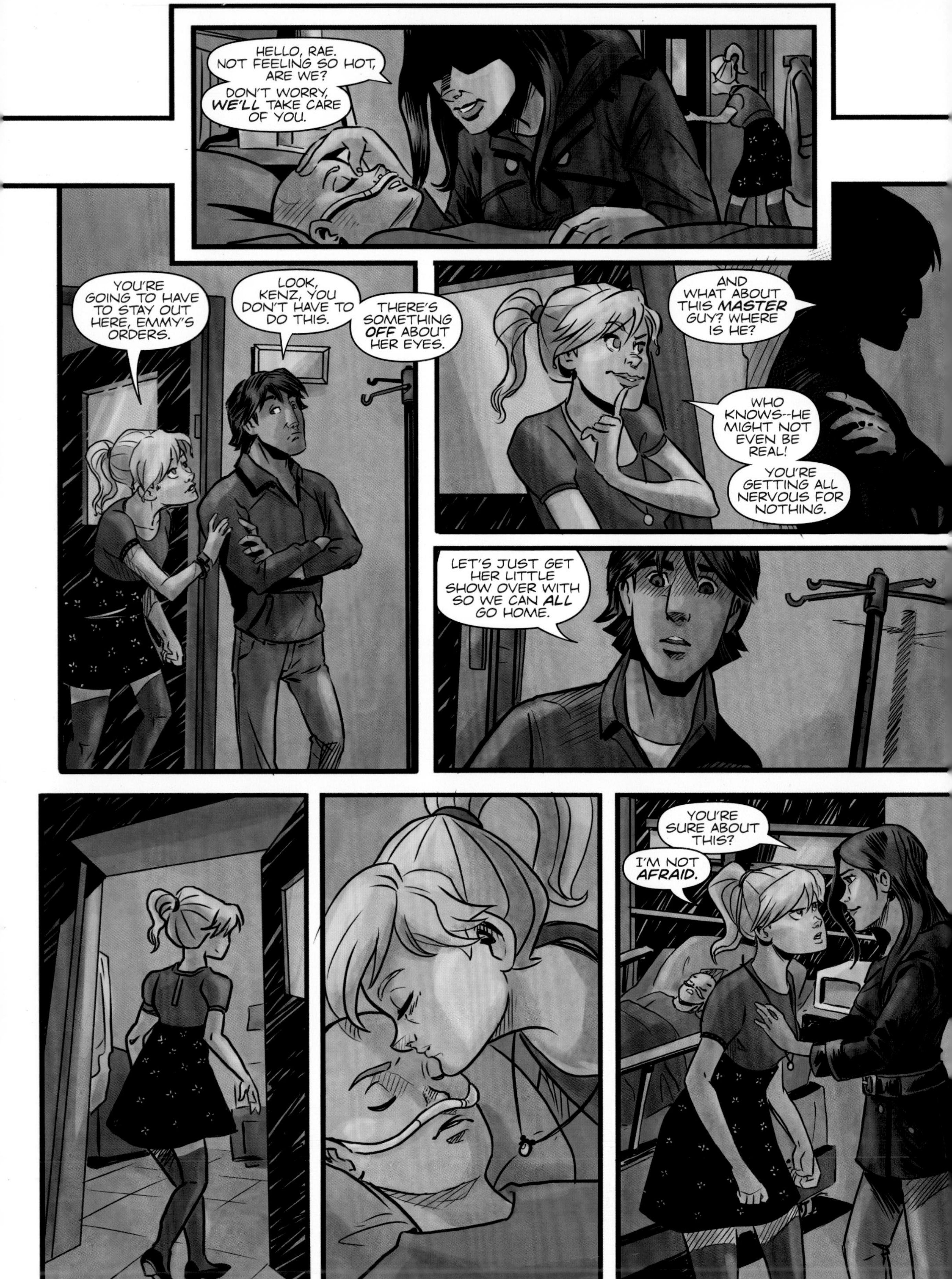
HELLO, RAE. NOT FEELING SO HOT, ARE WE?
DON'T WORRY, WE'LL TAKE CARE OF YOU.
YOU'RE GOING TO HAVE TO STAY OUT HERE, EMMY'S ORDERS.
LOOK, KENZ, YOU DON'T HAVE TO DO THIS.
THERE'S SOMETHING OFF ABOUT HER EYES.
AND WHAT ABOUT THIS MASTER GUY? WHERE IS HE?
WHO KNOWS--HE MIGHT NOT EVEN BE REAL!
YOU'RE GETTING ALL NERVOUS FOR NOTHING.
LET'S JUST GET HER LITTLE SHOW OVER WITH SO WE CAN ALL GO HOME.
YOU'RE SURE ABOUT THIS?
I'M NOT AFRAID.

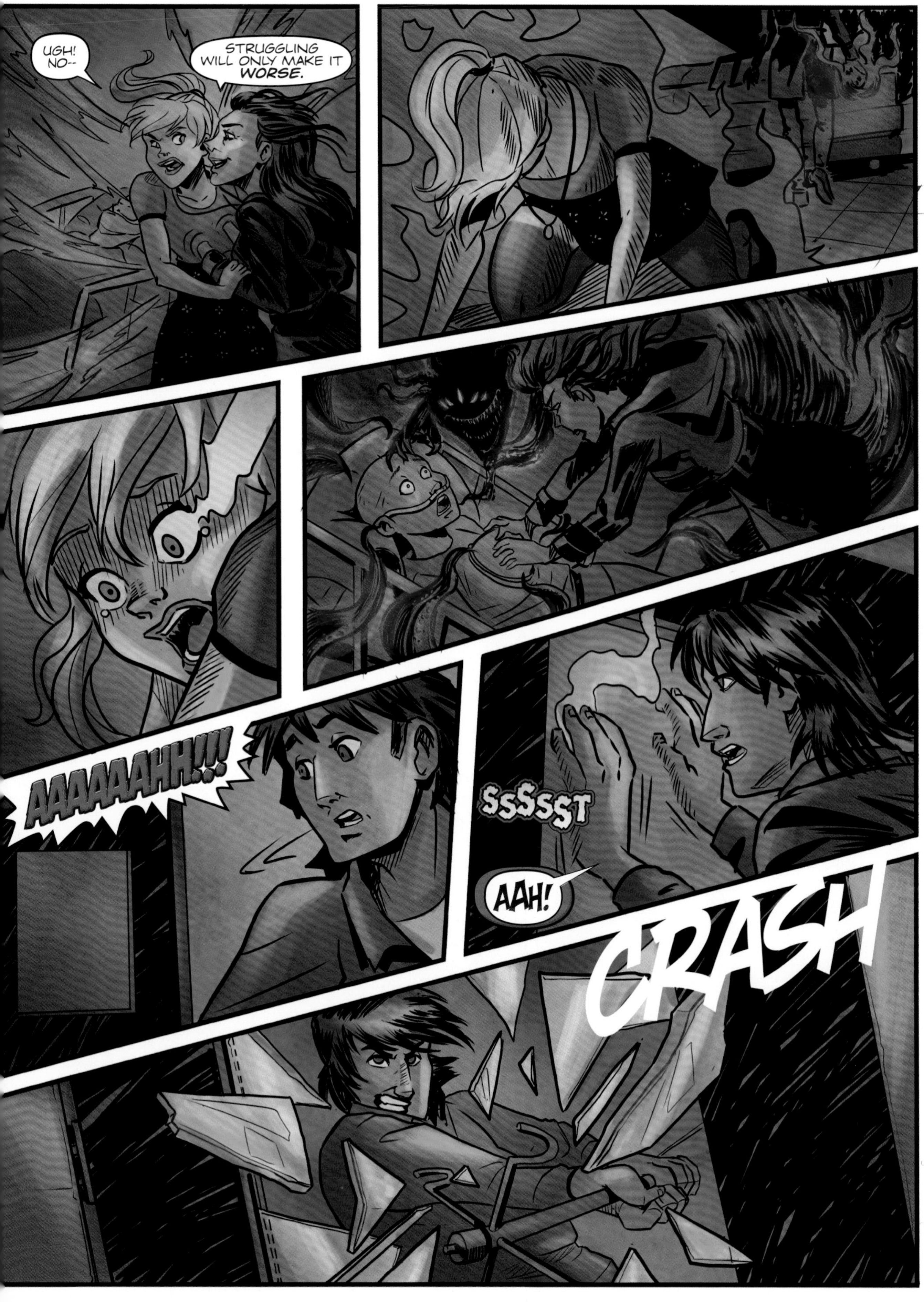
UGH! NO--
STRUGGLING WILL ONLY MAKE IT WORSE.
AAAAAAHH!!!
SSSSST
AAH!
CRASH

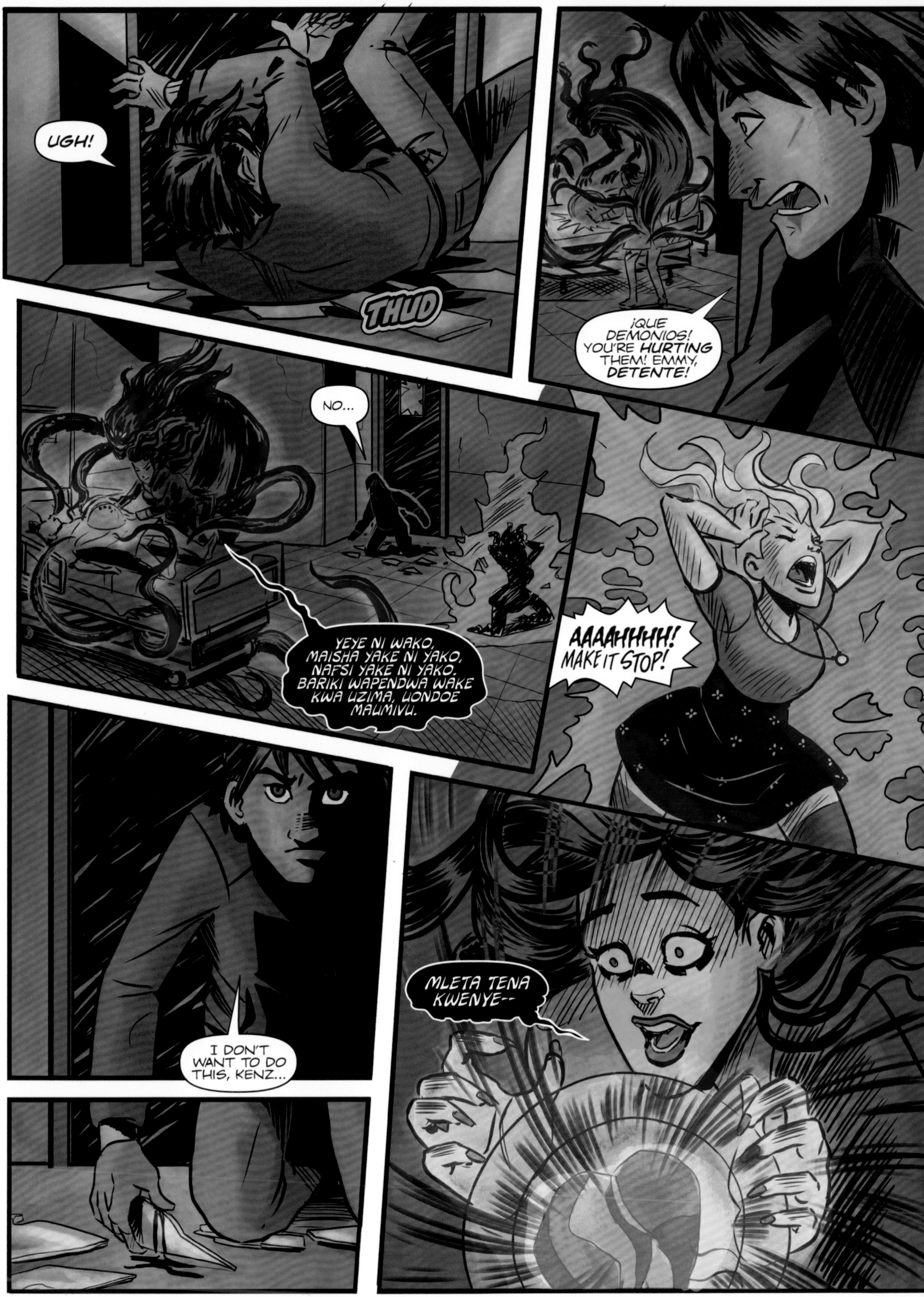

UGH!
THUD
¡QUE DEMONIOS! YOU'RE **HURTING** THEM! EMMY, **DETENTE!**
NO...
YEYE NI WAKO, MAISHA YAKE NI YAKO, NAFSI YAKE NI YAKO. BARIKI WAPENDWA WAKE KWA UZIMA, UONDOE MAUMIVU.
AAAAHHHH! MAKE IT STOP!
I DON'T WANT TO DO THIS, KENZ...
MLETA TENA KWENYE--

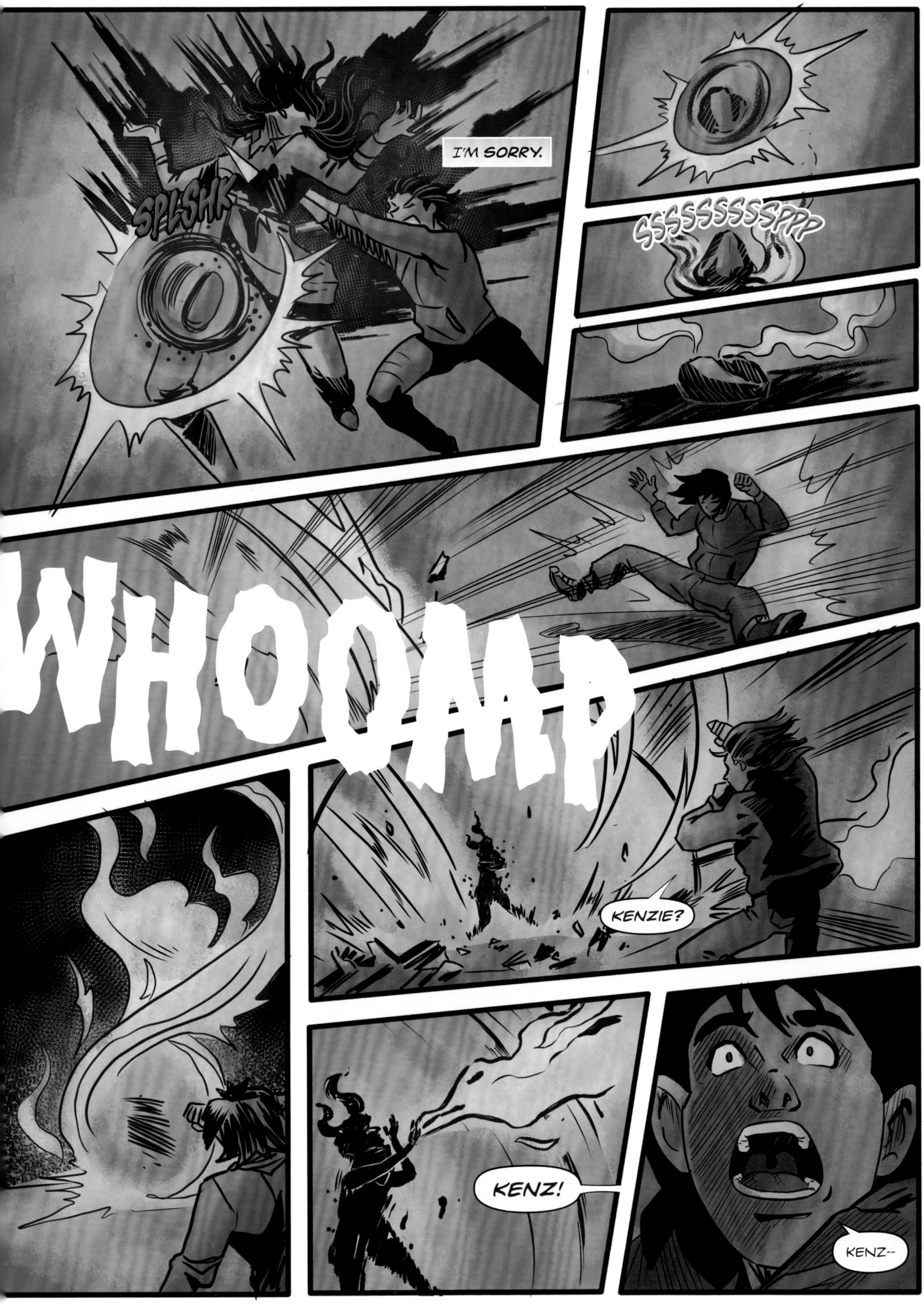
I'M SORRY.
SPLSHK
SSSSSSSSSSPPP
WHOOMP
KENZIE?
KENZ!
KENZ--

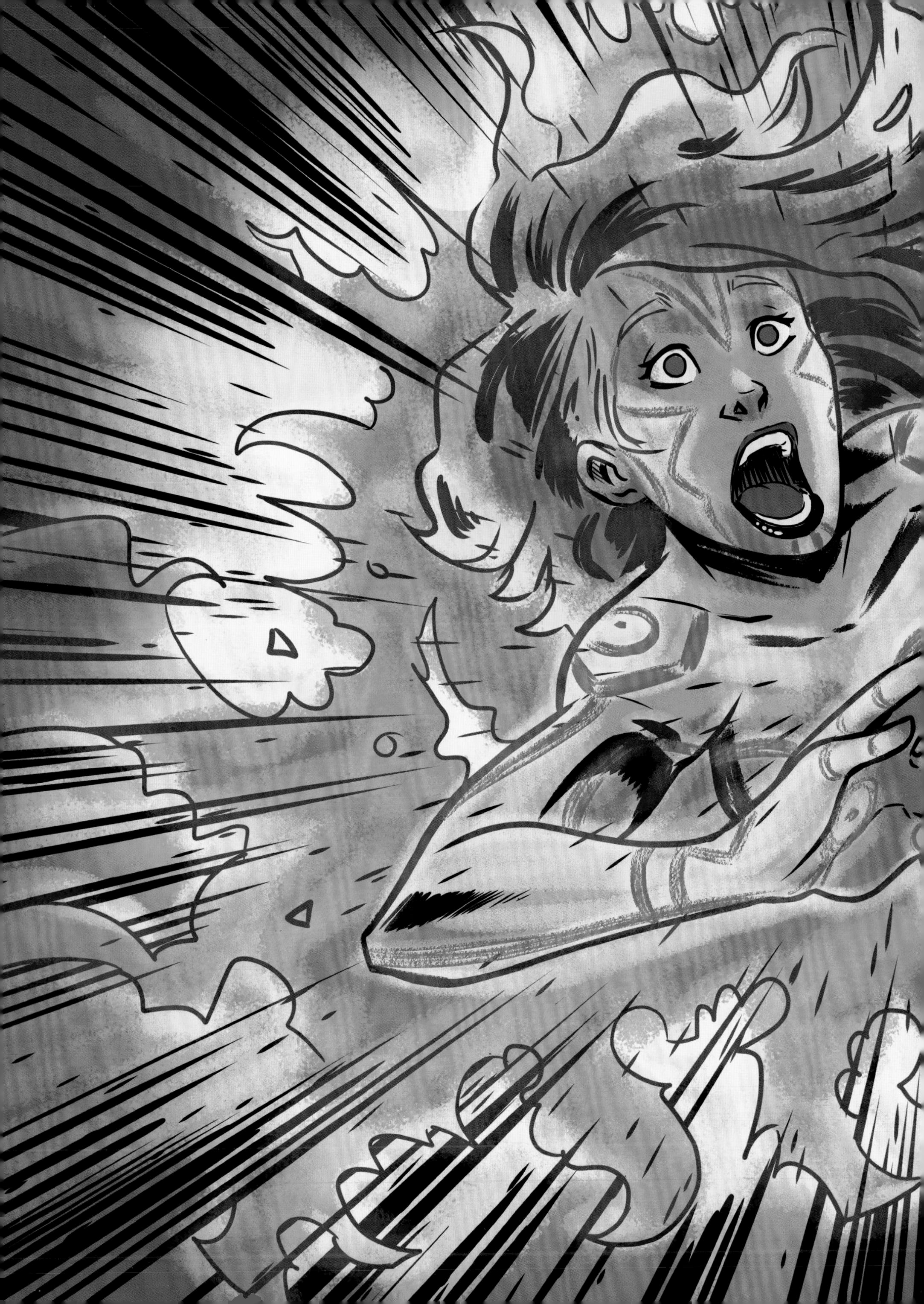

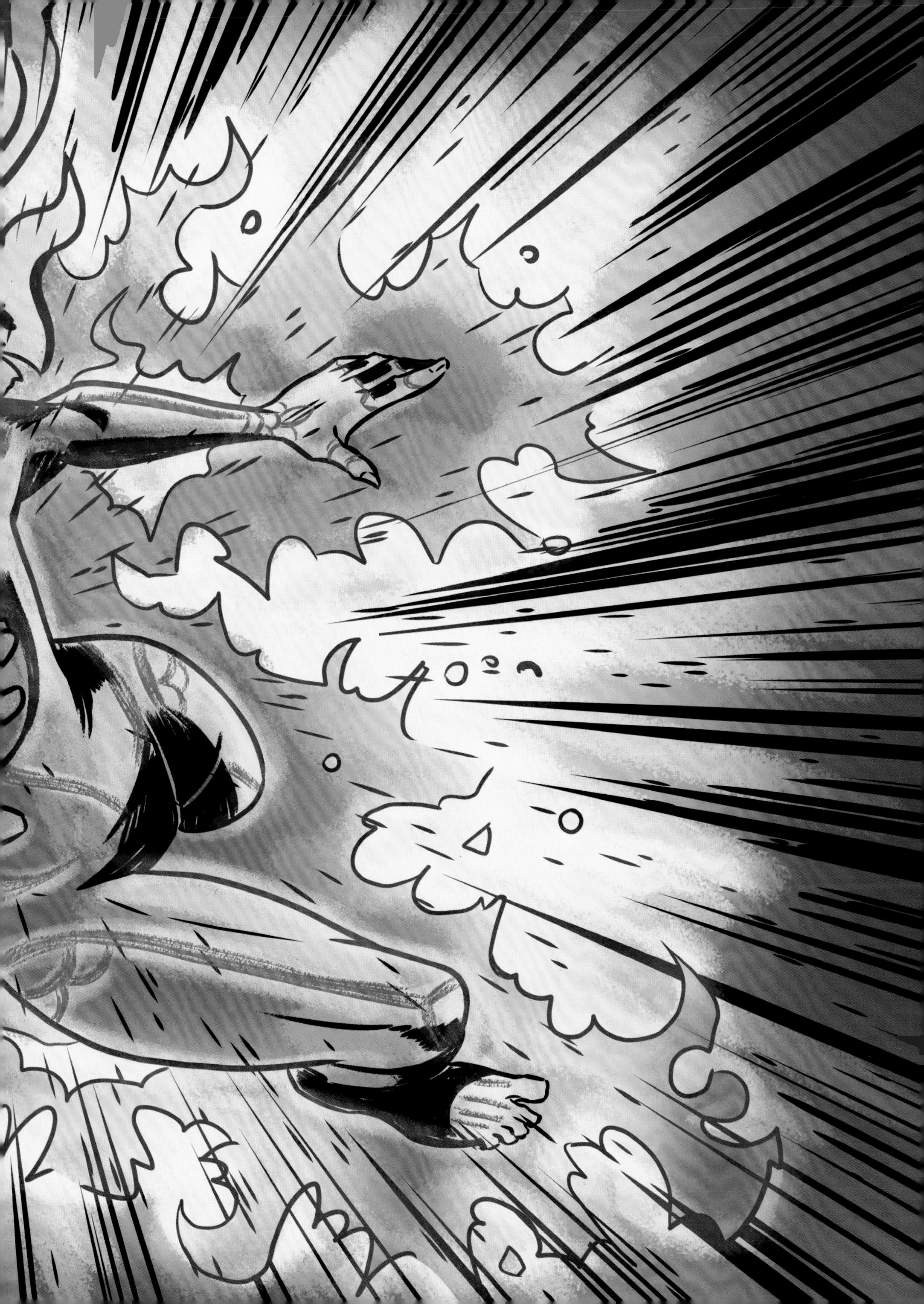

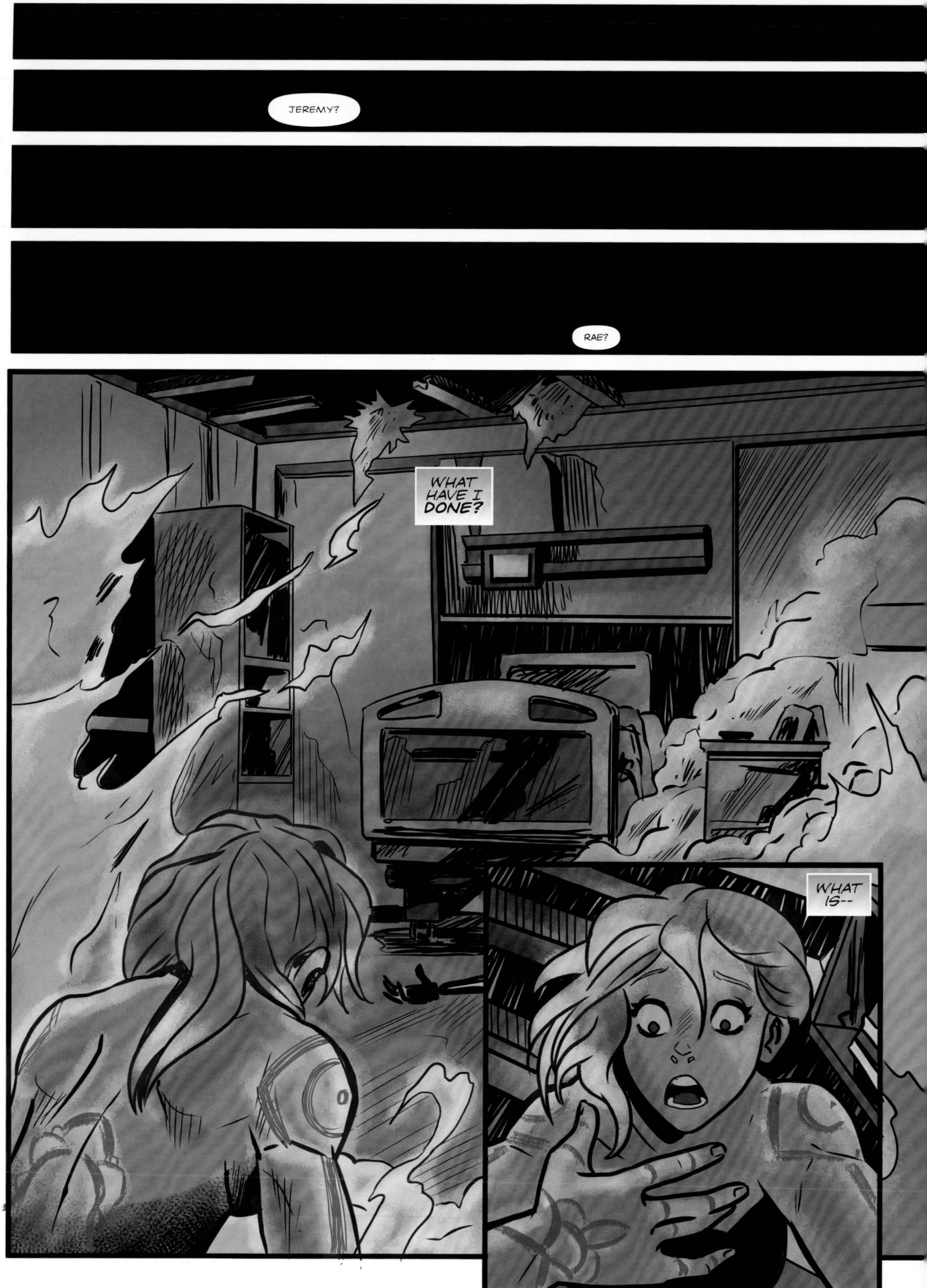
JEREMY?
RAE?
WHAT HAVE I DONE?
WHAT IS--

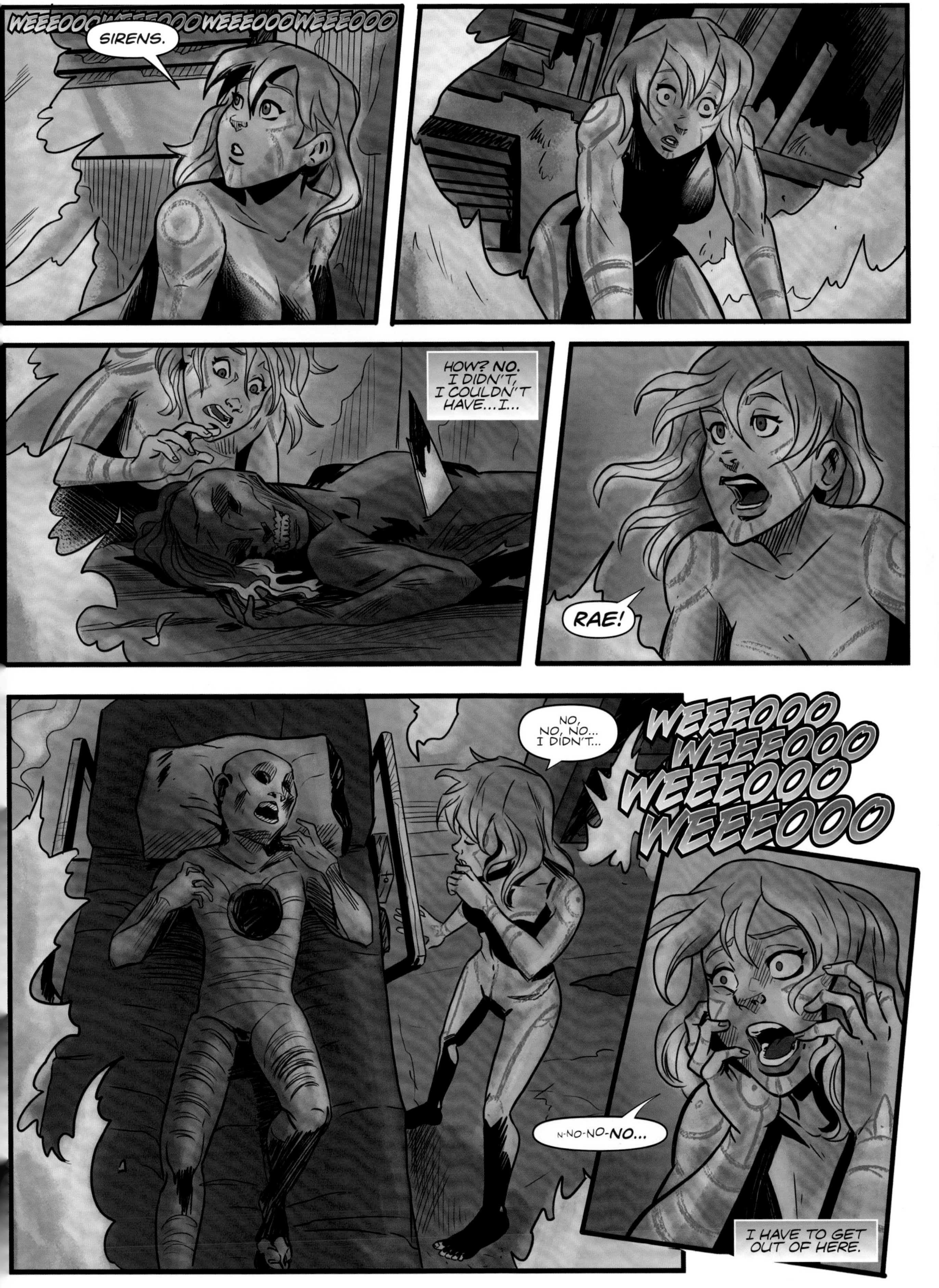
WEEEOOOWEEEOOOWEEEOOOWEEEOOO
SIRENS.
HOW? NO. I DIDN'T, I COULDN'T HAVE... I...
RAE!
NO, NO, NO... I DIDN'T...
WEEEOOO WEEEOOO WEEEOOO WEEEOOO
N-NO-NO-NO...
I HAVE TO GET OUT OF HERE.

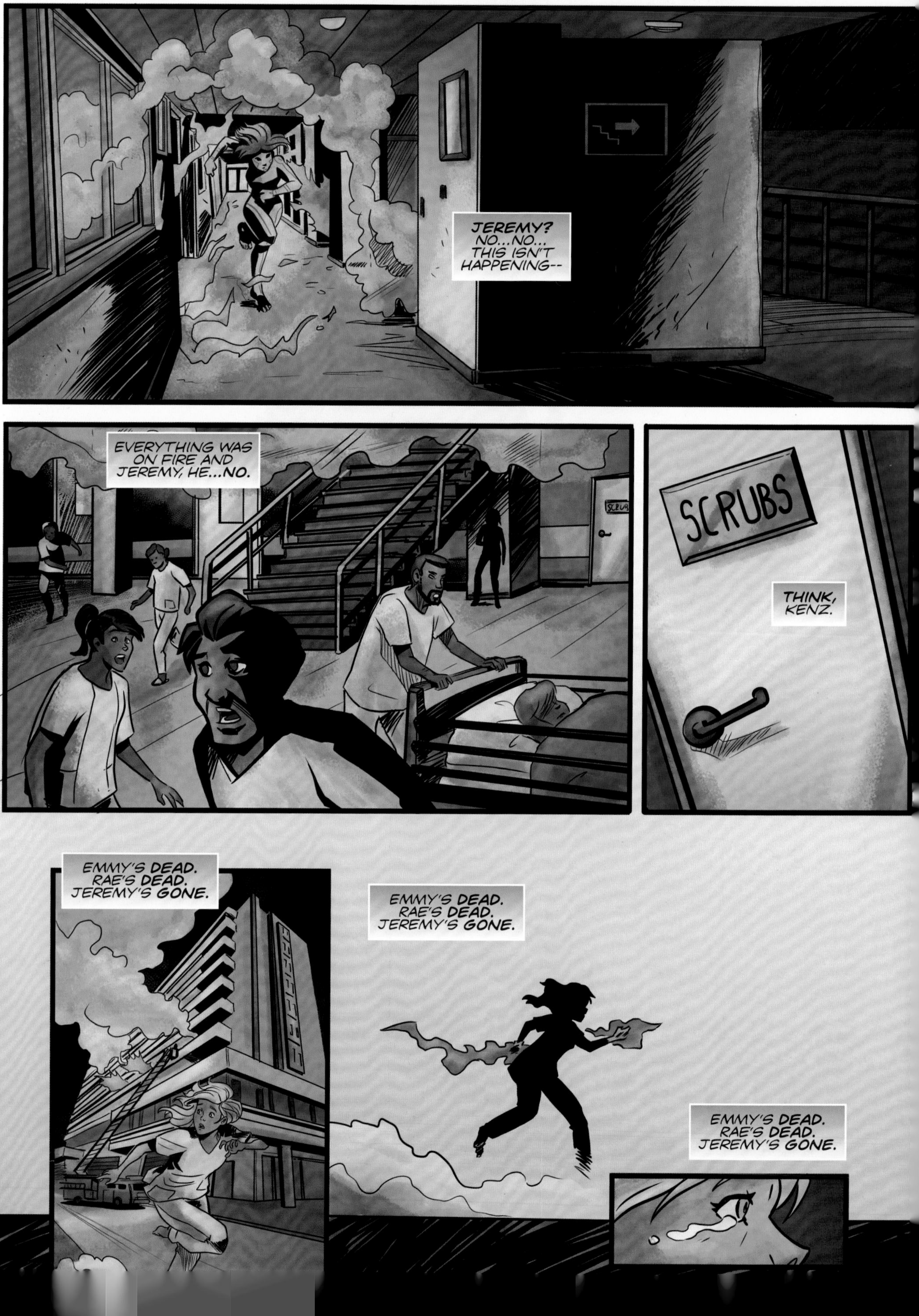
JEREMY? NO...NO... THIS ISN'T HAPPENING--
EVERYTHING WAS ON FIRE AND JEREMY, HE...NO.
SCRUBS
SCRUBS
THINK, KENZ.
EMMY'S DEAD. RAE'S DEAD. JEREMY'S GONE.
EMMY'S DEAD. RAE'S DEAD. JEREMY'S GONE.
EMMY'S DEAD. RAE'S DEAD. JEREMY'S GONE.

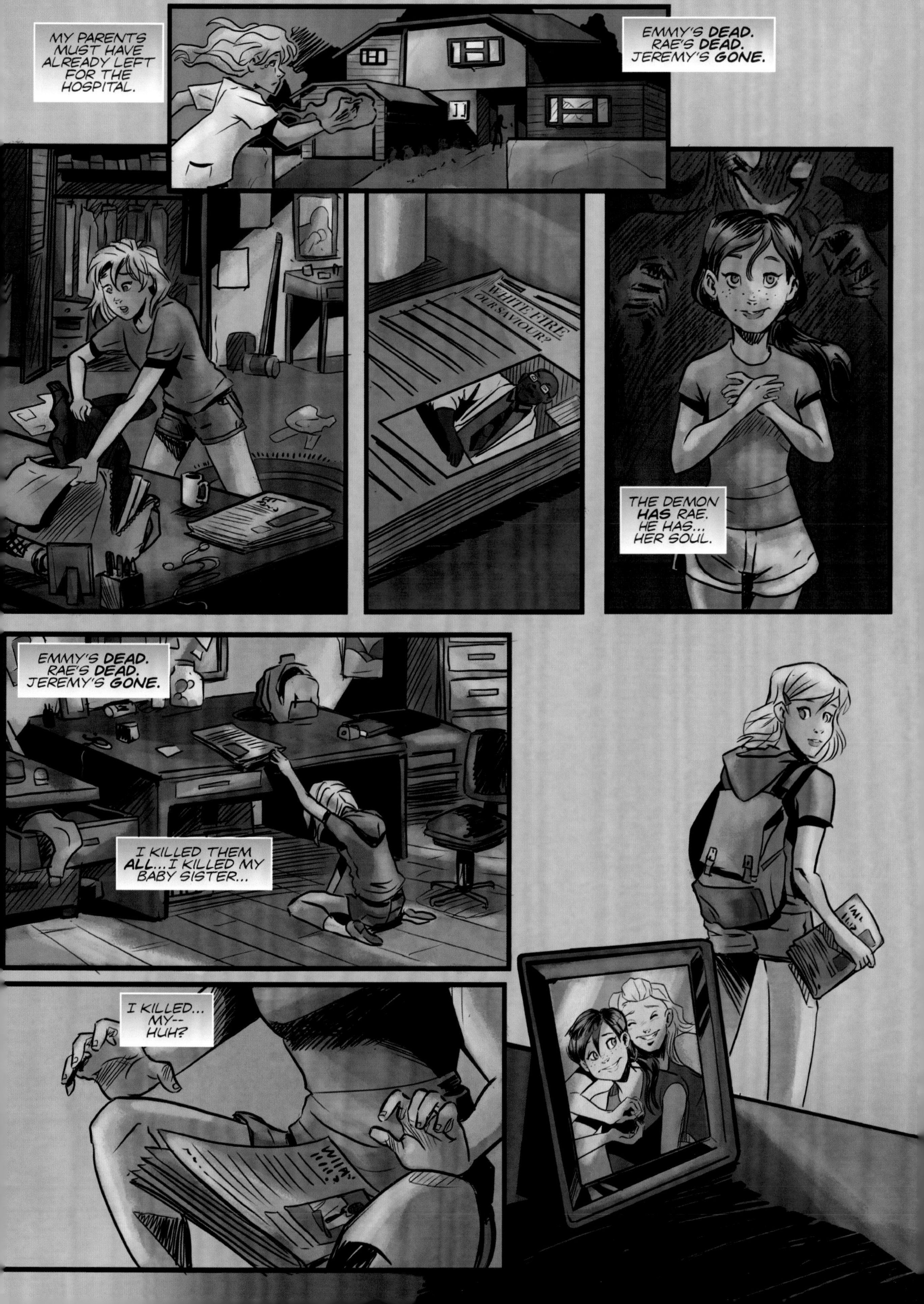

MY PARENTS MUST HAVE ALREADY LEFT FOR THE HOSPITAL.
EMMY'S DEAD. RAE'S DEAD. JEREMY'S GONE.
WHITE FIRE OUR SAVIOUR?
THE DEMON HAS RAE. HE HAS... HER SOUL.
EMMY'S DEAD. RAE'S DEAD. JEREMY'S GONE.
I KILLED THEM ALL... I KILLED MY BABY SISTER...
I KILLED... MY-- HUH?

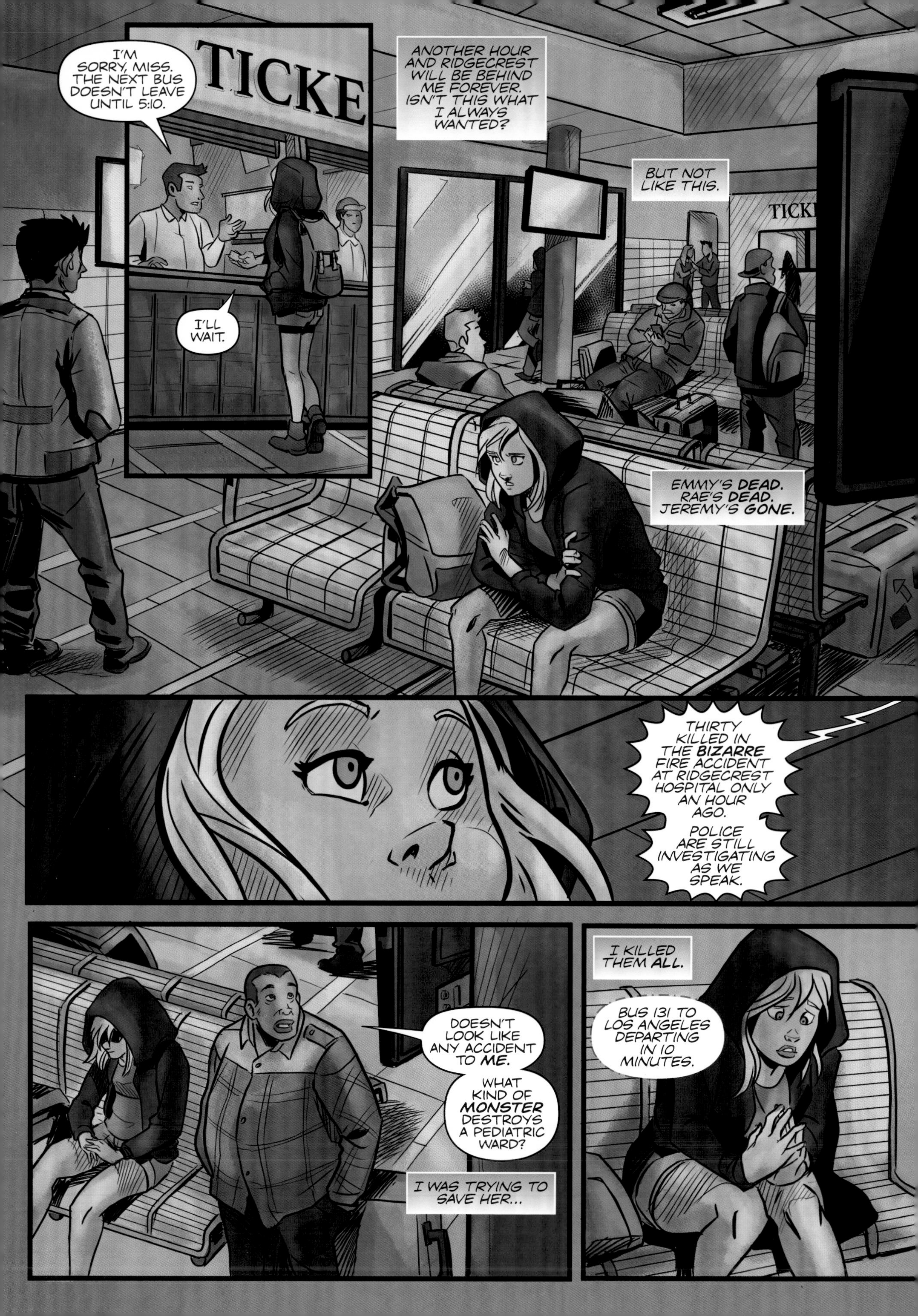
TICKE
I'M SORRY, MISS. THE NEXT BUS DOESN'T LEAVE UNTIL 5:10.
I'LL WAIT.
ANOTHER HOUR AND RIDGECREST WILL BE BEHIND ME FOREVER. ISN'T THIS WHAT I ALWAYS WANTED?
BUT NOT LIKE THIS.
EMMY'S DEAD. RAE'S DEAD. JEREMY'S GONE.
THIRTY KILLED IN THE BIZARRE FIRE ACCIDENT AT RIDGECREST HOSPITAL ONLY AN HOUR AGO.
POLICE ARE STILL INVESTIGATING AS WE SPEAK.
DOESN'T LOOK LIKE ANY ACCIDENT TO ME.
WHAT KIND OF MONSTER DESTROYS A PEDIATRIC WARD?
I WAS TRYING TO SAVE HER...
I KILLED THEM ALL.
BUS 131 TO LOS ANGELES DEPARTING IN 10 MINUTES.

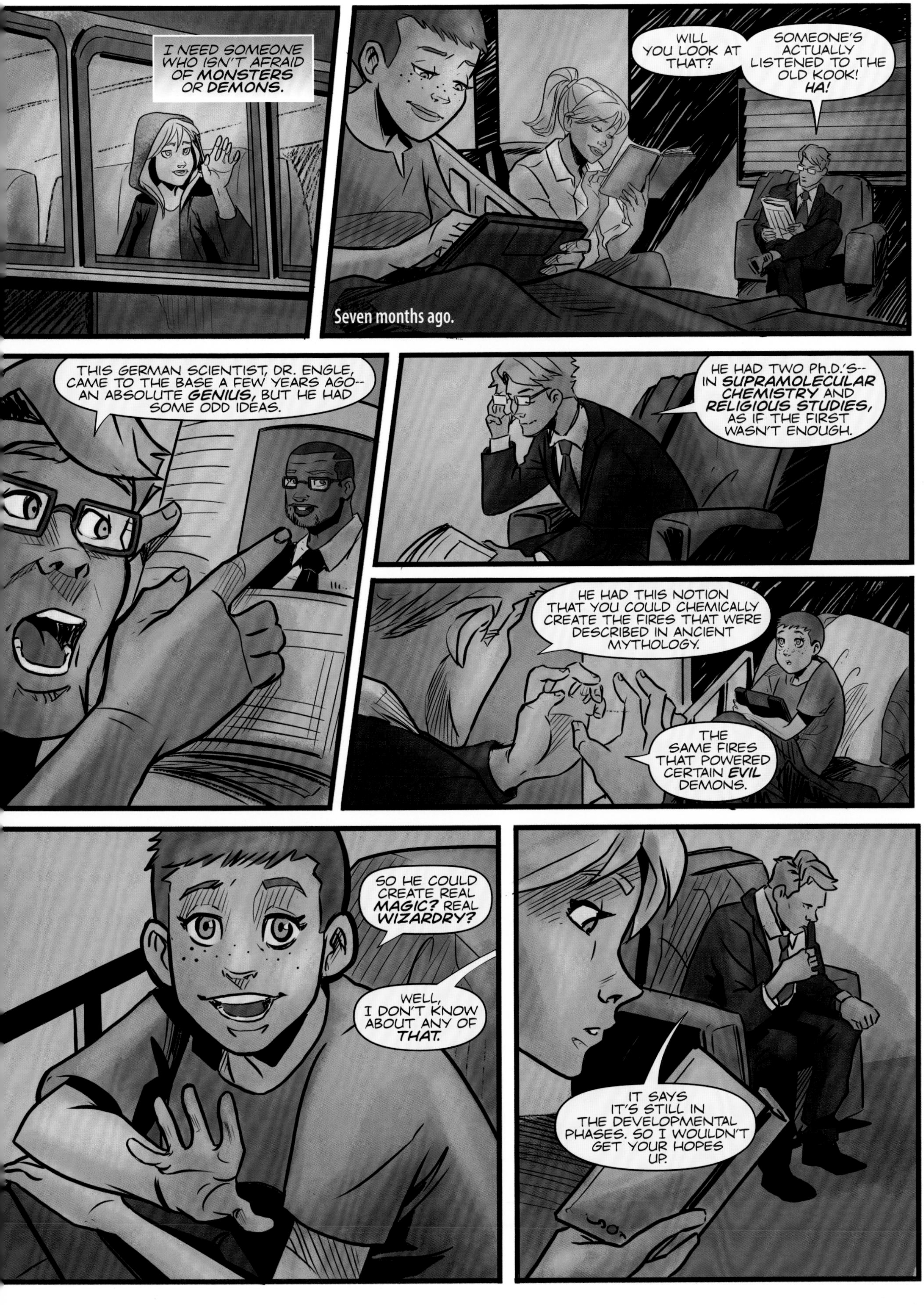
I NEED SOMEONE WHO ISN'T AFRAID OF MONSTERS OR DEMONS.
Seven months ago.
WILL YOU LOOK AT THAT?
SOMEONE'S ACTUALLY LISTENED TO THE OLD KOOK! HA!
THIS GERMAN SCIENTIST, DR. ENGLE, CAME TO THE BASE A FEW YEARS AGO-- AN ABSOLUTE GENIUS, BUT HE HAD SOME ODD IDEAS.
HE HAD TWO Ph.D.'S-- IN SUPRAMOLECULAR CHEMISTRY AND RELIGIOUS STUDIES, AS IF THE FIRST WASN'T ENOUGH.
HE HAD THIS NOTION THAT YOU COULD CHEMICALLY CREATE THE FIRES THAT WERE DESCRIBED IN ANCIENT MYTHOLOGY.
THE SAME FIRES THAT POWERED CERTAIN EVIL DEMONS.
SO HE COULD CREATE REAL MAGIC? REAL WIZARDRY?
WELL, I DON'T KNOW ABOUT ANY OF THAT.
IT SAYS IT'S STILL IN THE DEVELOPMENTAL PHASES. SO I WOULDN'T GET YOUR HOPES UP.

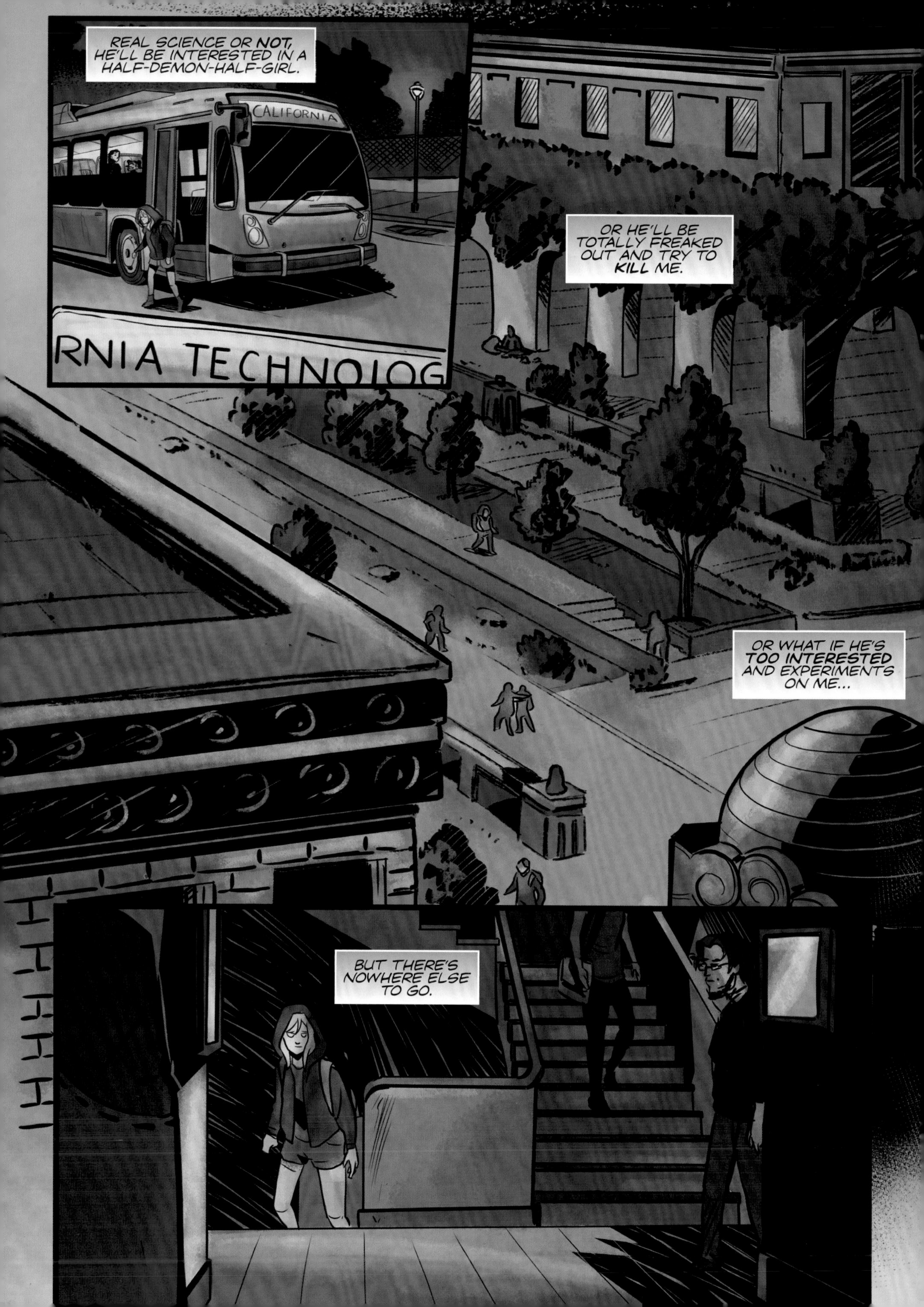
REAL SCIENCE OR NOT, HE'LL BE INTERESTED IN A HALF-DEMON-HALF-GIRL.
CALIFORNIA
RNIA TECHNOLOG
OR HE'LL BE TOTALLY FREAKED OUT AND TRY TO KILL ME.
OR WHAT IF HE'S TOO INTERESTED AND EXPERIMENTS ON ME...
BUT THERE'S NOWHERE ELSE TO GO.

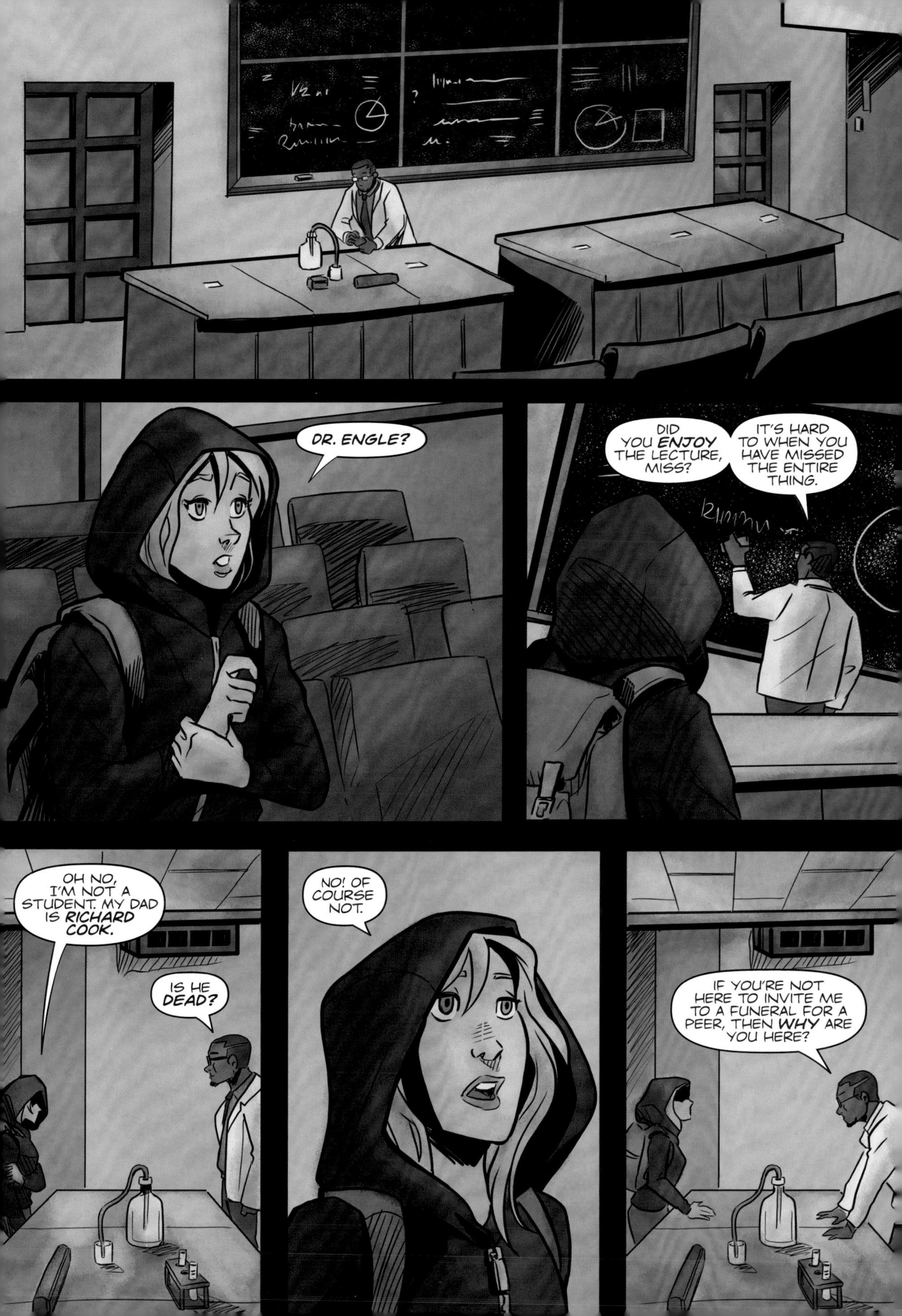
DR. ENGLE?
DID YOU ENJOY THE LECTURE, MISS?
IT'S HARD TO WHEN YOU HAVE MISSED THE ENTIRE THING.
OH NO, I'M NOT A STUDENT. MY DAD IS RICHARD COOK.
IS HE DEAD?
NO! OF COURSE NOT.
IF YOU'RE NOT HERE TO INVITE ME TO A FUNERAL FOR A PEER, THEN WHY ARE YOU HERE?

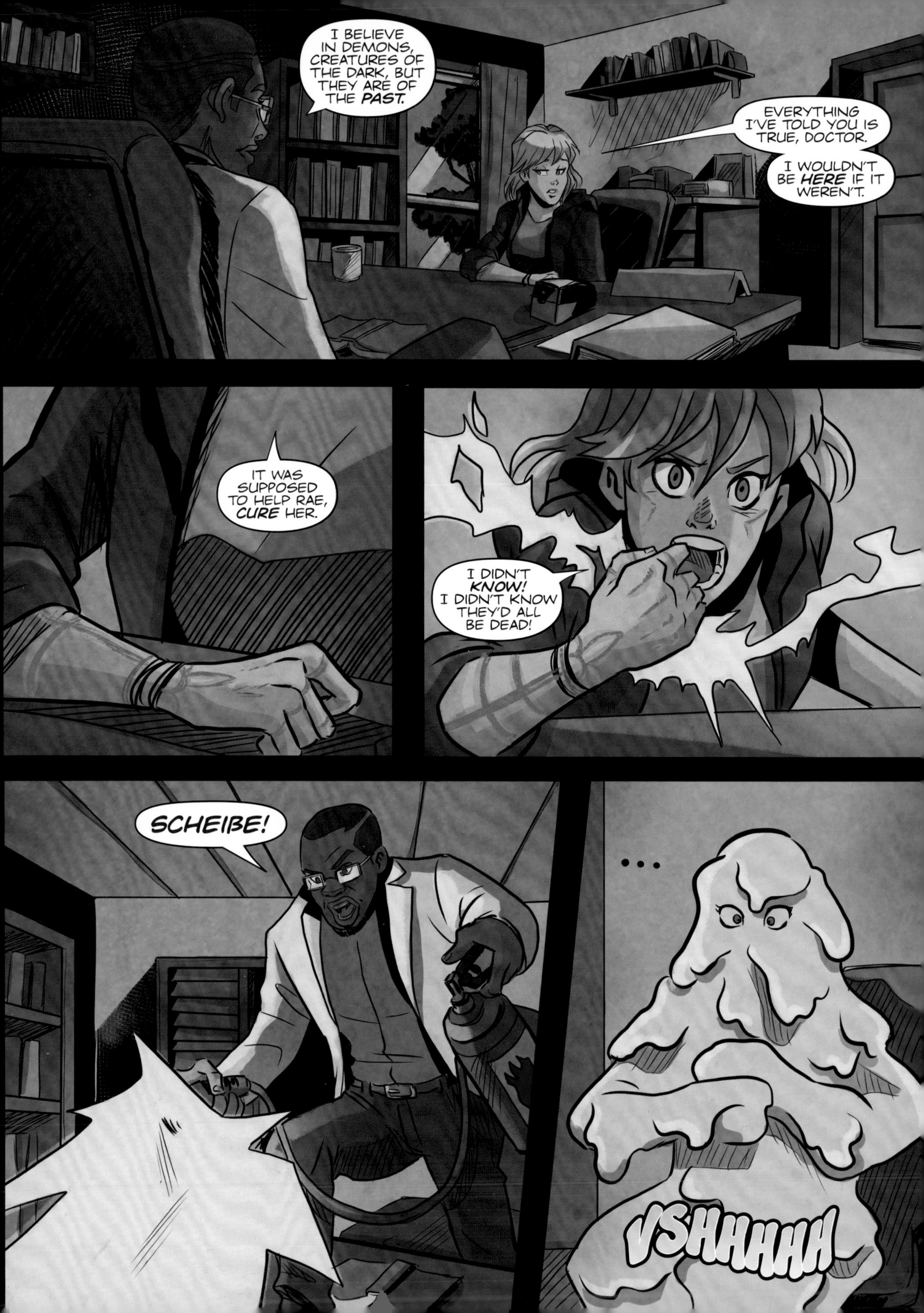
I BELIEVE IN DEMONS, CREATURES OF THE DARK, BUT THEY ARE OF THE *PAST.*
EVERYTHING I'VE TOLD YOU IS TRUE, DOCTOR.
I WOULDN'T BE *HERE* IF IT WEREN'T.
IT WAS SUPPOSED TO HELP RAE, *CURE* HER.
I DIDN'T *KNOW!* I DIDN'T KNOW THEY'D ALL BE DEAD!
SCHEIßE!
...
VSHHHHH

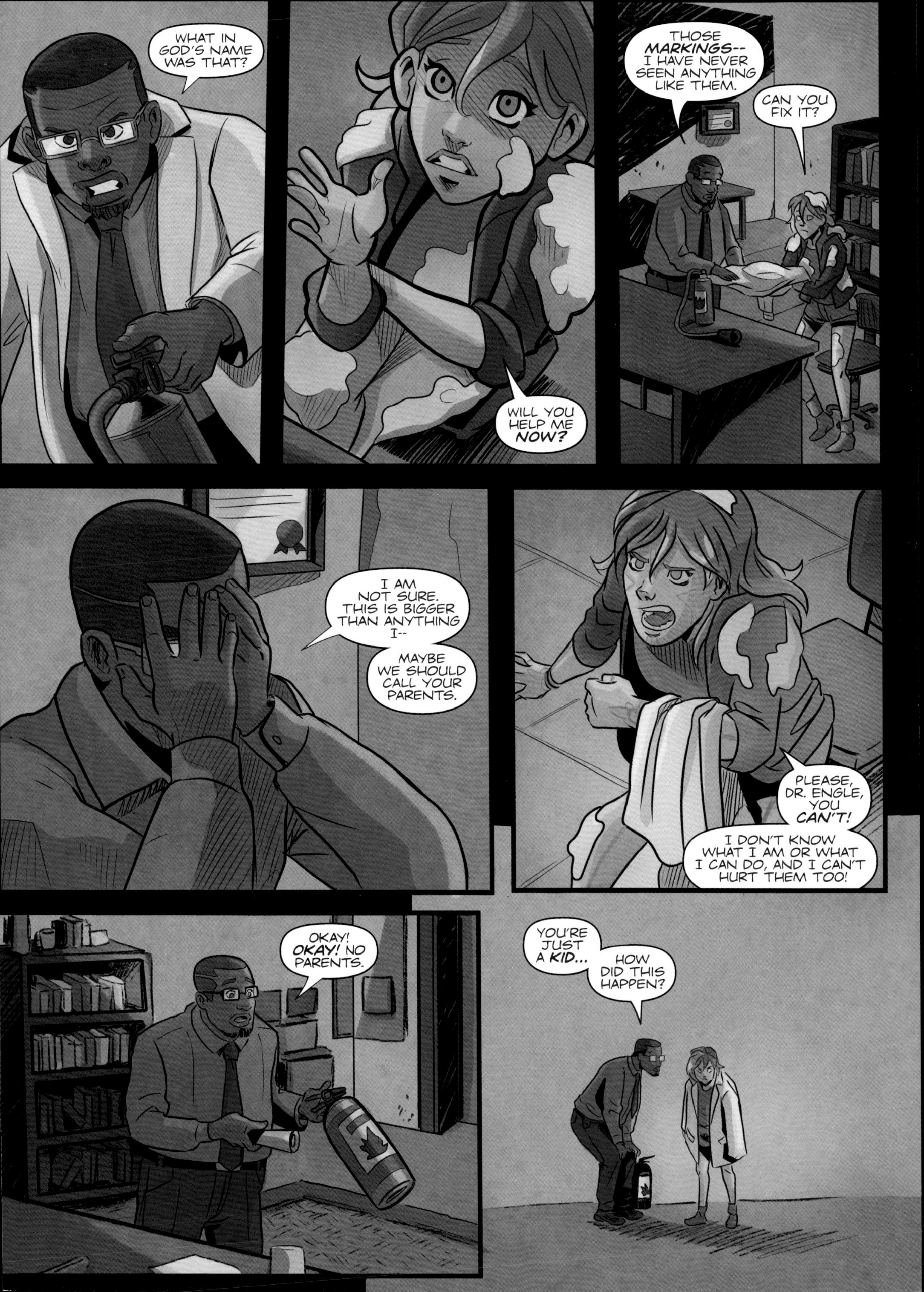
WHAT IN GOD'S NAME WAS THAT?
WILL YOU HELP ME NOW?
THOSE MARKINGS-- I HAVE NEVER SEEN ANYTHING LIKE THEM.
CAN YOU FIX IT?
I AM NOT SURE. THIS IS BIGGER THAN ANYTHING I--
MAYBE WE SHOULD CALL YOUR PARENTS.
PLEASE, DR. ENGLE, YOU CAN'T!
I DON'T KNOW WHAT I AM OR WHAT I CAN DO, AND I CAN'T HURT THEM TOO!
OKAY! OKAY! NO PARENTS.
YOU'RE JUST A KID...
HOW DID THIS HAPPEN?

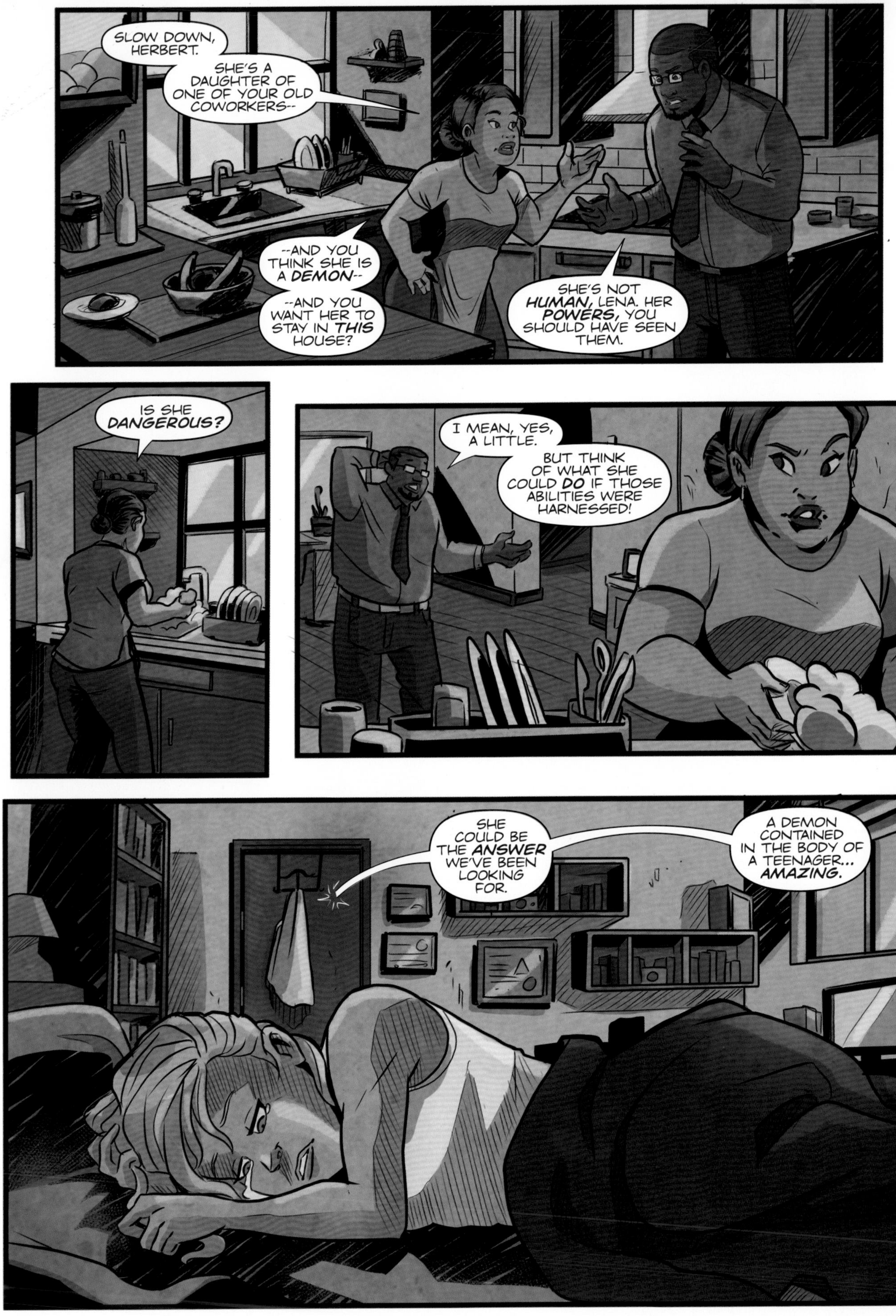

SLOW DOWN, HERBERT.
SHE'S A DAUGHTER OF ONE OF YOUR OLD COWORKERS--
--AND YOU THINK SHE IS A DEMON--
--AND YOU WANT HER TO STAY IN THIS HOUSE?
SHE'S NOT HUMAN, LENA. HER POWERS, YOU SHOULD HAVE SEEN THEM.
IS SHE DANGEROUS?
I MEAN, YES, A LITTLE.
BUT THINK OF WHAT SHE COULD DO IF THOSE ABILITIES WERE HARNESSED!
SHE COULD BE THE ANSWER WE'VE BEEN LOOKING FOR.
A DEMON CONTAINED IN THE BODY OF A TEENAGER... AMAZING.

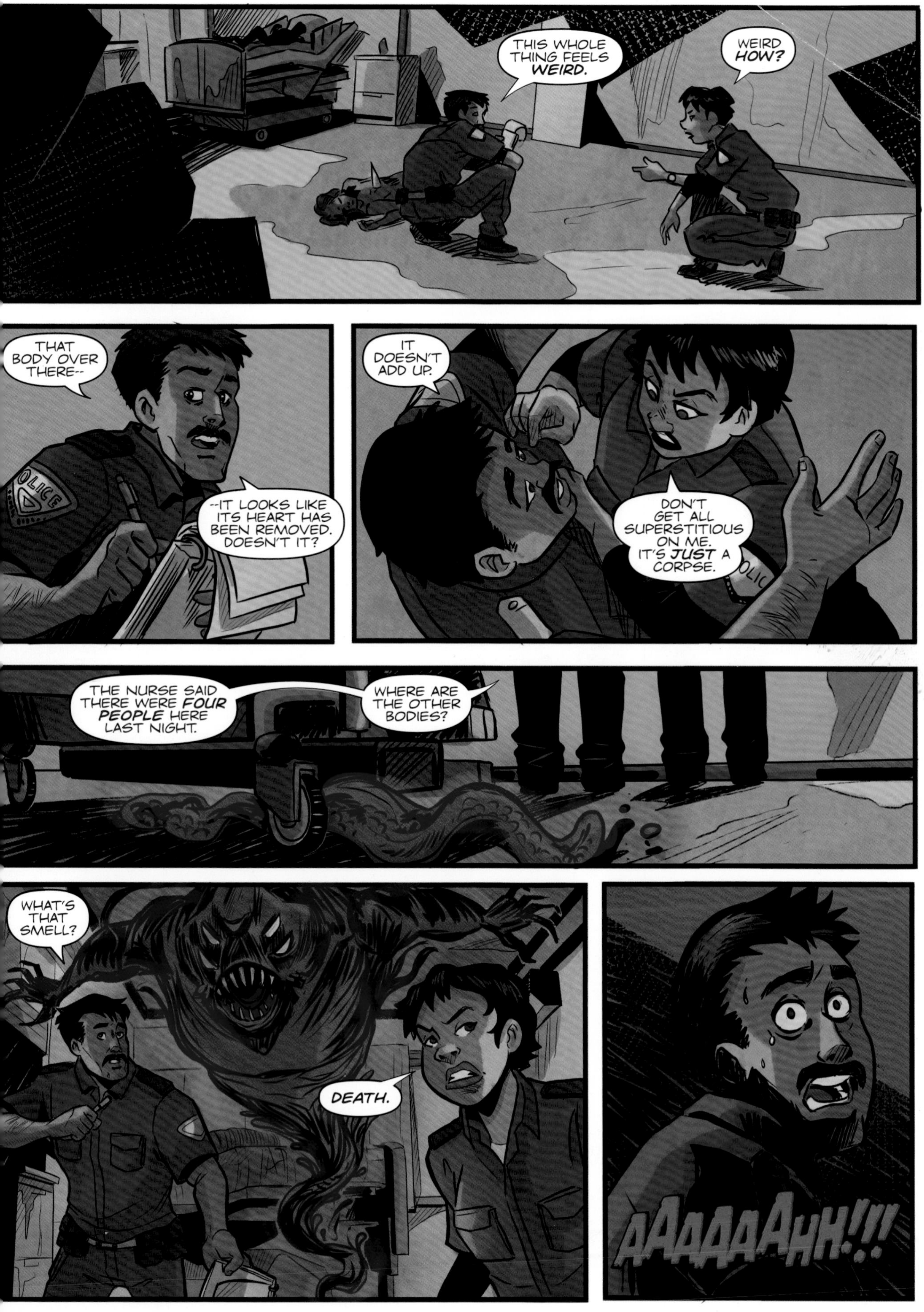
THIS WHOLE THING FEELS WEIRD.
WEIRD HOW?
THAT BODY OVER THERE--
--IT LOOKS LIKE ITS HEART HAS BEEN REMOVED. DOESN'T IT?
IT DOESN'T ADD UP.
DON'T GET ALL SUPERSTITIOUS ON ME. IT'S JUST A CORPSE.
THE NURSE SAID THERE WERE FOUR PEOPLE HERE LAST NIGHT.
WHERE ARE THE OTHER BODIES?
WHAT'S THAT SMELL?
DEATH.
AAAAAAHH!!!

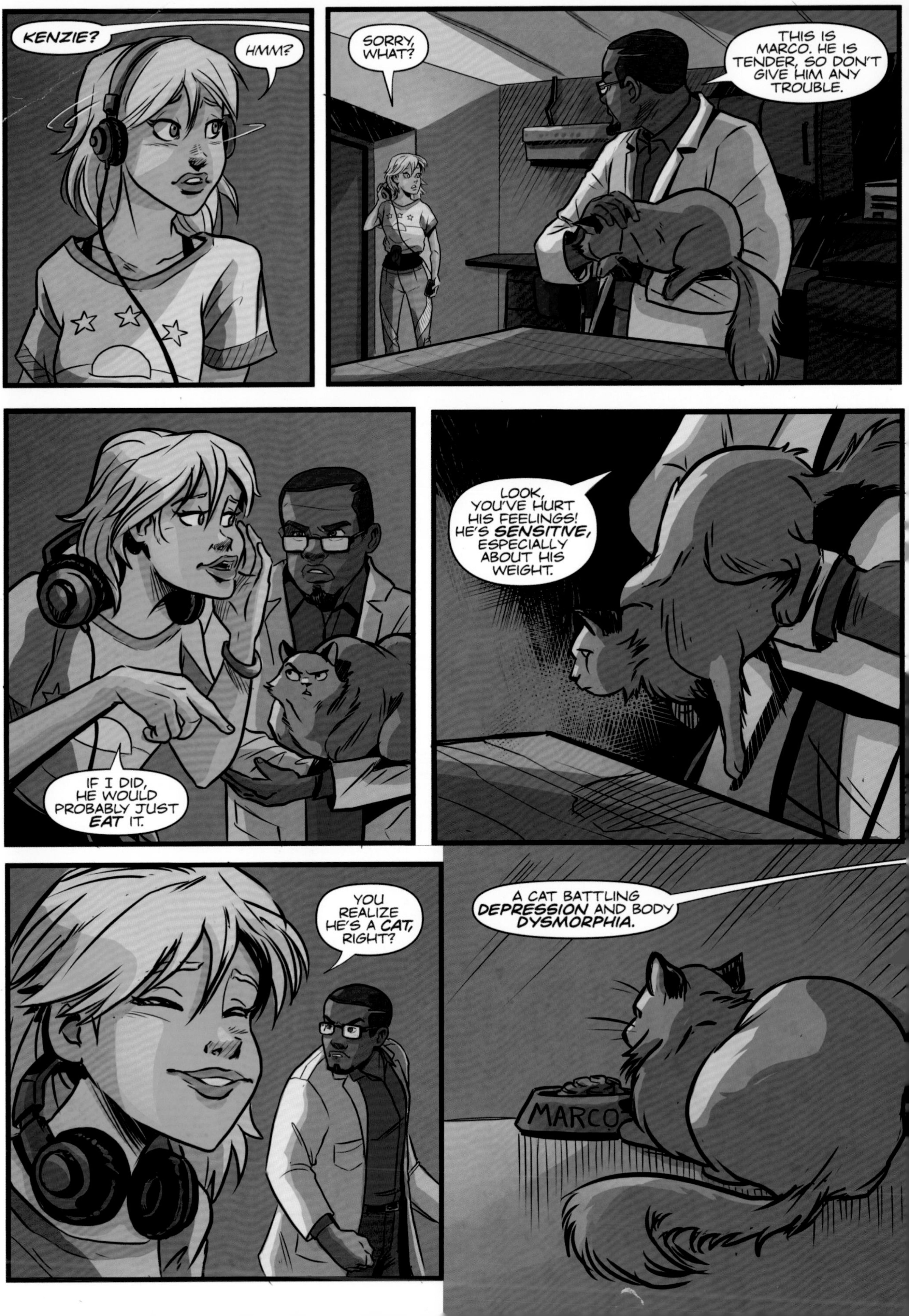
KENZIE?
HMM?
SORRY, WHAT?
THIS IS MARCO. HE IS TENDER, SO DON'T GIVE HIM ANY TROUBLE.
IF I DID, HE WOULD PROBABLY JUST EAT IT.
LOOK, YOU'VE HURT HIS FEELINGS! HE'S SENSITIVE, ESPECIALLY ABOUT HIS WEIGHT.
YOU REALIZE HE'S A CAT, RIGHT?
A CAT BATTLING DEPRESSION AND BODY DYSMORPHIA.
MARCO

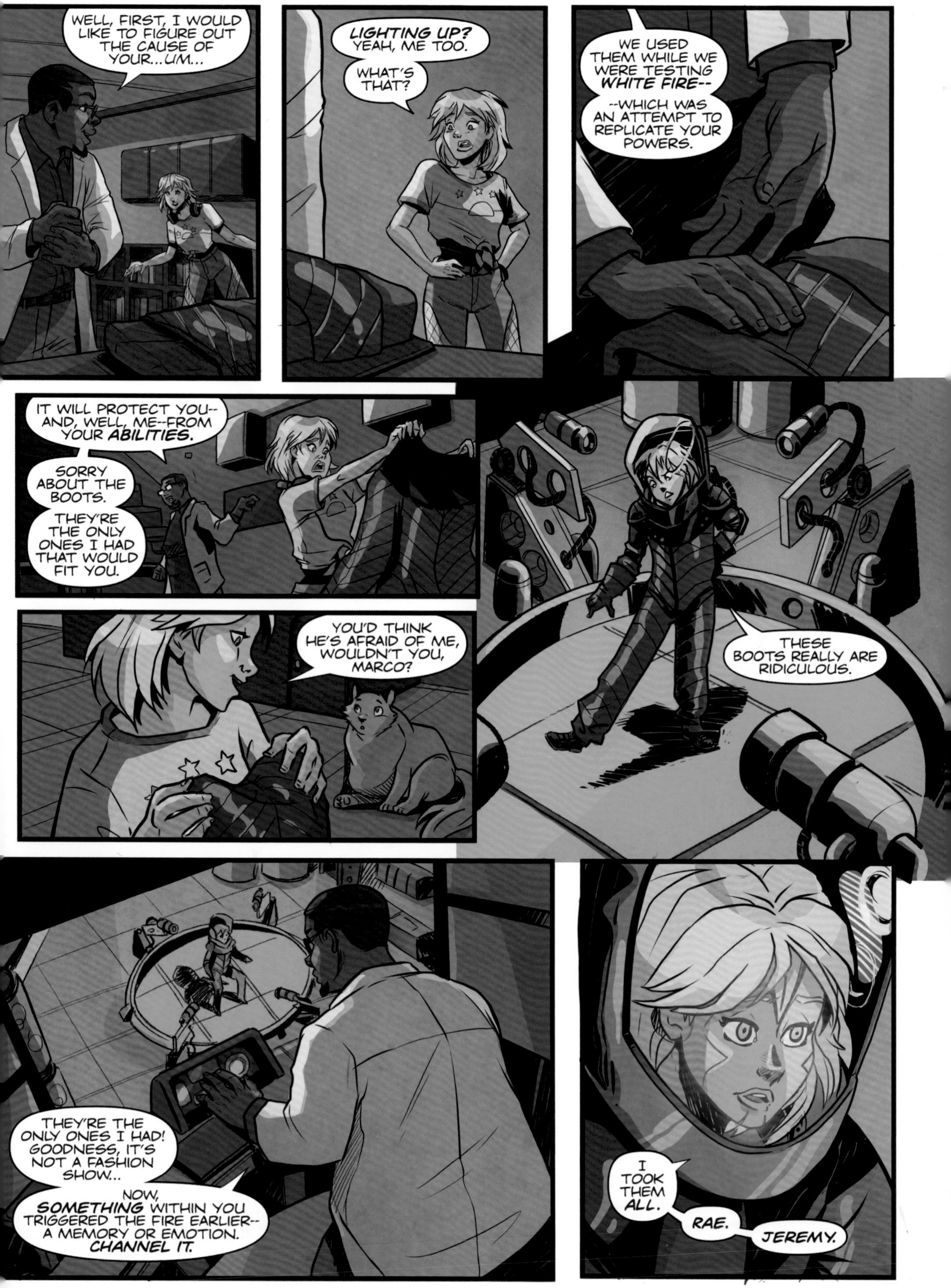
WELL, FIRST, I WOULD LIKE TO FIGURE OUT THE CAUSE OF YOUR...UM...
LIGHTING UP? YEAH, ME TOO.
WHAT'S THAT?
WE USED THEM WHILE WE WERE TESTING WHITE FIRE--
--WHICH WAS AN ATTEMPT TO REPLICATE YOUR POWERS.
IT WILL PROTECT YOU--AND, WELL, ME--FROM YOUR ABILITIES.
SORRY ABOUT THE BOOTS.
THEY'RE THE ONLY ONES I HAD THAT WOULD FIT YOU.
YOU'D THINK HE'S AFRAID OF ME, WOULDN'T YOU, MARCO?
THESE BOOTS REALLY ARE RIDICULOUS.
THEY'RE THE ONLY ONES I HAD! GOODNESS, IT'S NOT A FASHION SHOW...
NOW, SOMETHING WITHIN YOU TRIGGERED THE FIRE EARLIER--A MEMORY OR EMOTION. CHANNEL IT.
I TOOK THEM ALL.
RAE.
JEREMY.

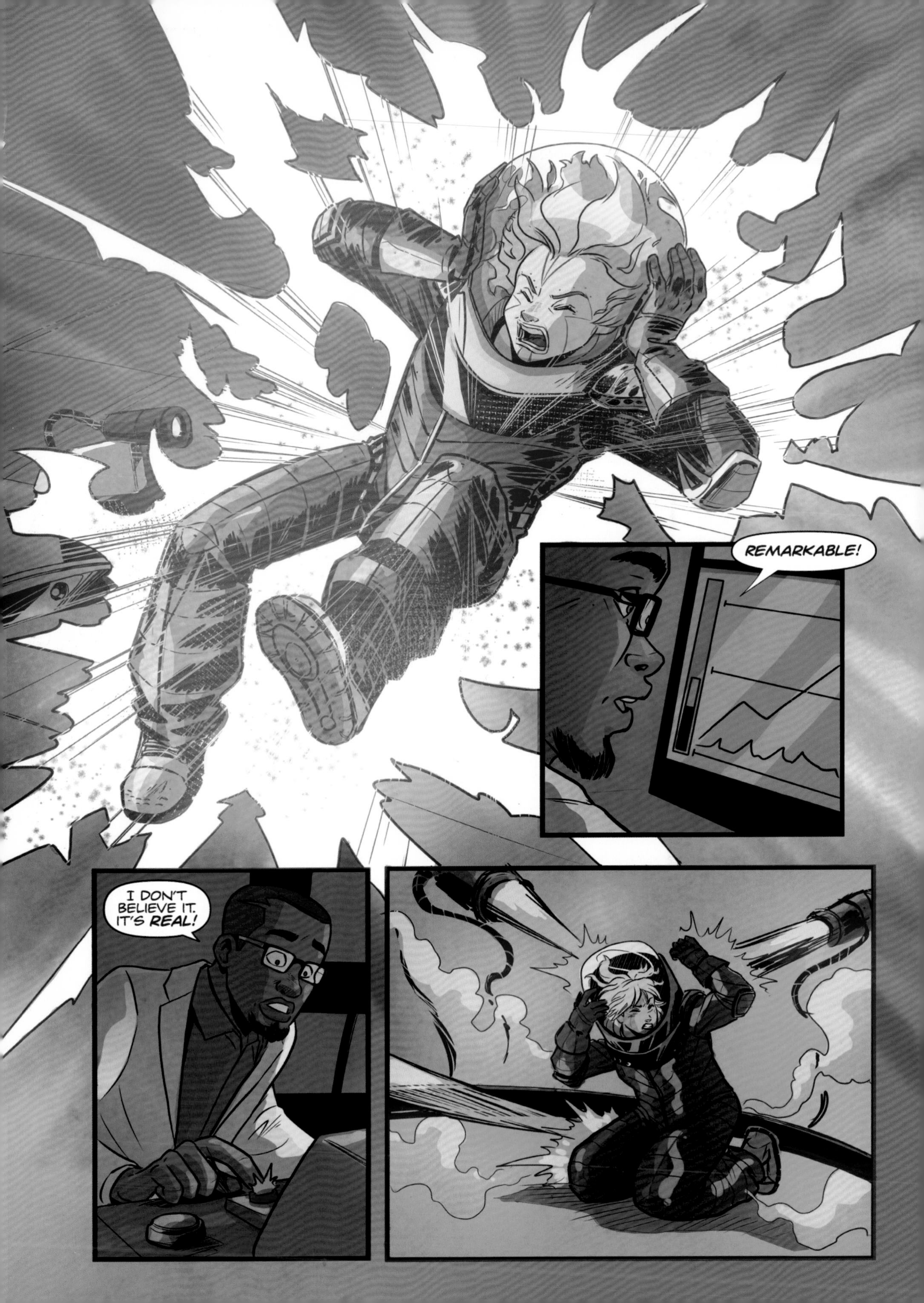
REMARKABLE!
I DON'T BELIEVE IT. IT'S REAL!

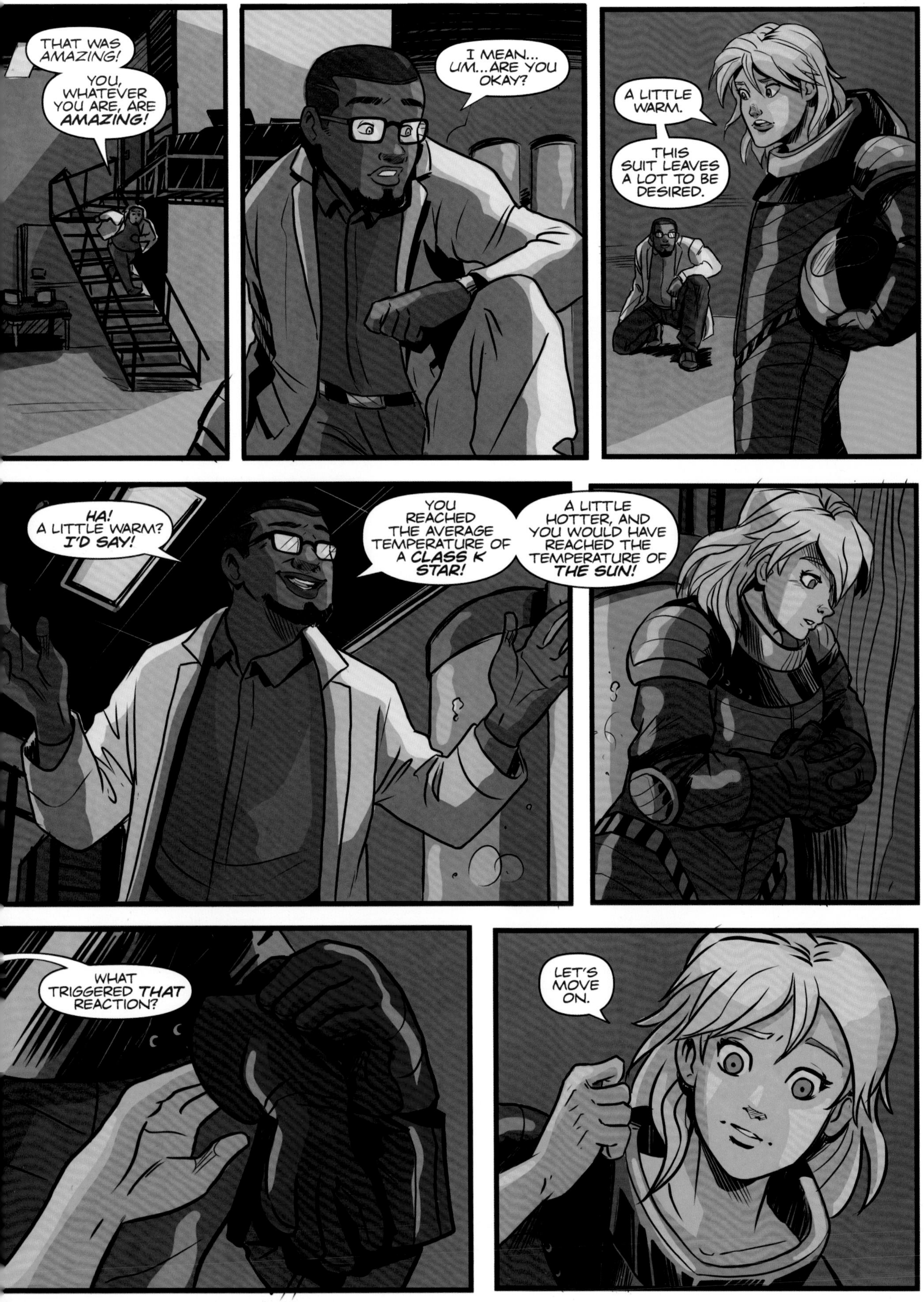

THAT WAS AMAZING!
YOU, WHATEVER YOU ARE, ARE AMAZING!
I MEAN... UM...ARE YOU OKAY?
A LITTLE WARM.
THIS SUIT LEAVES A LOT TO BE DESIRED.
HA! A LITTLE WARM? I'D SAY!
YOU REACHED THE AVERAGE TEMPERATURE OF A CLASS K STAR!
A LITTLE HOTTER, AND YOU WOULD HAVE REACHED THE TEMPERATURE OF THE SUN!
WHAT TRIGGERED THAT REACTION?
LET'S MOVE ON.

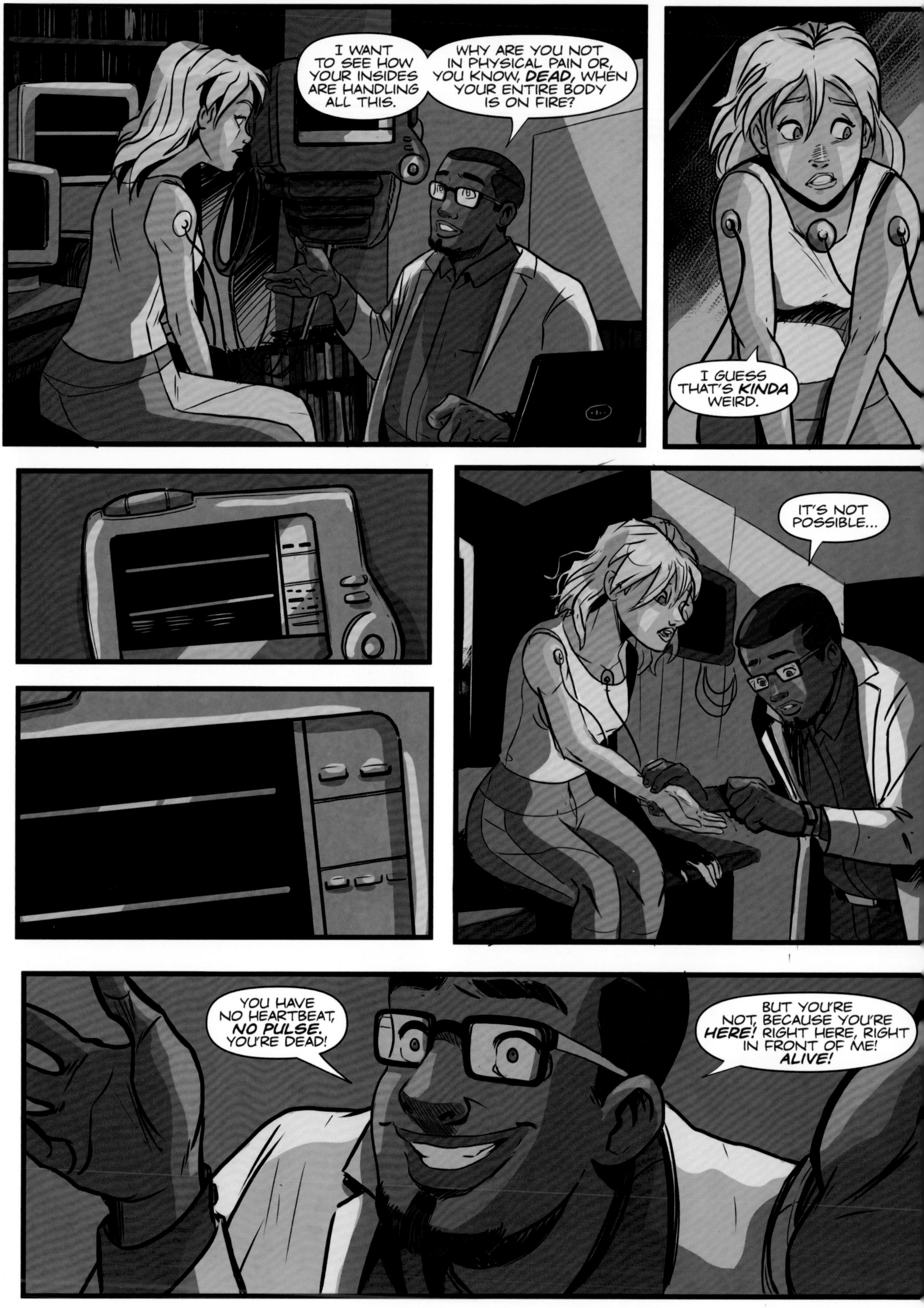
I WANT TO SEE HOW YOUR INSIDES ARE HANDLING ALL THIS.
WHY ARE YOU NOT IN PHYSICAL PAIN OR, YOU KNOW, DEAD, WHEN YOUR ENTIRE BODY IS ON FIRE?
I GUESS THAT'S KINDA WEIRD.
IT'S NOT POSSIBLE...
YOU HAVE NO HEARTBEAT, NO PULSE. YOU'RE DEAD!
BUT YOU'RE NOT, BECAUSE YOU'RE HERE! RIGHT HERE, RIGHT IN FRONT OF ME! ALIVE!

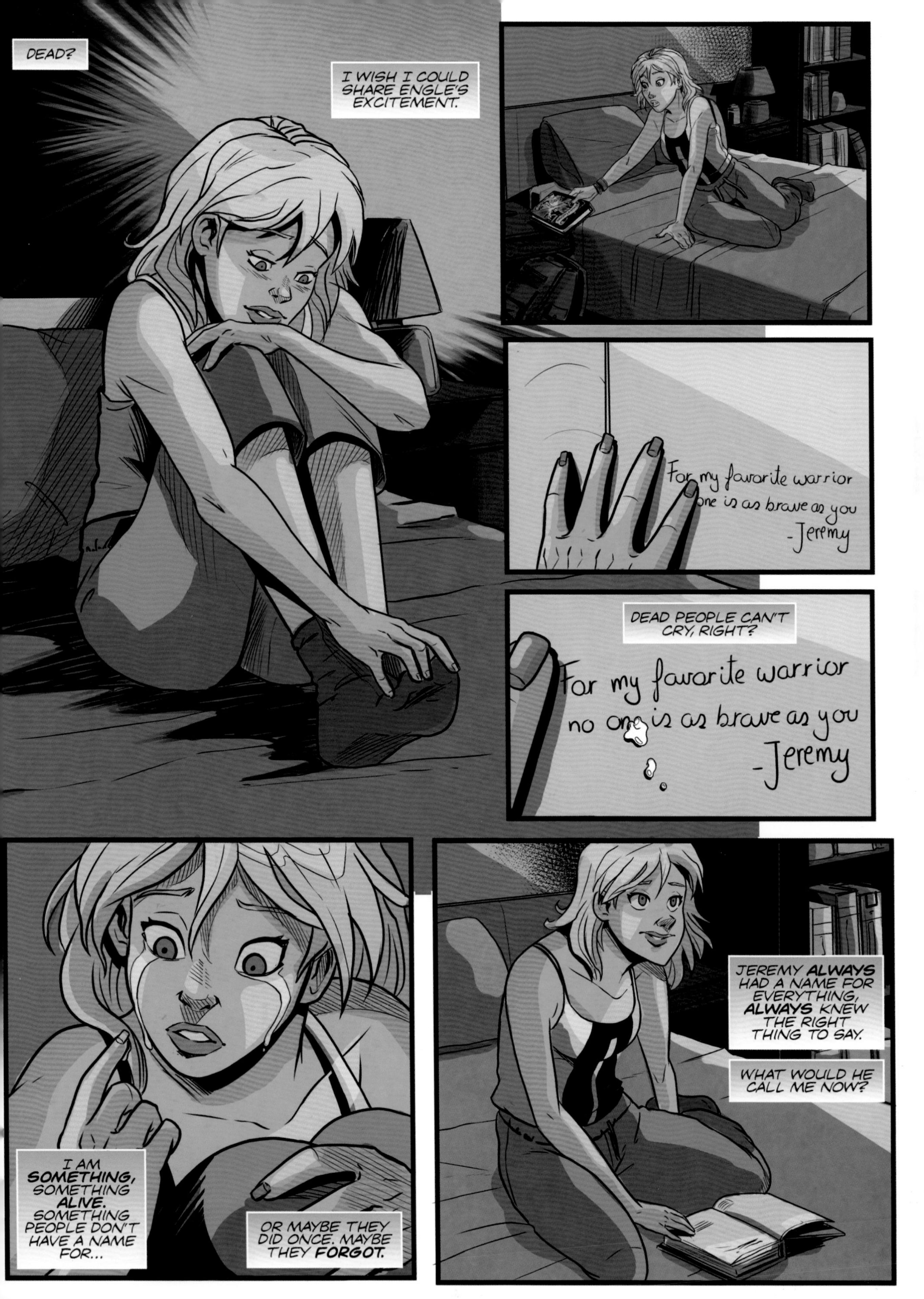
DEAD?
I WISH I COULD SHARE ENGLE'S EXCITEMENT.
For my favorite warrior
one is as brave as you
-Jeremy
DEAD PEOPLE CAN'T CRY, RIGHT?
For my favorite warrior
no one is as brave as you
-Jeremy
I AM SOMETHING, SOMETHING ALIVE. SOMETHING PEOPLE DON'T HAVE A NAME FOR...
OR MAYBE THEY DID ONCE. MAYBE THEY FORGOT.
JEREMY ALWAYS HAD A NAME FOR EVERYTHING, ALWAYS KNEW THE RIGHT THING TO SAY.
WHAT WOULD HE CALL ME NOW?

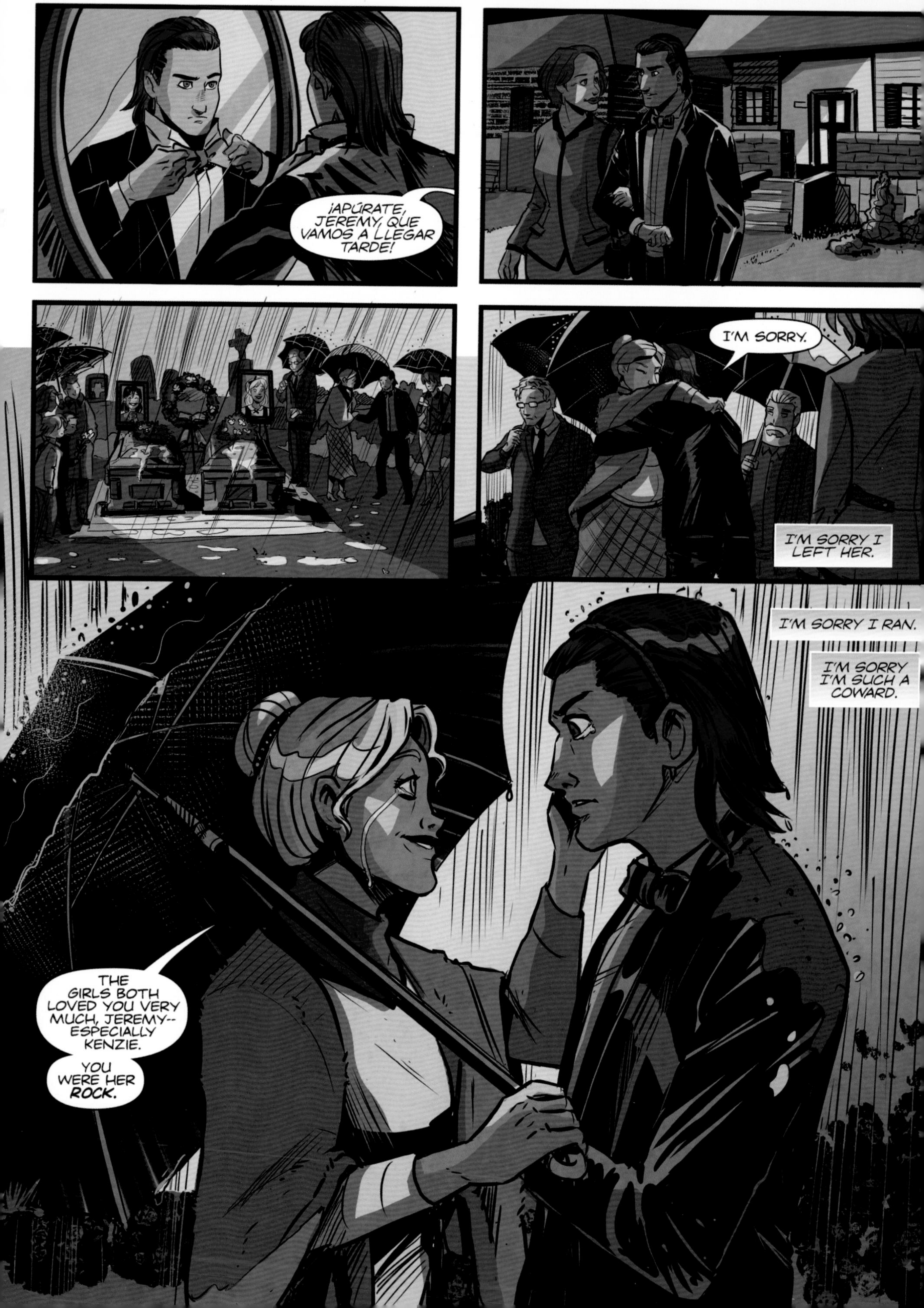
¡APÚRATE, JEREMY, QUE VAMOS A LLEGAR TARDE!
I'M SORRY.
I'M SORRY I LEFT HER.
I'M SORRY I RAN.
I'M SORRY I'M SUCH A COWARD.
THE GIRLS BOTH LOVED YOU VERY MUCH, JEREMY-- ESPECIALLY KENZIE.
YOU WERE HER **ROCK**.

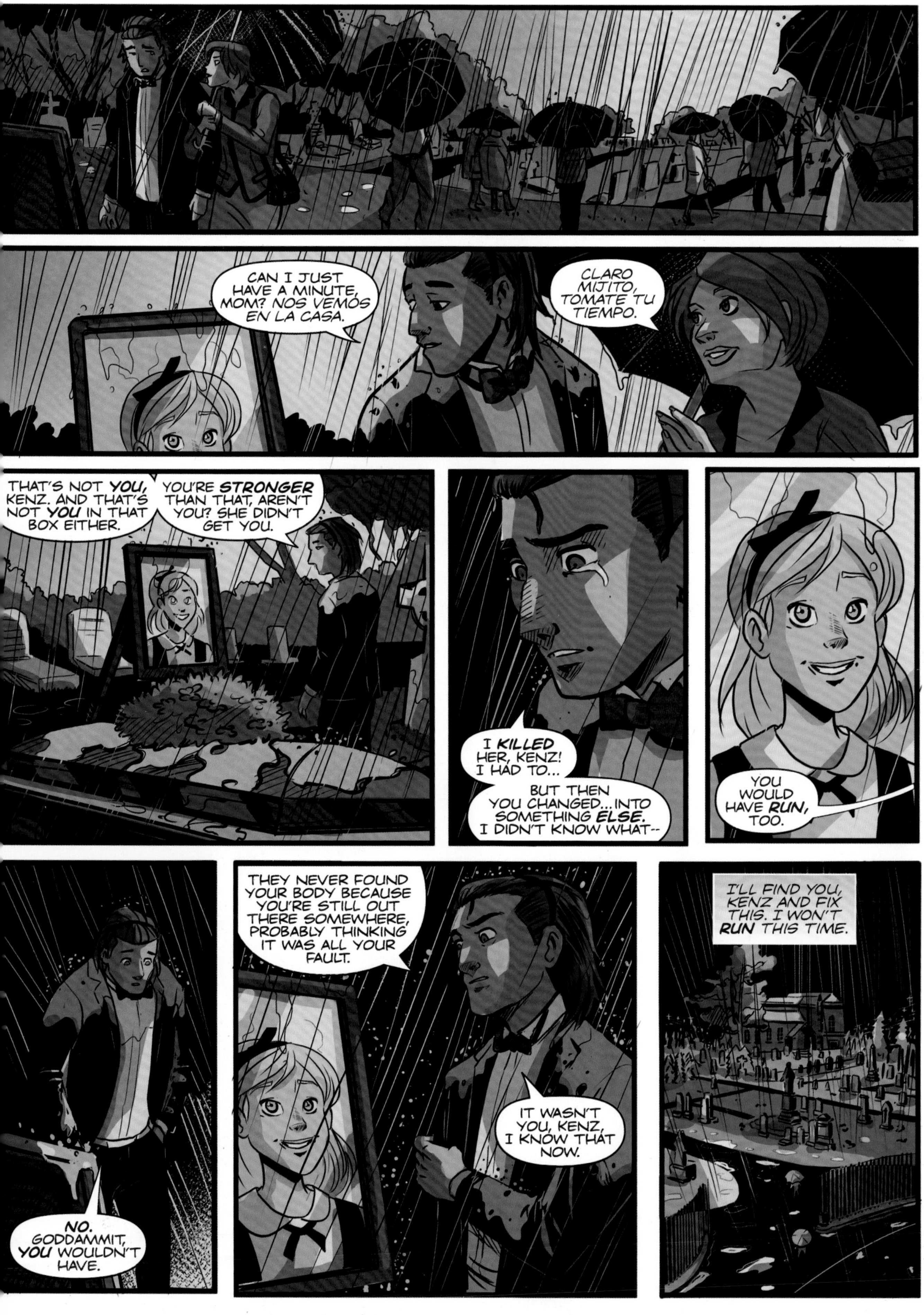
CAN I JUST HAVE A MINUTE, MOM? NOS VEMÓS EN LA CASA.
CLARO MIJITO, TOMATE TU TIEMPO.
THAT'S NOT *YOU*, KENZ. AND THAT'S NOT *YOU* IN THAT BOX EITHER.
YOU'RE *STRONGER* THAN THAT, AREN'T YOU? SHE DIDN'T GET YOU.
I *KILLED* HER, KENZ! I HAD TO...
BUT THEN YOU CHANGED...INTO SOMETHING *ELSE*. I DIDN'T KNOW WHAT--
YOU WOULD HAVE *RUN*, TOO.
NO. GODDAMMIT, *YOU* WOULDN'T HAVE.
THEY NEVER FOUND YOUR BODY BECAUSE YOU'RE STILL OUT THERE SOMEWHERE, PROBABLY THINKING IT WAS ALL YOUR FAULT.
IT WASN'T YOU, KENZ, I KNOW THAT NOW.
I'LL FIND YOU, KENZ AND FIX THIS. I WON'T *RUN* THIS TIME.

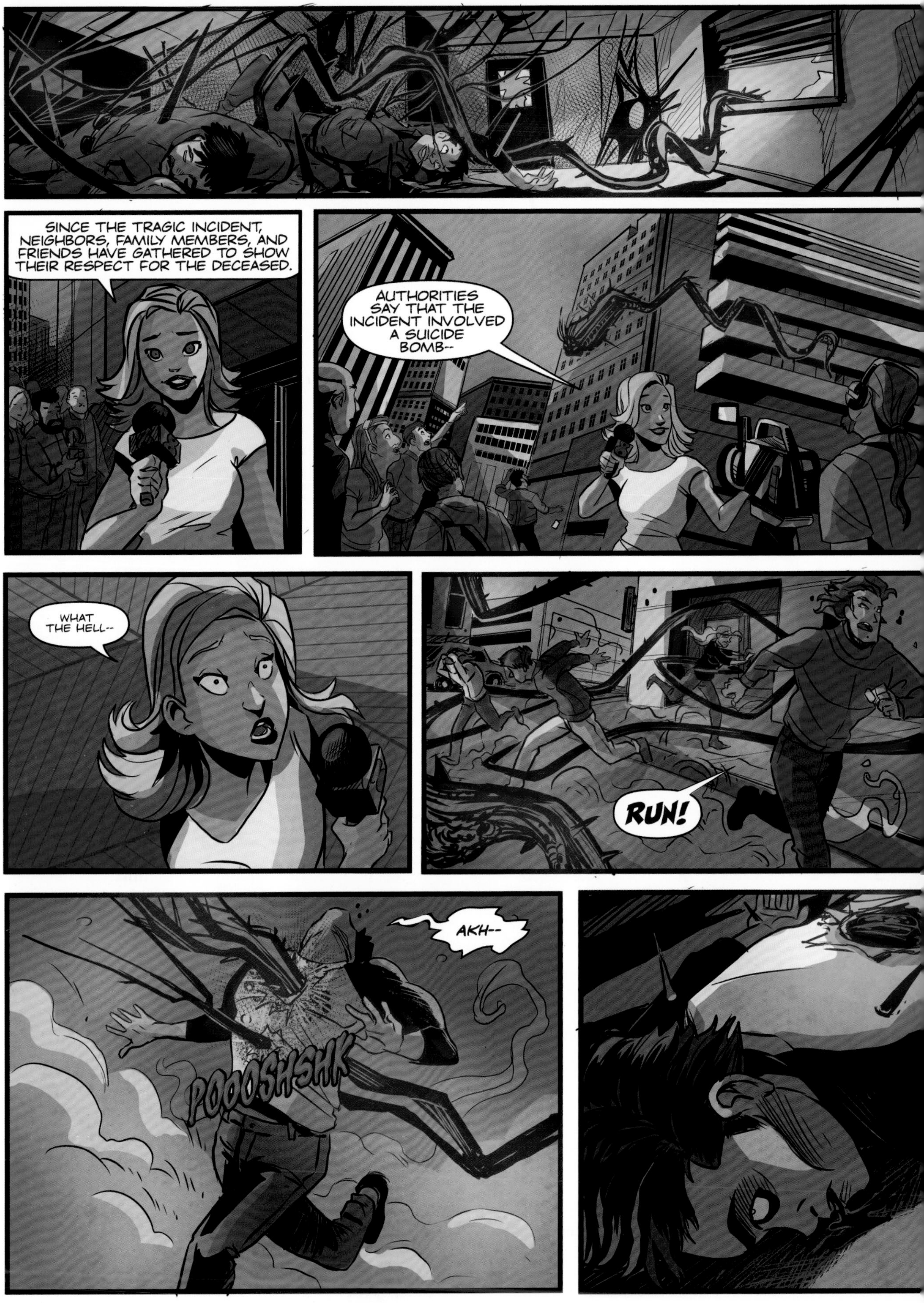
SINCE THE TRAGIC INCIDENT, NEIGHBORS, FAMILY MEMBERS, AND FRIENDS HAVE GATHERED TO SHOW THEIR RESPECT FOR THE DECEASED.
AUTHORITIES SAY THAT THE INCIDENT INVOLVED A SUICIDE BOMB--
WHAT THE HELL--
RUN!
AKH--
POOOSHSHK

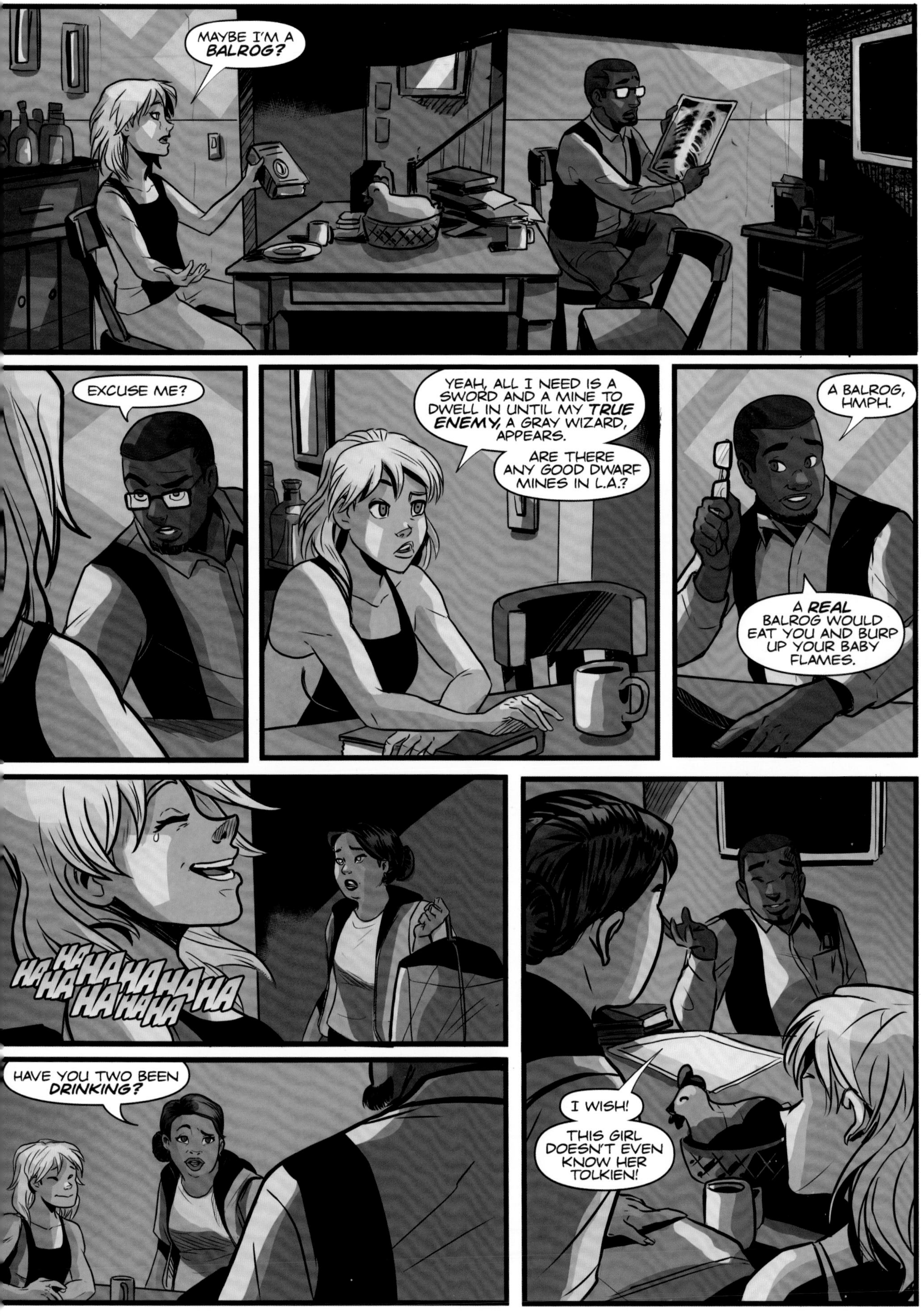
MAYBE I'M A **BALROG?**
EXCUSE ME?
YEAH, ALL I NEED IS A SWORD AND A MINE TO DWELL IN UNTIL MY **TRUE ENEMY,** A GRAY WIZARD, APPEARS.
ARE THERE ANY GOOD DWARF MINES IN L.A.?
A BALROG, HMPH.
A **REAL** BALROG WOULD EAT YOU AND BURP UP YOUR BABY FLAMES.
HAHAHAHAHAHAHA HAHAHAHAHA
HAVE YOU TWO BEEN **DRINKING?**
I WISH!
THIS GIRL DOESN'T EVEN KNOW HER TOLKIEN!

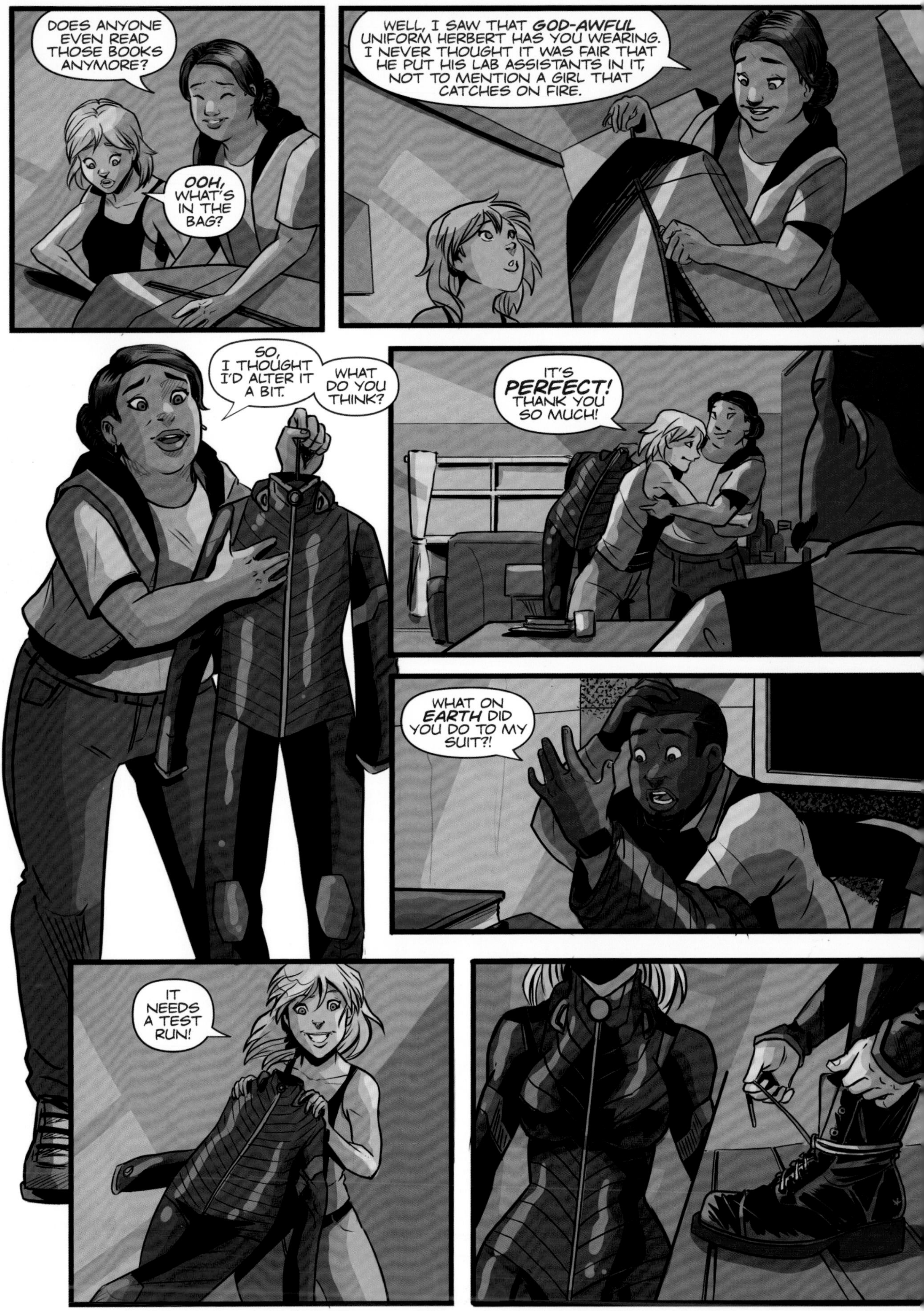
DOES ANYONE EVEN READ THOSE BOOKS ANYMORE?
OOH, WHAT'S IN THE BAG?
WELL, I SAW THAT GOD-AWFUL UNIFORM HERBERT HAS YOU WEARING. I NEVER THOUGHT IT WAS FAIR THAT HE PUT HIS LAB ASSISTANTS IN IT, NOT TO MENTION A GIRL THAT CATCHES ON FIRE.
SO, I THOUGHT I'D ALTER IT A BIT.
WHAT DO YOU THINK?
IT'S PERFECT! THANK YOU SO MUCH!
WHAT ON EARTH DID YOU DO TO MY SUIT?!
IT NEEDS A TEST RUN!

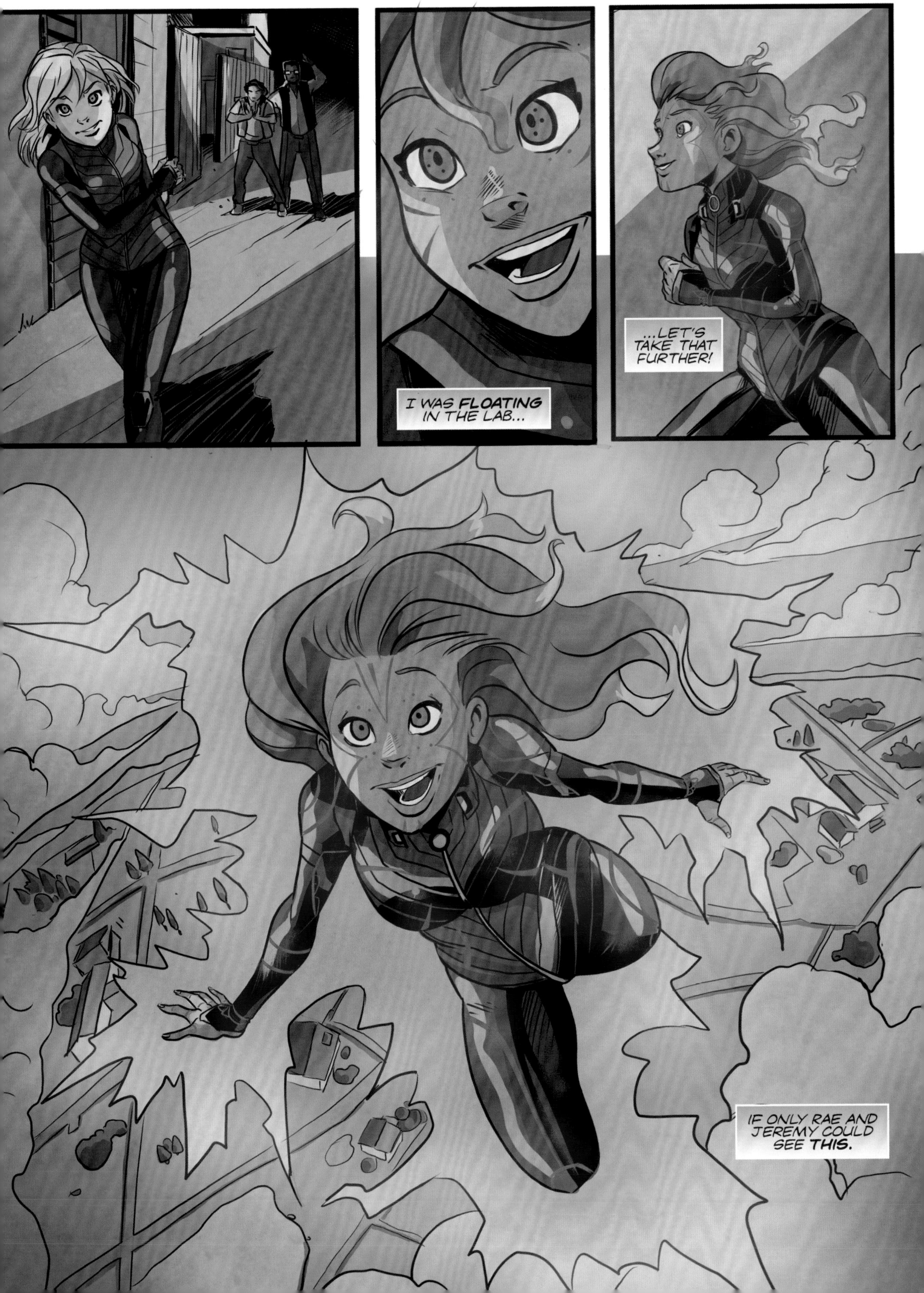
I WAS FLOATING IN THE LAB...
...LET'S TAKE THAT FURTHER!
IF ONLY RAE AND JEREMY COULD SEE THIS.

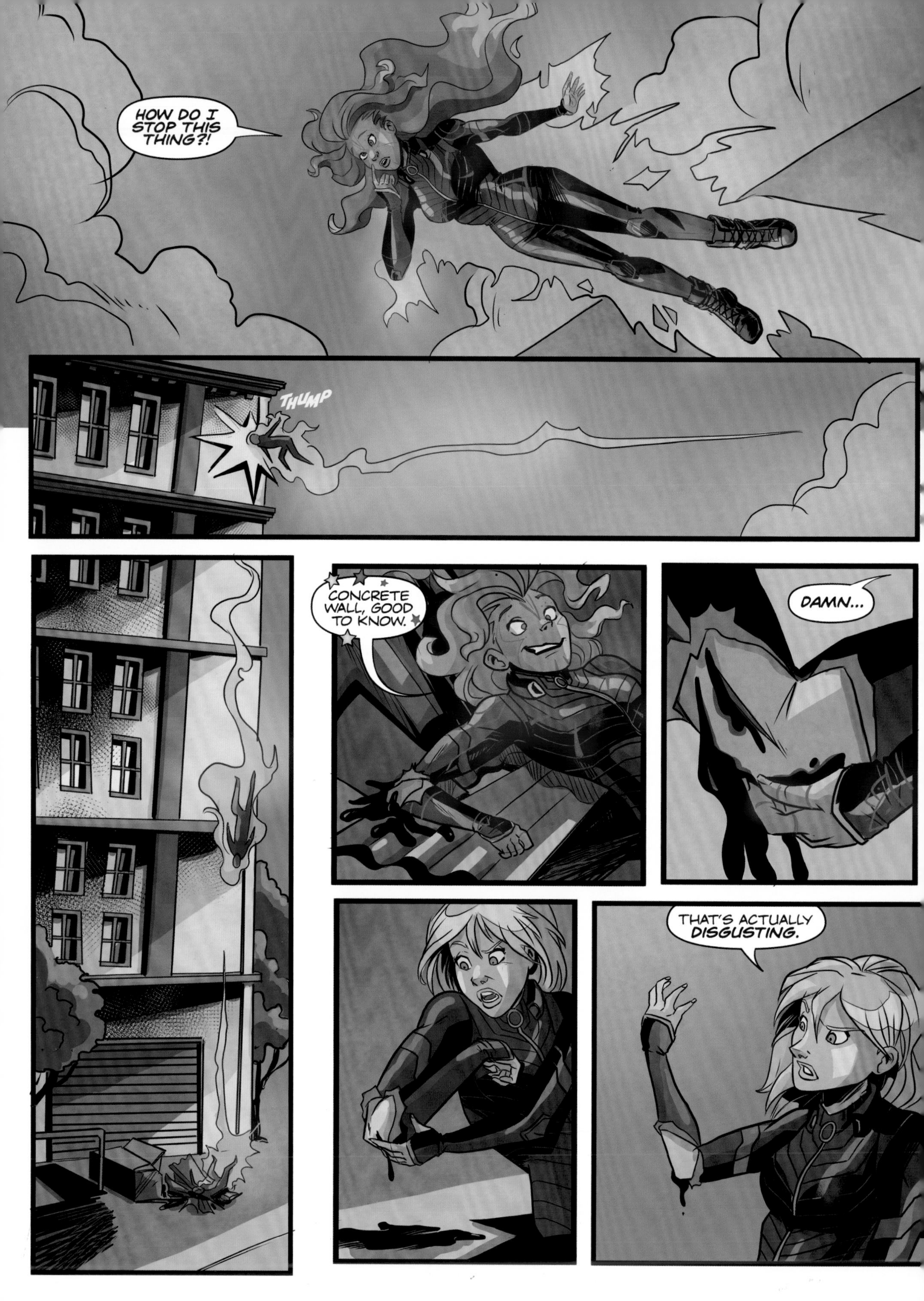
HOW DO I STOP THIS THING?!
THUMP
CONCRETE WALL, GOOD TO KNOW.
DAMN...
THAT'S ACTUALLY DISGUSTING.

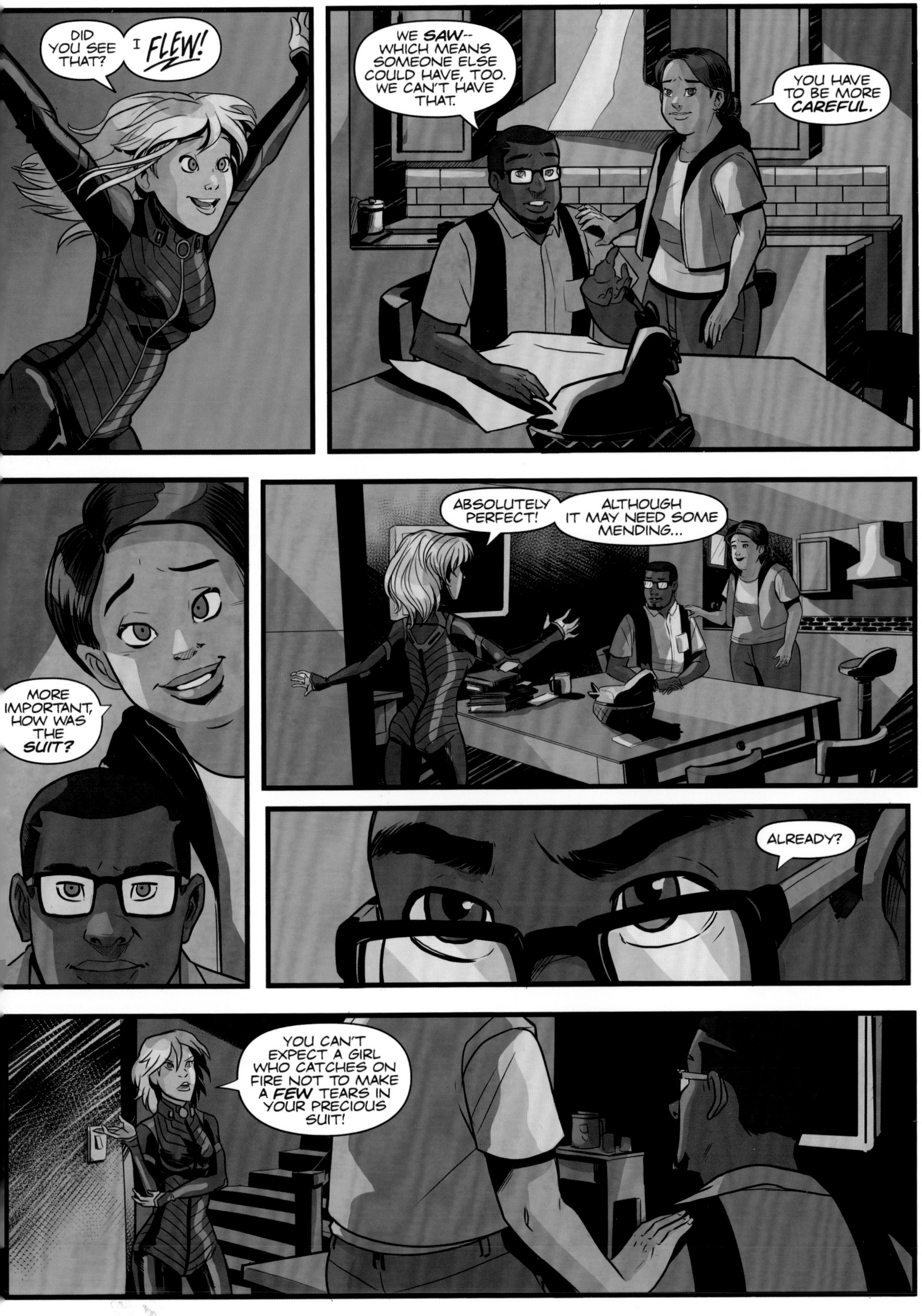
DID YOU SEE THAT?
I FLEW!
WE SAW-- WHICH MEANS SOMEONE ELSE COULD HAVE, TOO. WE CAN'T HAVE THAT.
YOU HAVE TO BE MORE CAREFUL.
MORE IMPORTANT, HOW WAS THE SUIT?
ABSOLUTELY PERFECT!
ALTHOUGH IT MAY NEED SOME MENDING...
ALREADY?
YOU CAN'T EXPECT A GIRL WHO CATCHES ON FIRE NOT TO MAKE A FEW TEARS IN YOUR PRECIOUS SUIT!

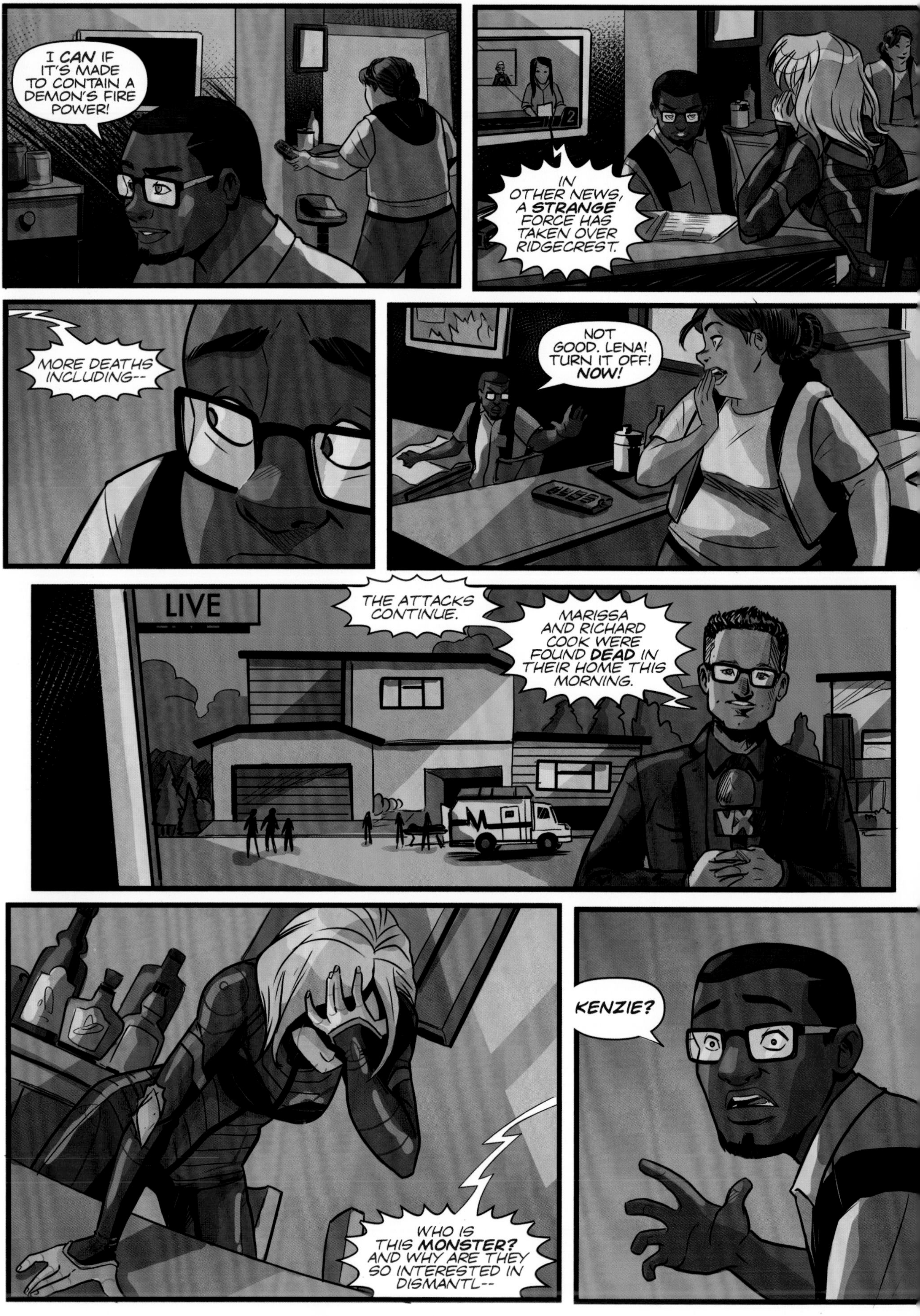
I CAN IF IT'S MADE TO CONTAIN A DEMON'S FIRE POWER!
IN OTHER NEWS, A STRANGE FORCE HAS TAKEN OVER RIDGECREST.
MORE DEATHS INCLUDING--
NOT GOOD. LENA! TURN IT OFF! NOW!
LIVE
THE ATTACKS CONTINUE.
MARISSA AND RICHARD COOK WERE FOUND DEAD IN THEIR HOME THIS MORNING.
WHO IS THIS MONSTER? AND WHY ARE THEY SO INTERESTED IN DISMANTL--
KENZIE?

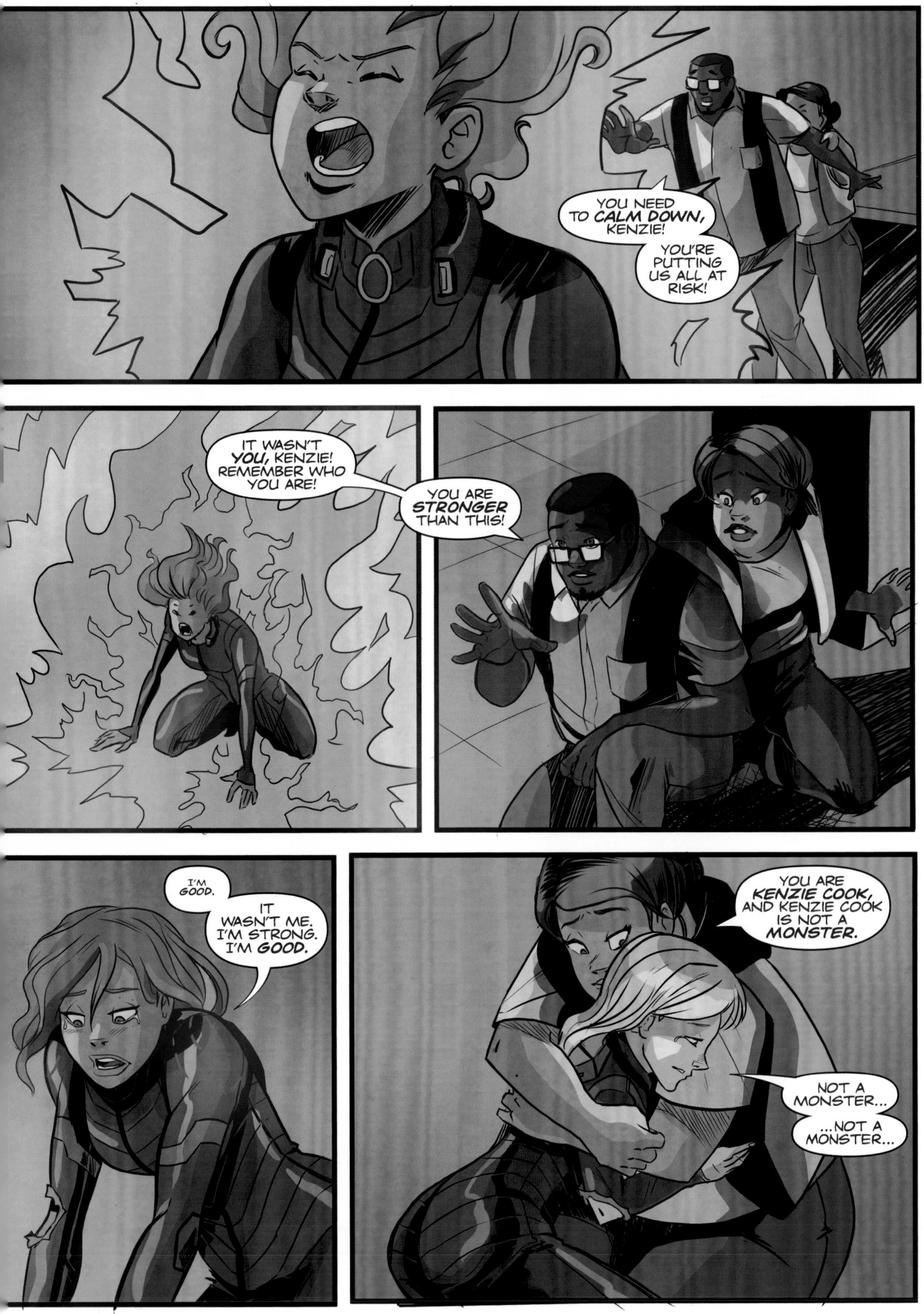
YOU NEED TO CALM DOWN, KENZIE!
YOU'RE PUTTING US ALL AT RISK!
IT WASN'T YOU, KENZIE! REMEMBER WHO YOU ARE!
YOU ARE STRONGER THAN THIS!
I'M GOOD.
IT WASN'T ME. I'M STRONG. I'M GOOD.
YOU ARE KENZIE COOK, AND KENZIE COOK IS NOT A MONSTER.
NOT A MONSTER...
...NOT A MONSTER...

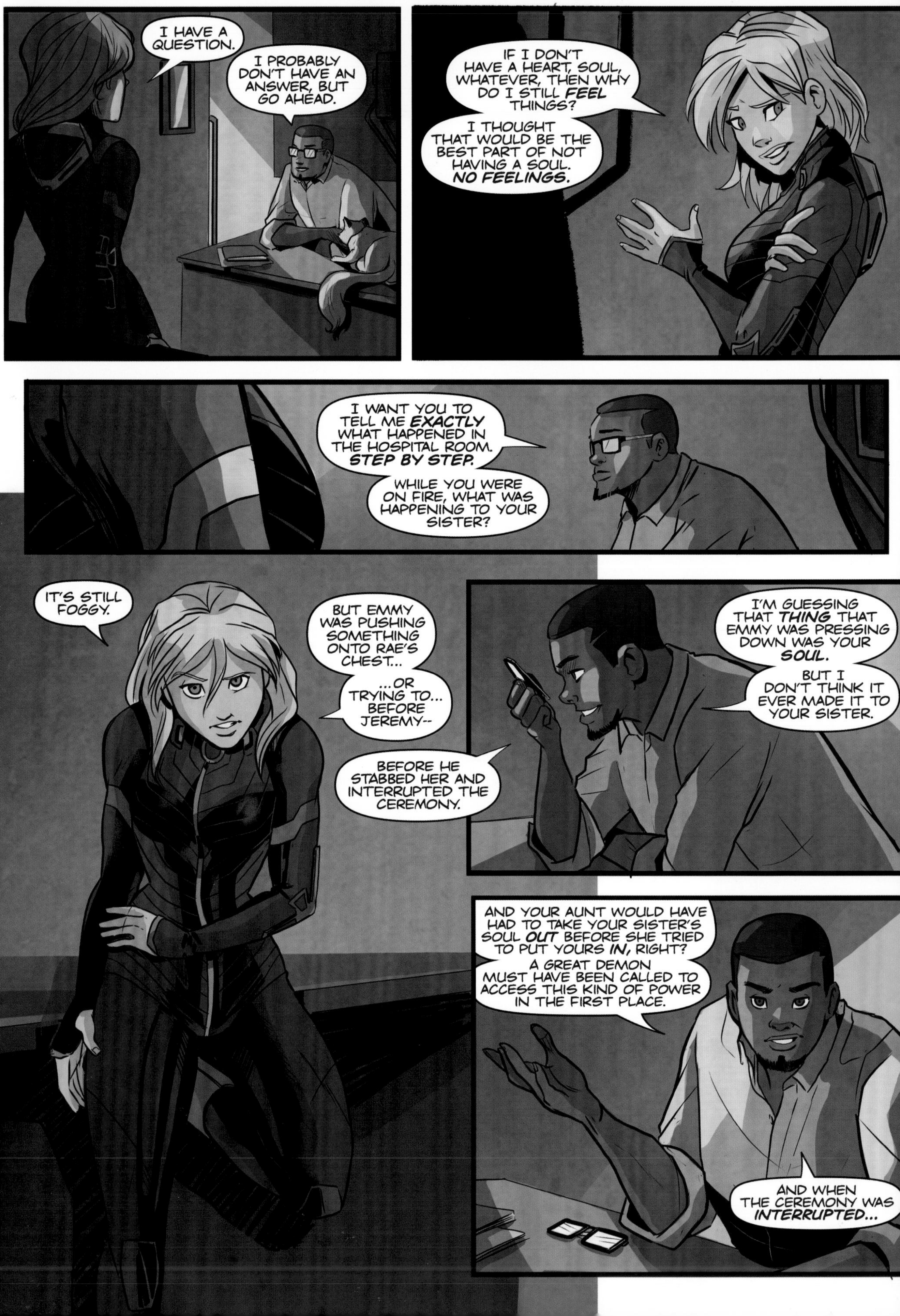
I HAVE A QUESTION.
I PROBABLY DON'T HAVE AN ANSWER, BUT GO AHEAD.
IF I DON'T HAVE A HEART, SOUL, WHATEVER, THEN WHY DO I STILL FEEL THINGS?
I THOUGHT THAT WOULD BE THE BEST PART OF NOT HAVING A SOUL. NO FEELINGS.
I WANT YOU TO TELL ME EXACTLY WHAT HAPPENED IN THE HOSPITAL ROOM. STEP BY STEP.
WHILE YOU WERE ON FIRE, WHAT WAS HAPPENING TO YOUR SISTER?
IT'S STILL FOGGY.
BUT EMMY WAS PUSHING SOMETHING ONTO RAE'S CHEST...
...OR TRYING TO... BEFORE JEREMY--
BEFORE HE STABBED HER AND INTERRUPTED THE CEREMONY.
I'M GUESSING THAT THING THAT EMMY WAS PRESSING DOWN WAS YOUR SOUL.
BUT I DON'T THINK IT EVER MADE IT TO YOUR SISTER.
AND YOUR AUNT WOULD HAVE HAD TO TAKE YOUR SISTER'S SOUL OUT BEFORE SHE TRIED TO PUT YOURS IN, RIGHT?
A GREAT DEMON MUST HAVE BEEN CALLED TO ACCESS THIS KIND OF POWER IN THE FIRST PLACE.
AND WHEN THE CEREMONY WAS INTERRUPTED...

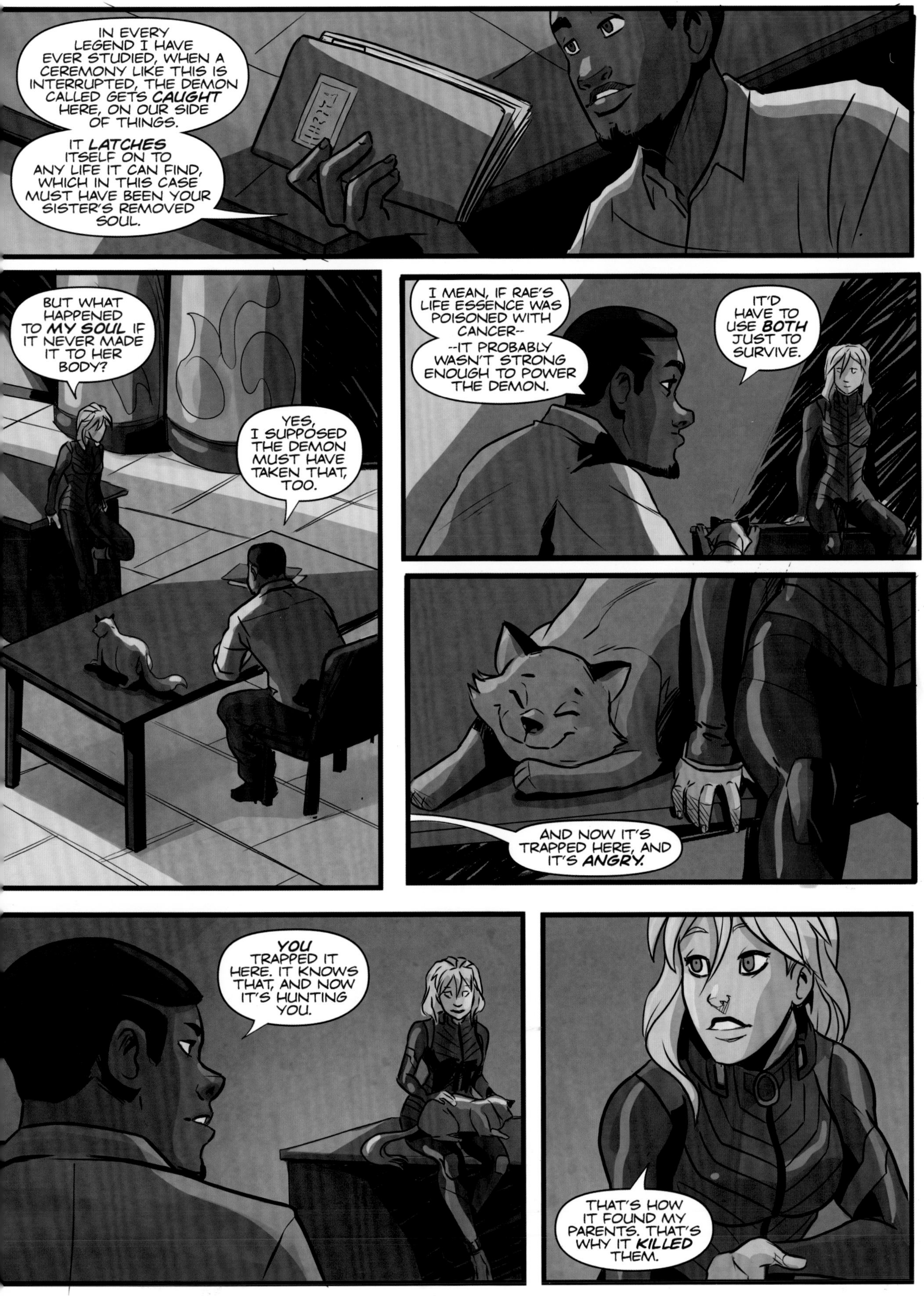
IN EVERY LEGEND I HAVE EVER STUDIED, WHEN A CEREMONY LIKE THIS IS INTERRUPTED, THE DEMON CALLED GETS CAUGHT HERE, ON OUR SIDE OF THINGS.
IT LATCHES ITSELF ON TO ANY LIFE IT CAN FIND, WHICH IN THIS CASE MUST HAVE BEEN YOUR SISTER'S REMOVED SOUL.
BUT WHAT HAPPENED TO MY SOUL IF IT NEVER MADE IT TO HER BODY?
YES, I SUPPOSED THE DEMON MUST HAVE TAKEN THAT, TOO.
I MEAN, IF RAE'S LIFE ESSENCE WAS POISONED WITH CANCER--
--IT PROBABLY WASN'T STRONG ENOUGH TO POWER THE DEMON.
IT'D HAVE TO USE BOTH JUST TO SURVIVE.
AND NOW IT'S TRAPPED HERE, AND IT'S ANGRY.
YOU TRAPPED IT HERE. IT KNOWS THAT, AND NOW IT'S HUNTING YOU.
THAT'S HOW IT FOUND MY PARENTS. THAT'S WHY IT KILLED THEM.

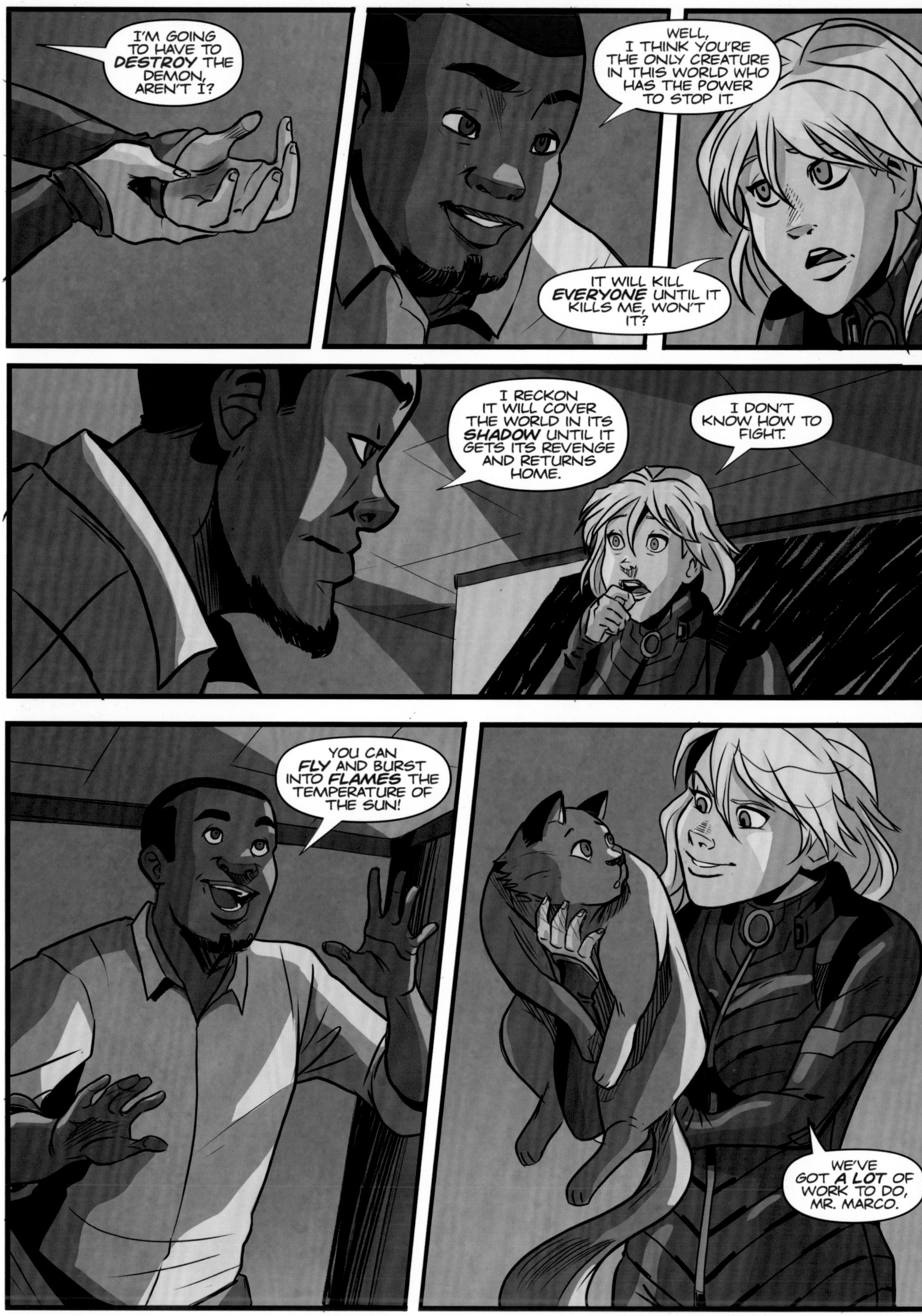

I'M GOING TO HAVE TO DESTROY THE DEMON, AREN'T I?
WELL, I THINK YOU'RE THE ONLY CREATURE IN THIS WORLD WHO HAS THE POWER TO STOP IT.
IT WILL KILL EVERYONE UNTIL IT KILLS ME, WON'T IT?
I RECKON IT WILL COVER THE WORLD IN ITS SHADOW UNTIL IT GETS ITS REVENGE AND RETURNS HOME.
I DON'T KNOW HOW TO FIGHT.
YOU CAN FLY AND BURST INTO FLAMES THE TEMPERATURE OF THE SUN!
WE'VE GOT A LOT OF WORK TO DO, MR. MARCO.

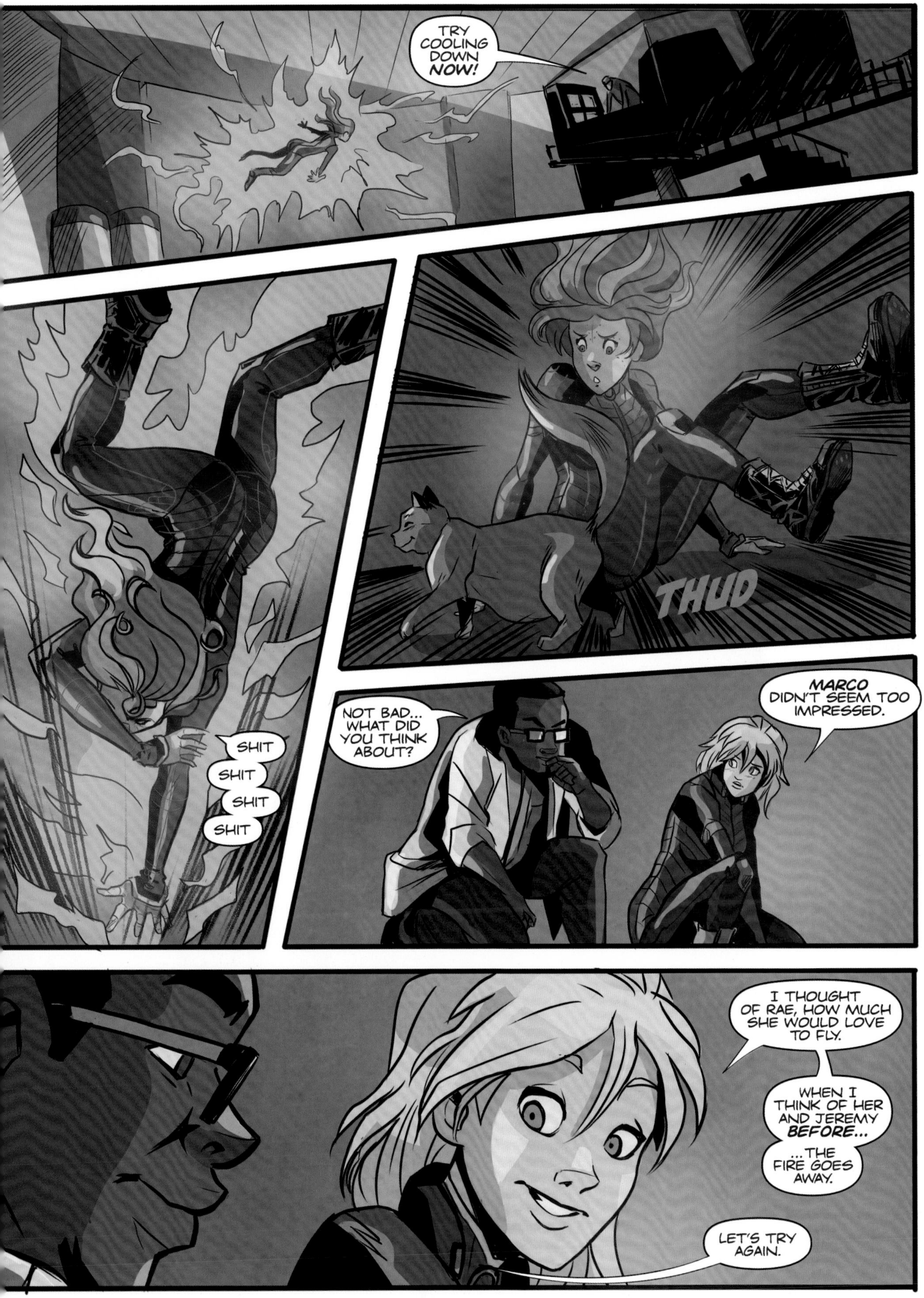
TRY COOLING DOWN NOW!
SHIT
SHIT
SHIT
SHIT
THUD
NOT BAD... WHAT DID YOU THINK ABOUT?
MARCO DIDN'T SEEM TOO IMPRESSED.
I THOUGHT OF RAE, HOW MUCH SHE WOULD LOVE TO FLY.
WHEN I THINK OF HER AND JEREMY BEFORE...
...THE FIRE GOES AWAY.
LET'S TRY AGAIN.

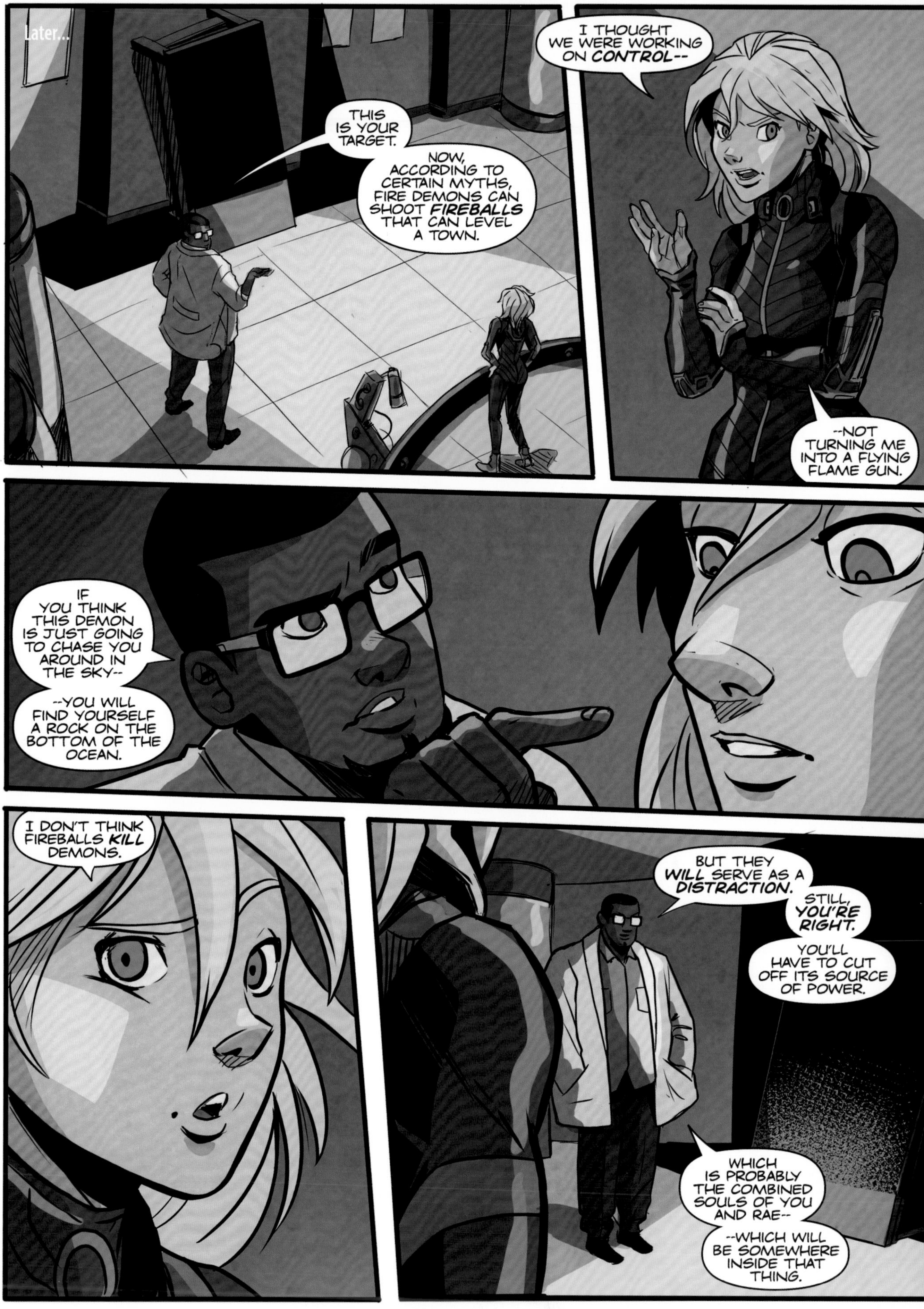
Later...
THIS IS YOUR TARGET.
NOW, ACCORDING TO CERTAIN MYTHS, FIRE DEMONS CAN SHOOT FIREBALLS THAT CAN LEVEL A TOWN.
I THOUGHT WE WERE WORKING ON CONTROL--
--NOT TURNING ME INTO A FLYING FLAME GUN.
IF YOU THINK THIS DEMON IS JUST GOING TO CHASE YOU AROUND IN THE SKY--
--YOU WILL FIND YOURSELF A ROCK ON THE BOTTOM OF THE OCEAN.
I DON'T THINK FIREBALLS KILL DEMONS.
BUT THEY WILL SERVE AS A DISTRACTION.
STILL, YOU'RE RIGHT.
YOU'LL HAVE TO CUT OFF ITS SOURCE OF POWER.
WHICH IS PROBABLY THE COMBINED SOULS OF YOU AND RAE--
--WHICH WILL BE SOMEWHERE INSIDE THAT THING.

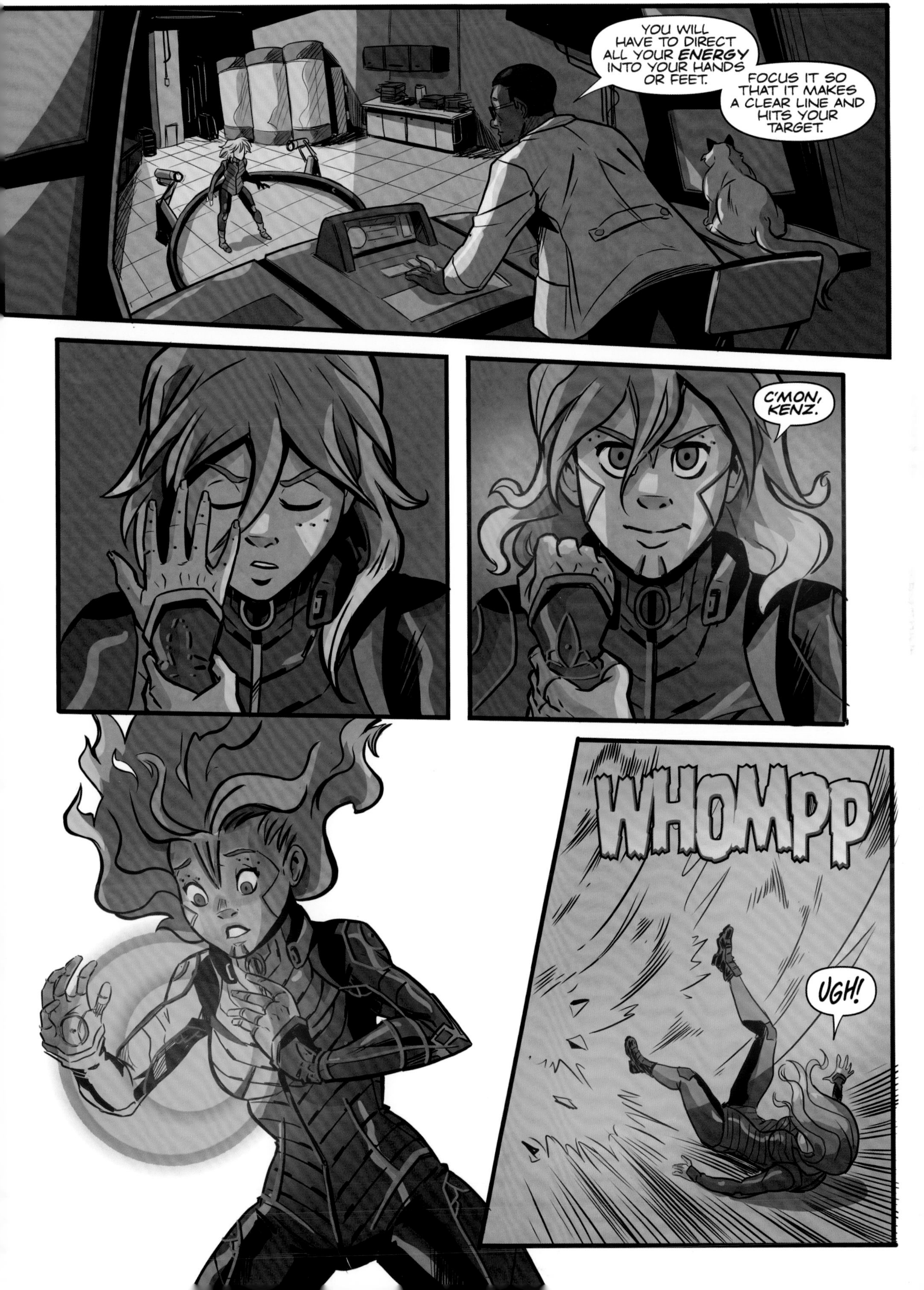
YOU WILL HAVE TO DIRECT ALL YOUR ENERGY INTO YOUR HANDS OR FEET.
FOCUS IT SO THAT IT MAKES A CLEAR LINE AND HITS YOUR TARGET.
C'MON, KENZ.
WHOMPP
UGH!

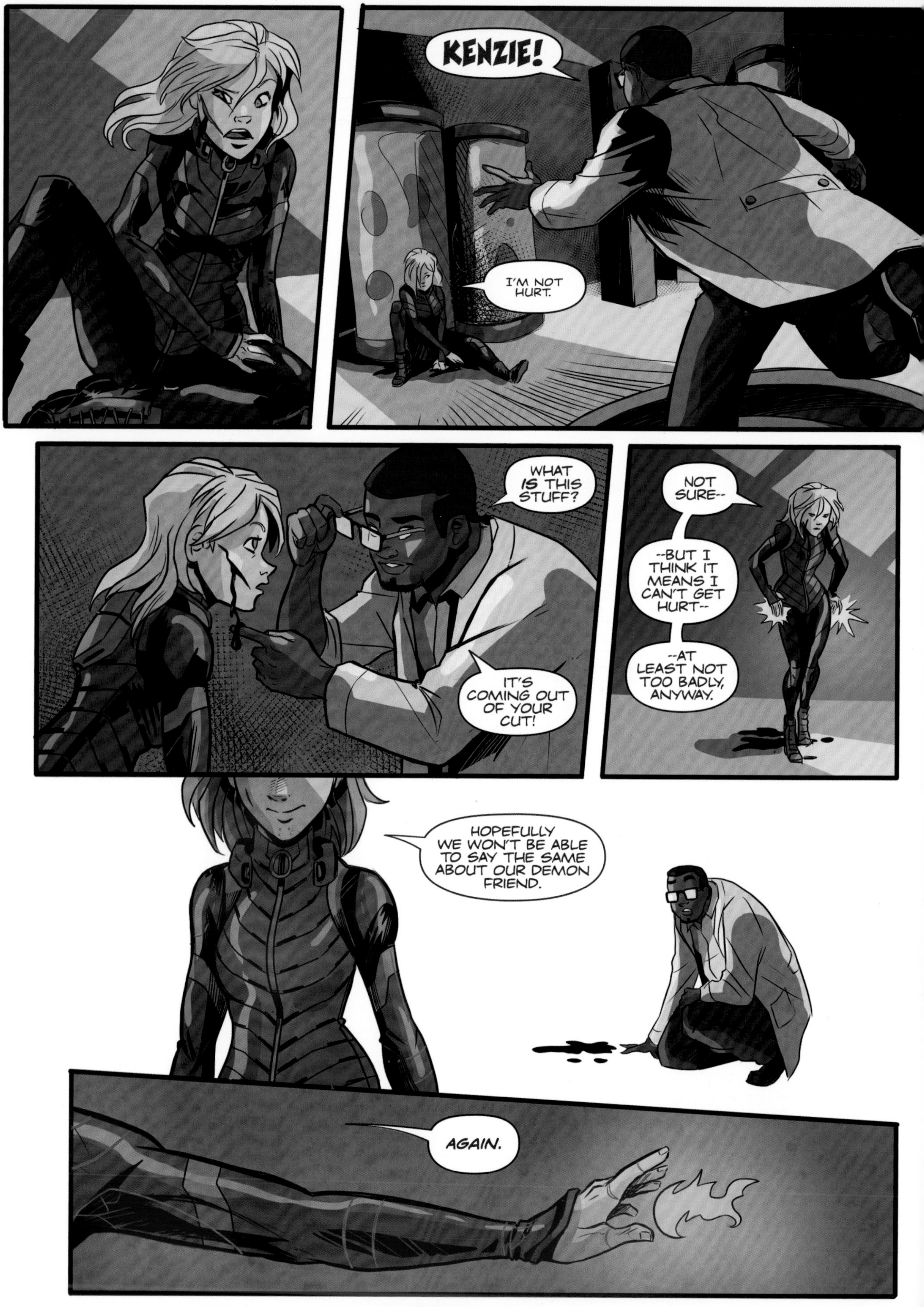
KENZIE!
I'M NOT HURT.
WHAT IS THIS STUFF?
IT'S COMING OUT OF YOUR CUT!
NOT SURE--
--BUT I THINK IT MEANS I CAN'T GET HURT--
--AT LEAST NOT TOO BADLY, ANYWAY.
HOPEFULLY WE WON'T BE ABLE TO SAY THE SAME ABOUT OUR DEMON FRIEND.
AGAIN.

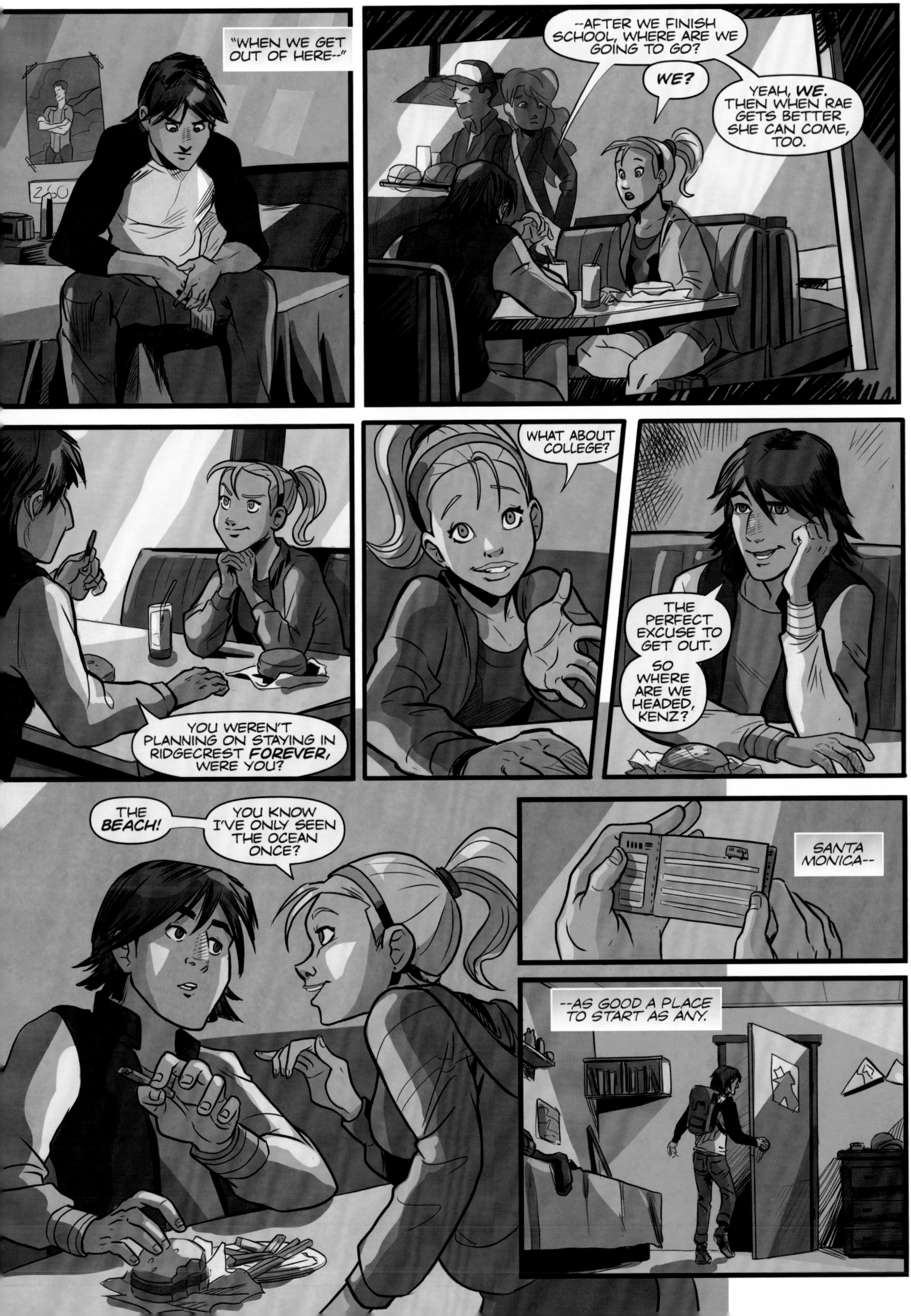
"WHEN WE GET OUT OF HERE--"
--AFTER WE FINISH SCHOOL, WHERE ARE WE GOING TO GO?
WE?
YEAH, **WE.** THEN WHEN RAE GETS BETTER SHE CAN COME, TOO.
YOU WEREN'T PLANNING ON STAYING IN RIDGECREST ***FOREVER,*** WERE YOU?
WHAT ABOUT COLLEGE?
THE PERFECT EXCUSE TO GET OUT.
SO WHERE ARE WE HEADED, KENZ?
THE ***BEACH!***
YOU KNOW I'VE ONLY SEEN THE OCEAN ONCE?
SANTA MONICA--
--AS GOOD A PLACE TO START AS ANY.

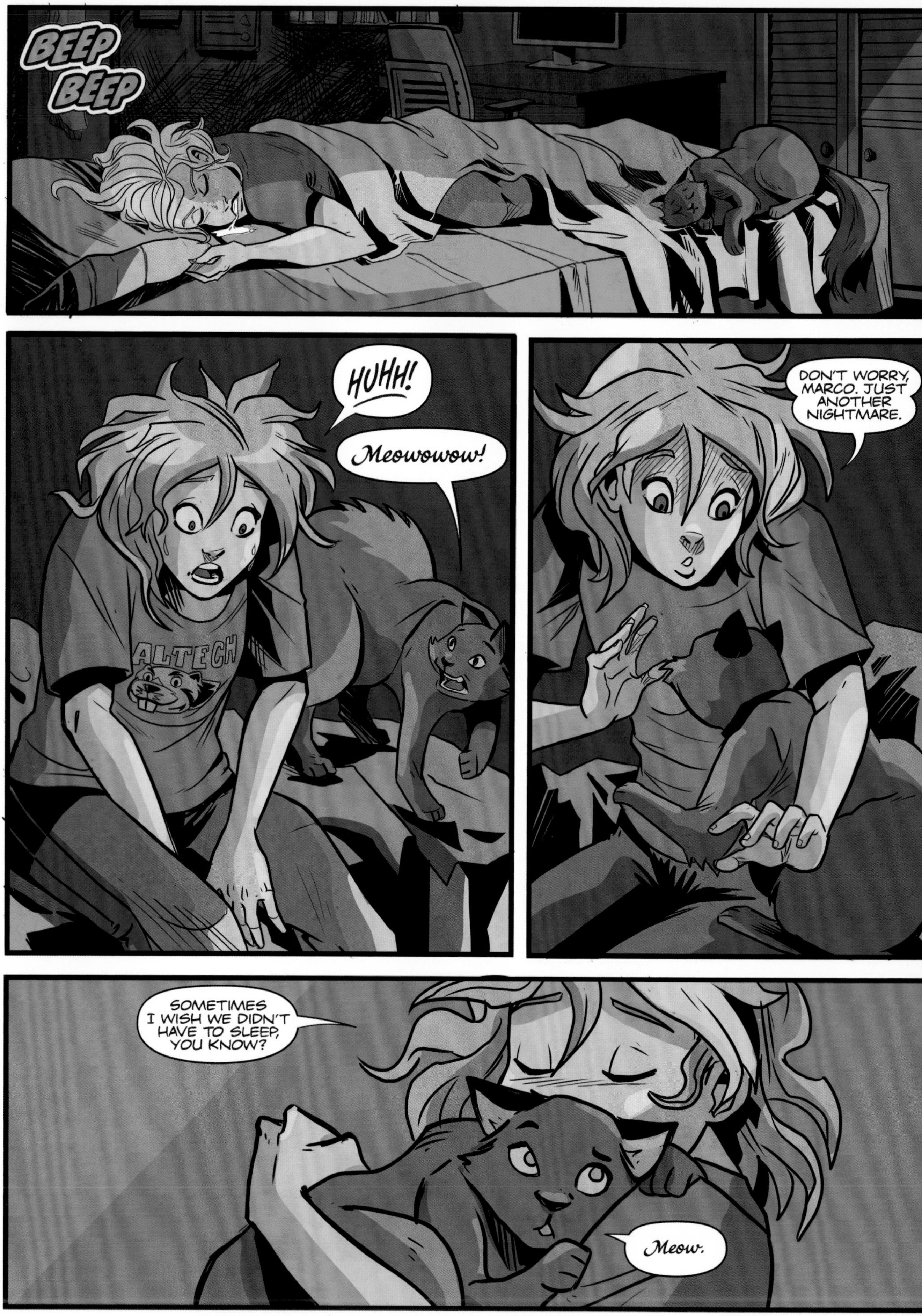
BEEP BEEP
HUHH!
Meowowow!
DON'T WORRY, MARCO. JUST ANOTHER NIGHTMARE.
SOMETIMES I WISH WE DIDN'T HAVE TO SLEEP, YOU KNOW?
Meow.
ALTECH

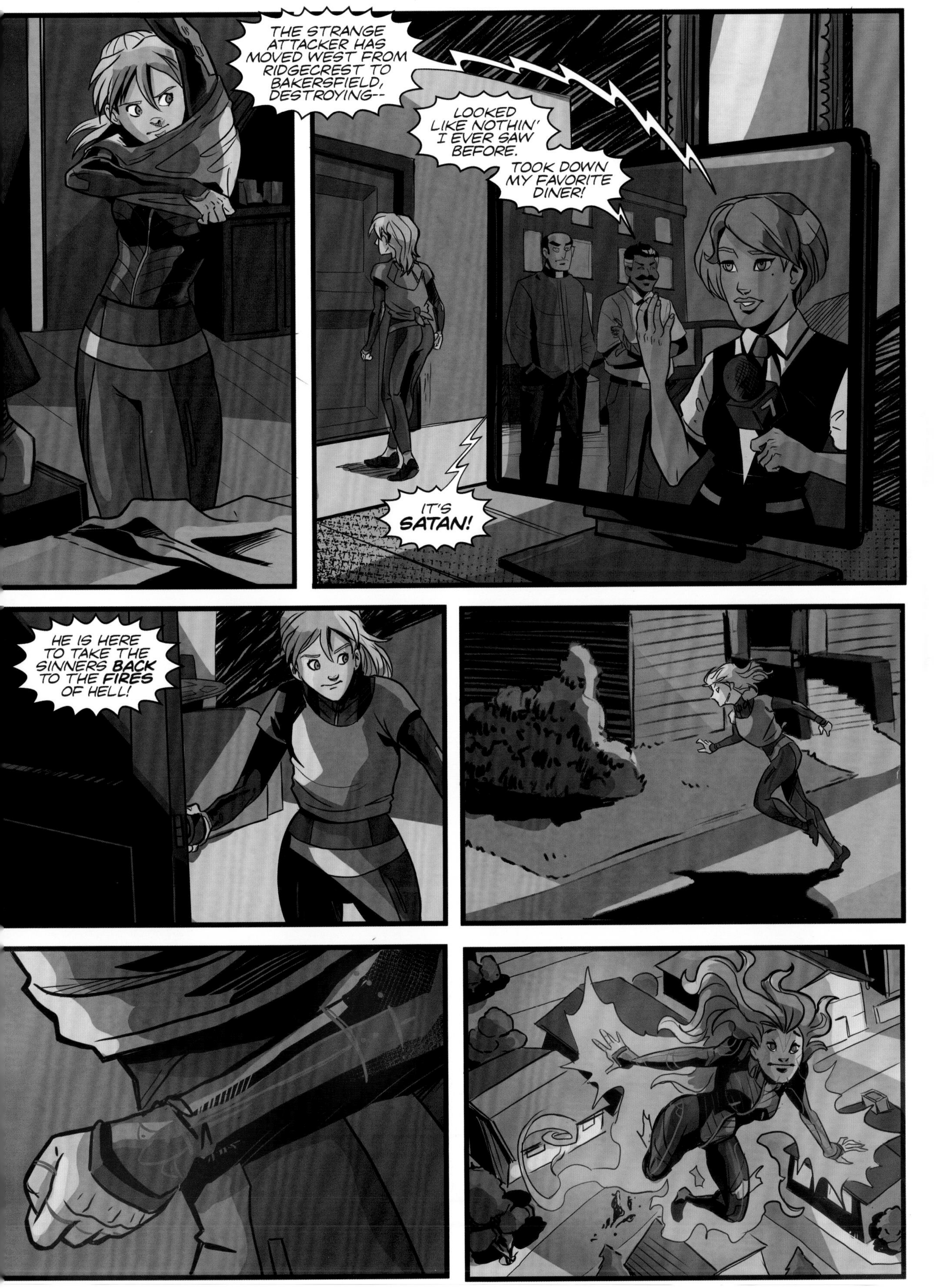
THE STRANGE ATTACKER HAS MOVED WEST FROM RIDGECREST TO BAKERSFIELD, DESTROYING--
LOOKED LIKE NOTHIN' I EVER SAW BEFORE.
TOOK DOWN MY FAVORITE DINER!
IT'S **SATAN!**
HE IS HERE TO TAKE THE SINNERS **BACK** TO THE **FIRES** OF HELL!

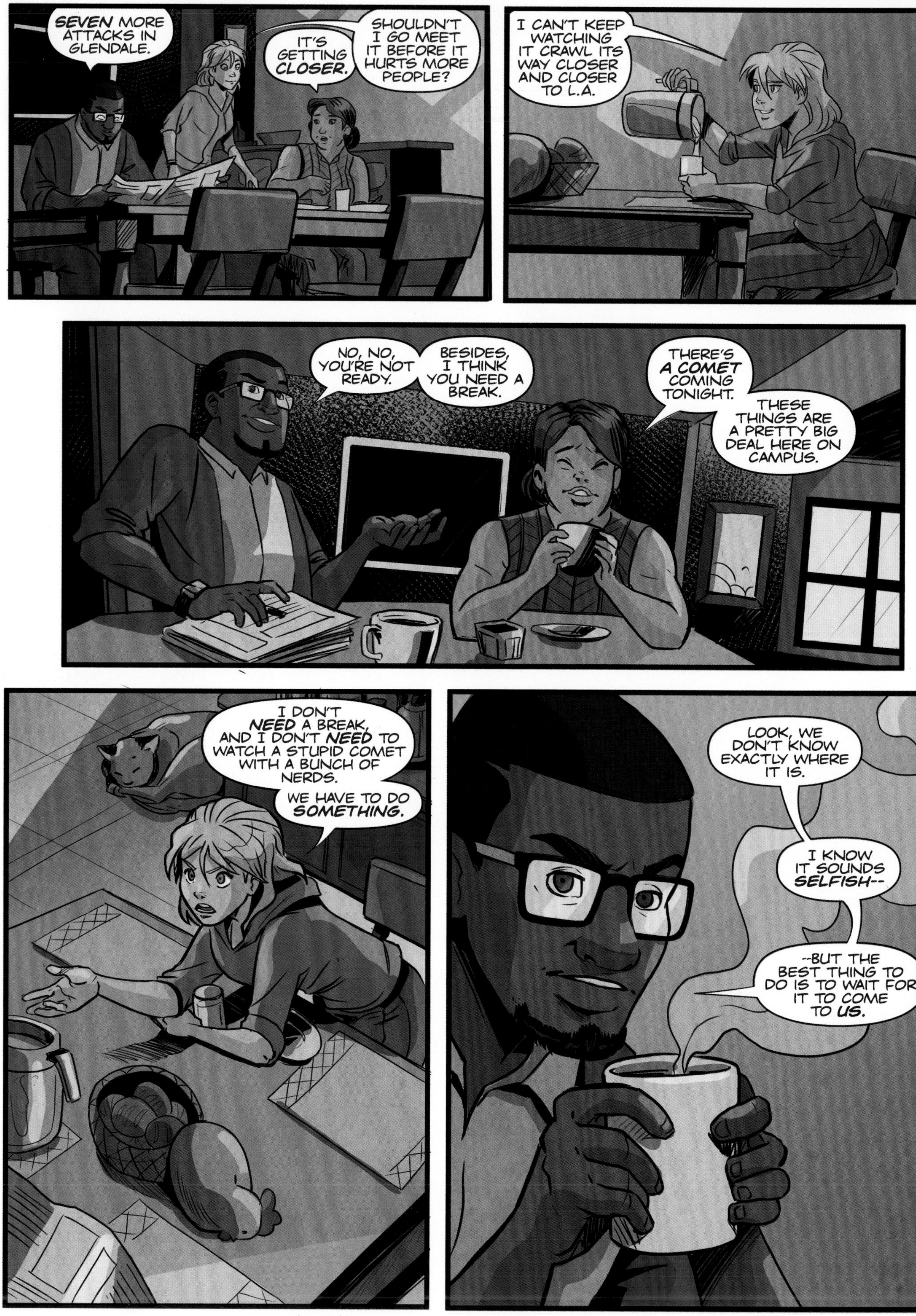
SEVEN MORE ATTACKS IN GLENDALE.
IT'S GETTING CLOSER.
SHOULDN'T I GO MEET IT BEFORE IT HURTS MORE PEOPLE?
I CAN'T KEEP WATCHING IT CRAWL ITS WAY CLOSER AND CLOSER TO L.A.
NO, NO, YOU'RE NOT READY.
BESIDES, I THINK YOU NEED A BREAK.
THERE'S A COMET COMING TONIGHT.
THESE THINGS ARE A PRETTY BIG DEAL HERE ON CAMPUS.
I DON'T NEED A BREAK, AND I DON'T NEED TO WATCH A STUPID COMET WITH A BUNCH OF NERDS.
WE HAVE TO DO SOMETHING.
LOOK, WE DON'T KNOW EXACTLY WHERE IT IS.
I KNOW IT SOUNDS SELFISH--
--BUT THE BEST THING TO DO IS TO WAIT FOR IT TO COME TO US.

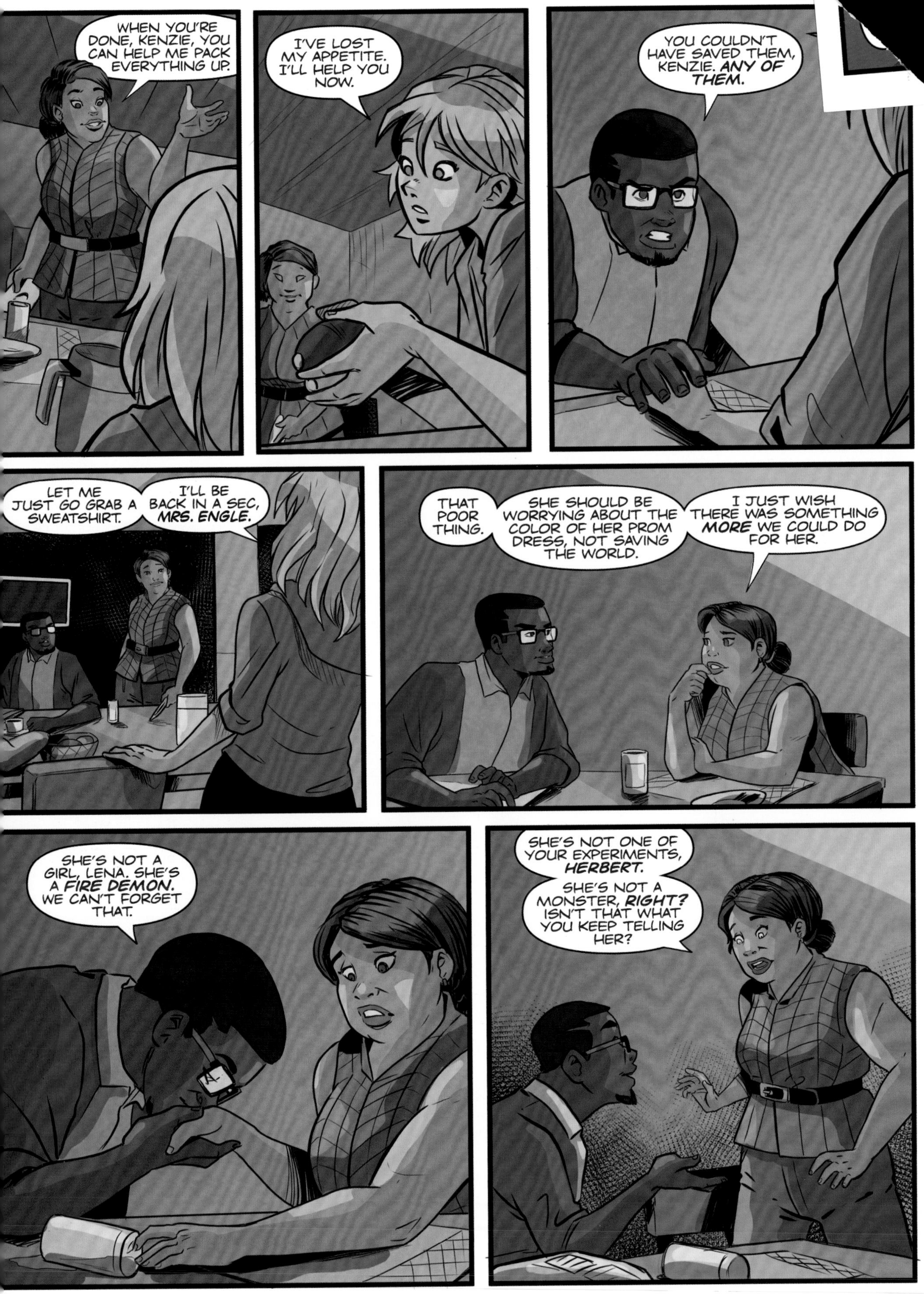
WHEN YOU'RE DONE, KENZIE, YOU CAN HELP ME PACK EVERYTHING UP.
I'VE LOST MY APPETITE. I'LL HELP YOU NOW.
YOU COULDN'T HAVE SAVED THEM, KENZIE. ***ANY OF THEM.***
LET ME JUST GO GRAB A SWEATSHIRT.
I'LL BE BACK IN A SEC, ***MRS. ENGLE.***
THAT POOR THING.
SHE SHOULD BE WORRYING ABOUT THE COLOR OF HER PROM DRESS, NOT SAVING THE WORLD.
I JUST WISH THERE WAS SOMETHING ***MORE*** WE COULD DO FOR HER.
SHE'S NOT A GIRL, LENA. SHE'S A ***FIRE DEMON.*** WE CAN'T FORGET THAT.
SHE'S NOT ONE OF YOUR EXPERIMENTS, ***HERBERT.***
SHE'S NOT A MONSTER, ***RIGHT?*** ISN'T THAT WHAT YOU KEEP TELLING HER?

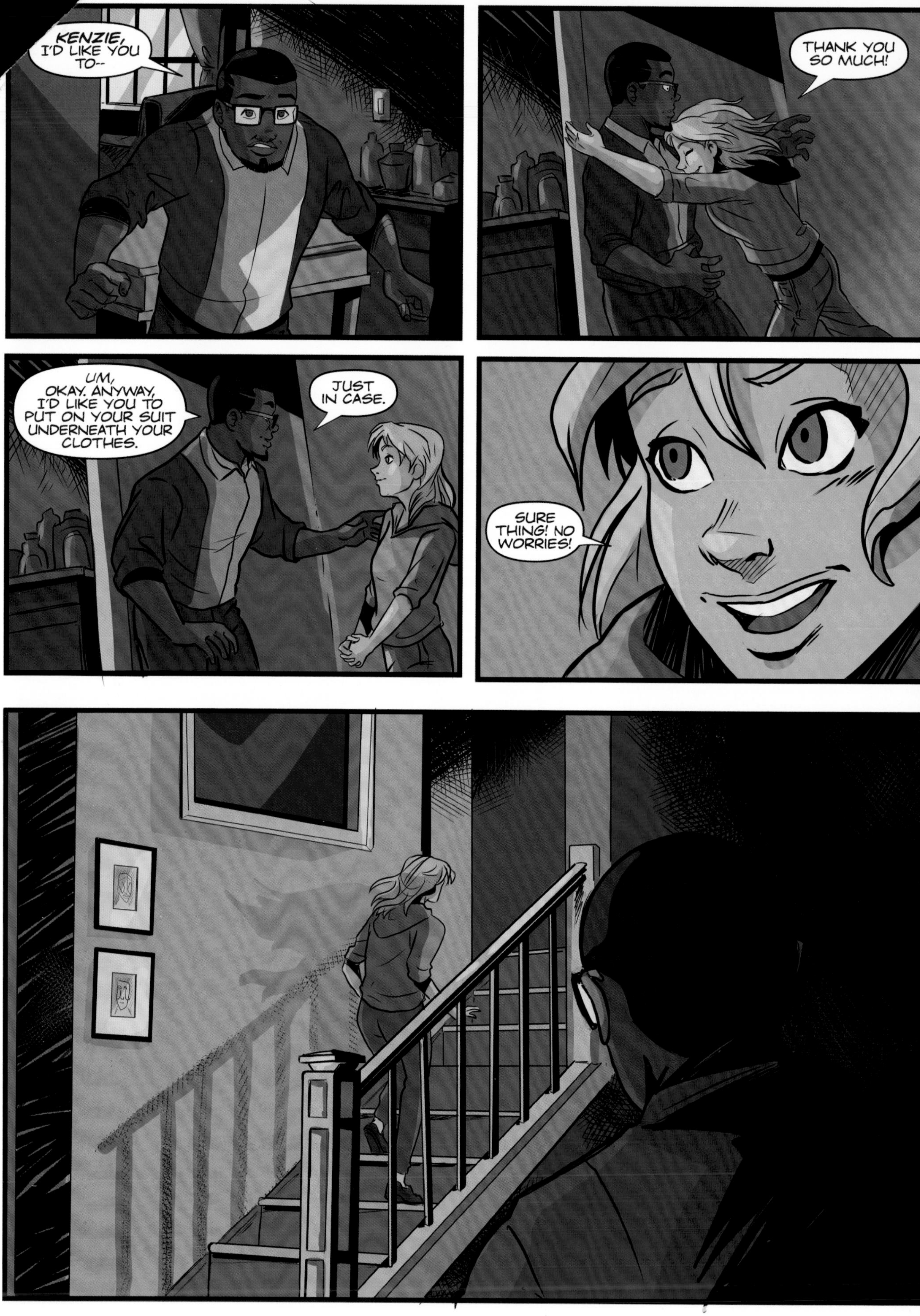
KENZIE, I'D LIKE YOU TO--
THANK YOU SO MUCH!
UM, OKAY. ANYWAY, I'D LIKE YOU TO PUT ON YOUR SUIT UNDERNEATH YOUR CLOTHES.
JUST IN CASE.
SURE THING! NO WORRIES!

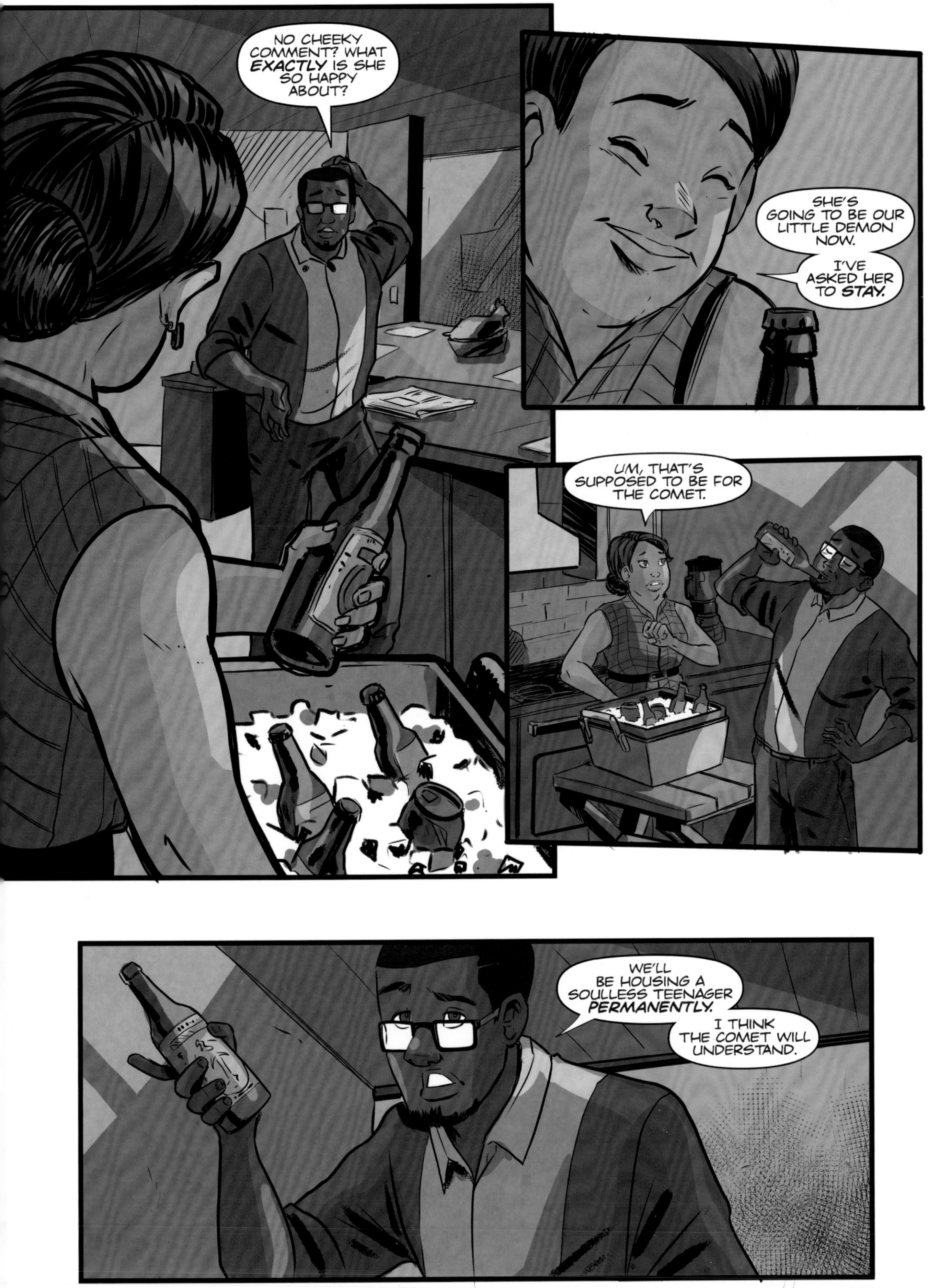
NO CHEEKY COMMENT? WHAT **EXACTLY** IS SHE SO HAPPY ABOUT?
SHE'S GOING TO BE OUR LITTLE DEMON NOW.
I'VE ASKED HER TO **STAY.**
UM, THAT'S SUPPOSED TO BE FOR THE COMET.
WE'LL BE HOUSING A SOULLESS TEENAGER **PERMANENTLY.**
I THINK THE COMET WILL UNDERSTAND.

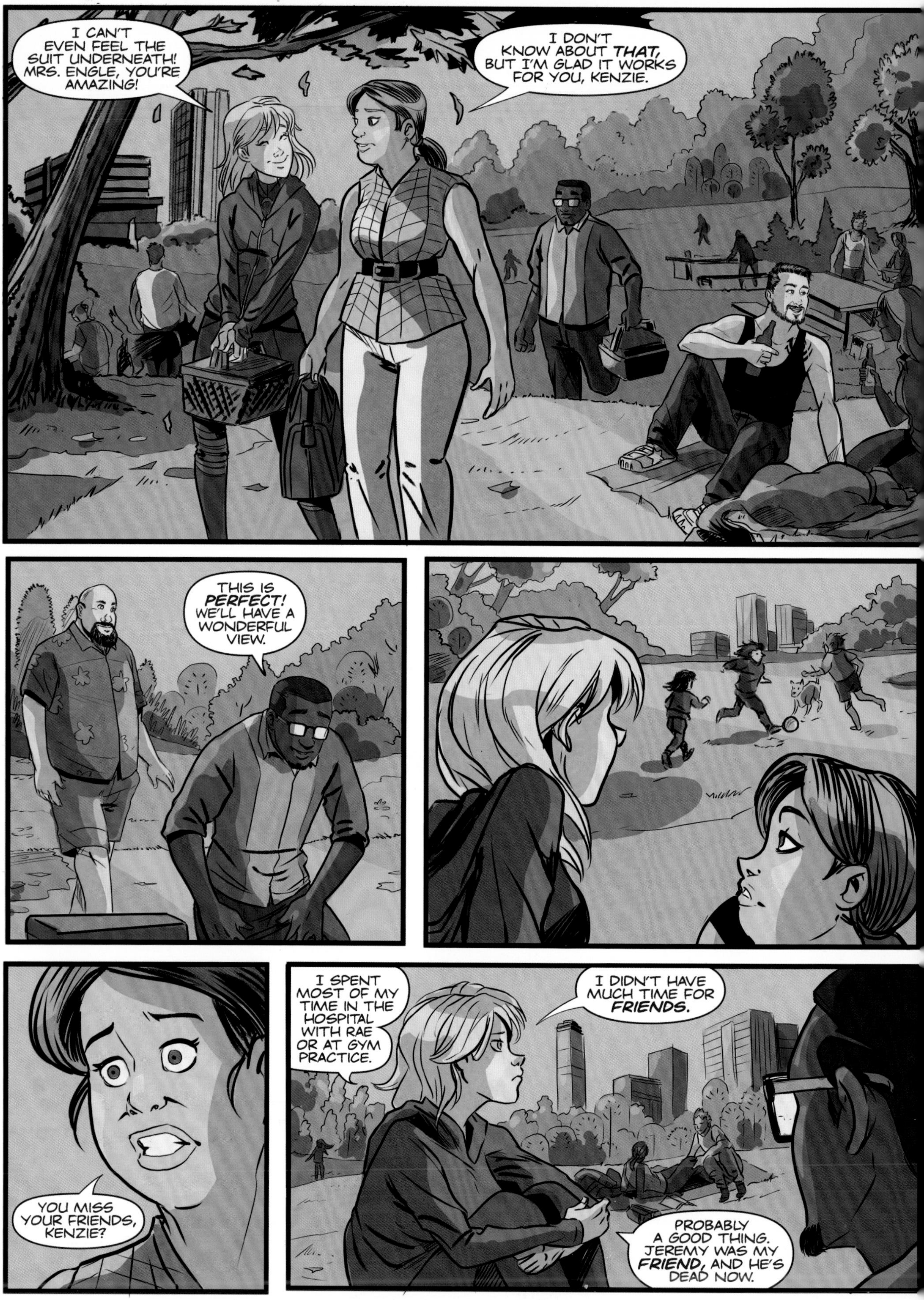
I CAN'T EVEN FEEL THE SUIT UNDERNEATH! MRS. ENGLE, YOU'RE AMAZING!
I DON'T KNOW ABOUT THAT, BUT I'M GLAD IT WORKS FOR YOU, KENZIE.
THIS IS PERFECT! WE'LL HAVE A WONDERFUL VIEW.
YOU MISS YOUR FRIENDS, KENZIE?
I SPENT MOST OF MY TIME IN THE HOSPITAL WITH RAE OR AT GYM PRACTICE.
I DIDN'T HAVE MUCH TIME FOR FRIENDS.
PROBABLY A GOOD THING. JEREMY WAS MY FRIEND, AND HE'S DEAD NOW.

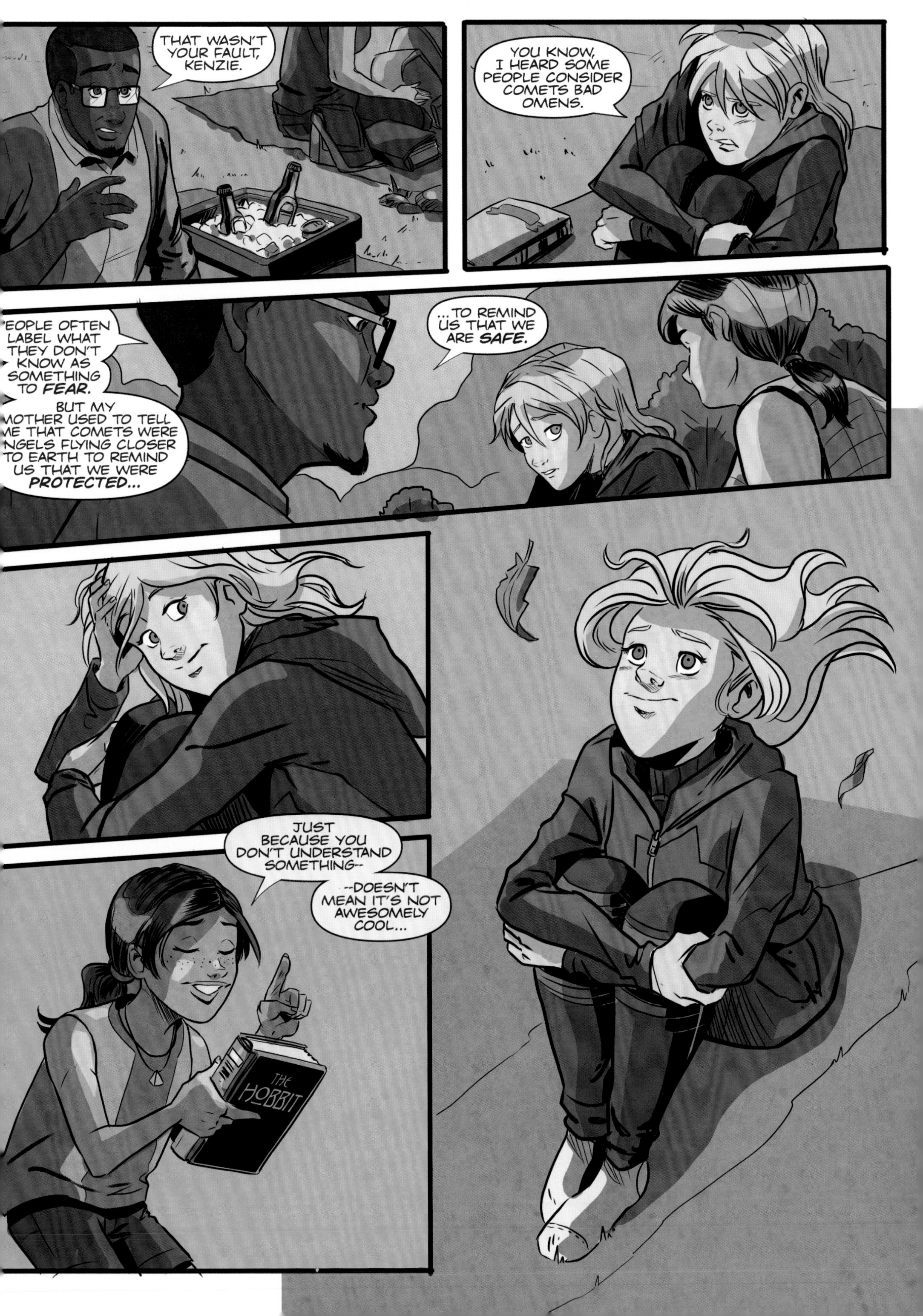
THAT WASN'T YOUR FAULT, KENZIE.
YOU KNOW, I HEARD SOME PEOPLE CONSIDER COMETS BAD OMENS.
PEOPLE OFTEN LABEL WHAT THEY DON'T KNOW AS SOMETHING TO FEAR.
BUT MY MOTHER USED TO TELL ME THAT COMETS WERE ANGELS FLYING CLOSER TO EARTH TO REMIND US THAT WE WERE PROTECTED...
...TO REMIND US THAT WE ARE SAFE.
JUST BECAUSE YOU DON'T UNDERSTAND SOMETHING--
--DOESN'T MEAN IT'S NOT AWESOMELY COOL...
THE HOBBIT

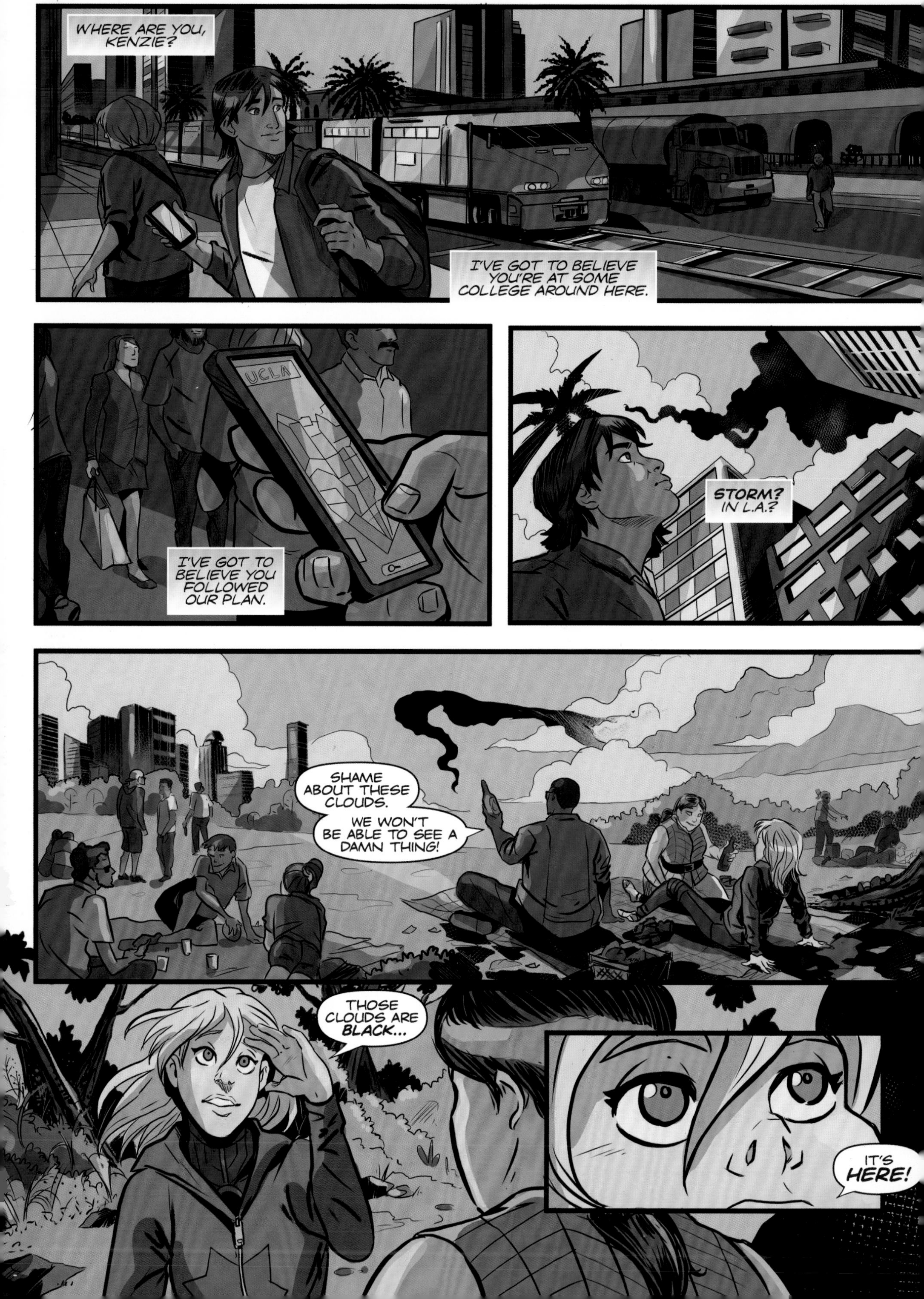
WHERE ARE YOU, KENZIE?
I'VE GOT TO BELIEVE YOU'RE AT SOME COLLEGE AROUND HERE.
UCLA
I'VE GOT TO BELIEVE YOU FOLLOWED OUR PLAN.
STORM? IN L.A.?
SHAME ABOUT THESE CLOUDS.
WE WON'T BE ABLE TO SEE A DAMN THING!
THOSE CLOUDS ARE BLACK...
IT'S HERE!

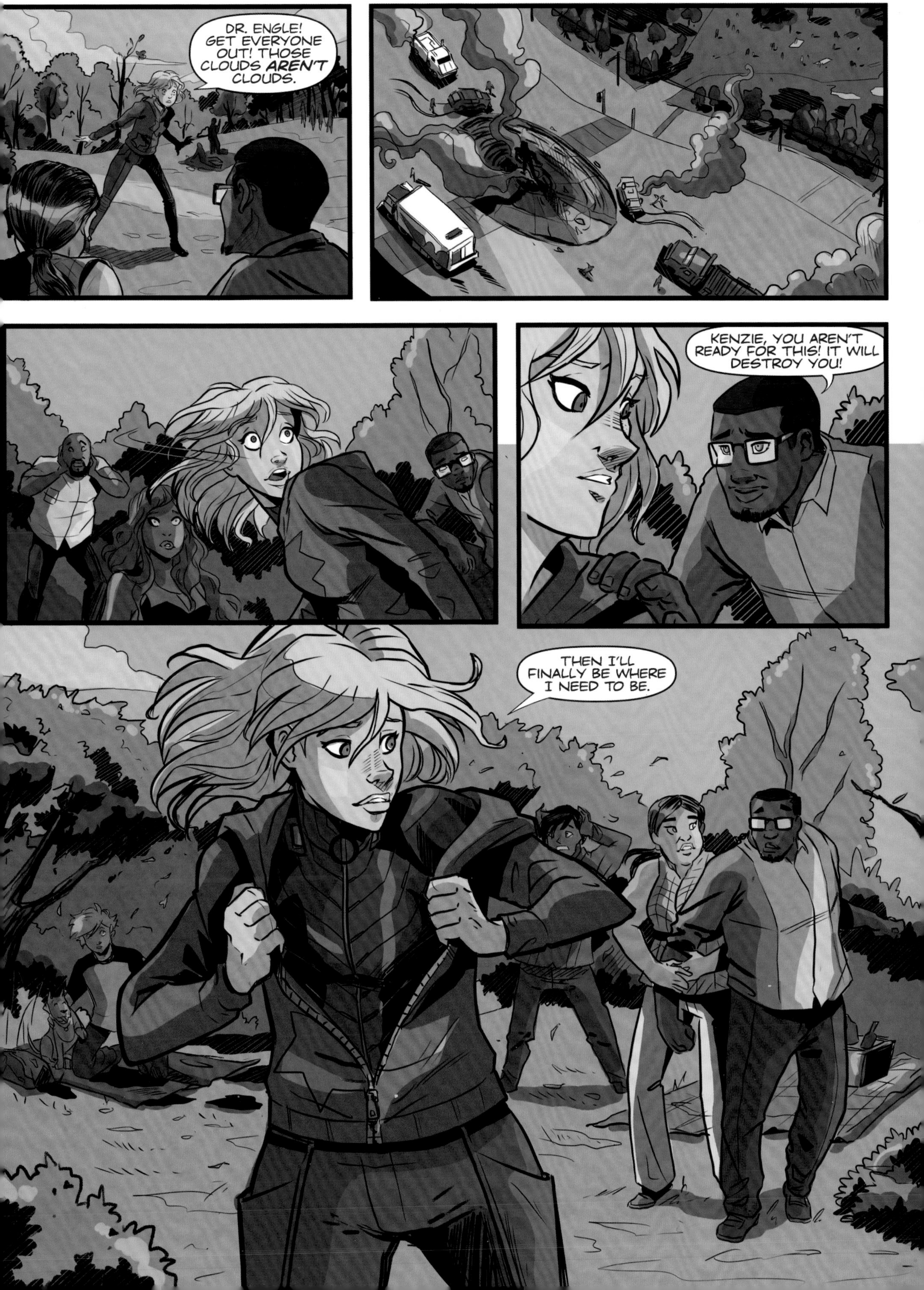
DR. ENGLE! GET EVERYONE OUT! THOSE CLOUDS ***AREN'T*** CLOUDS.
KENZIE, YOU AREN'T READY FOR THIS! IT WILL DESTROY YOU!
THEN I'LL FINALLY BE WHERE I NEED TO BE.

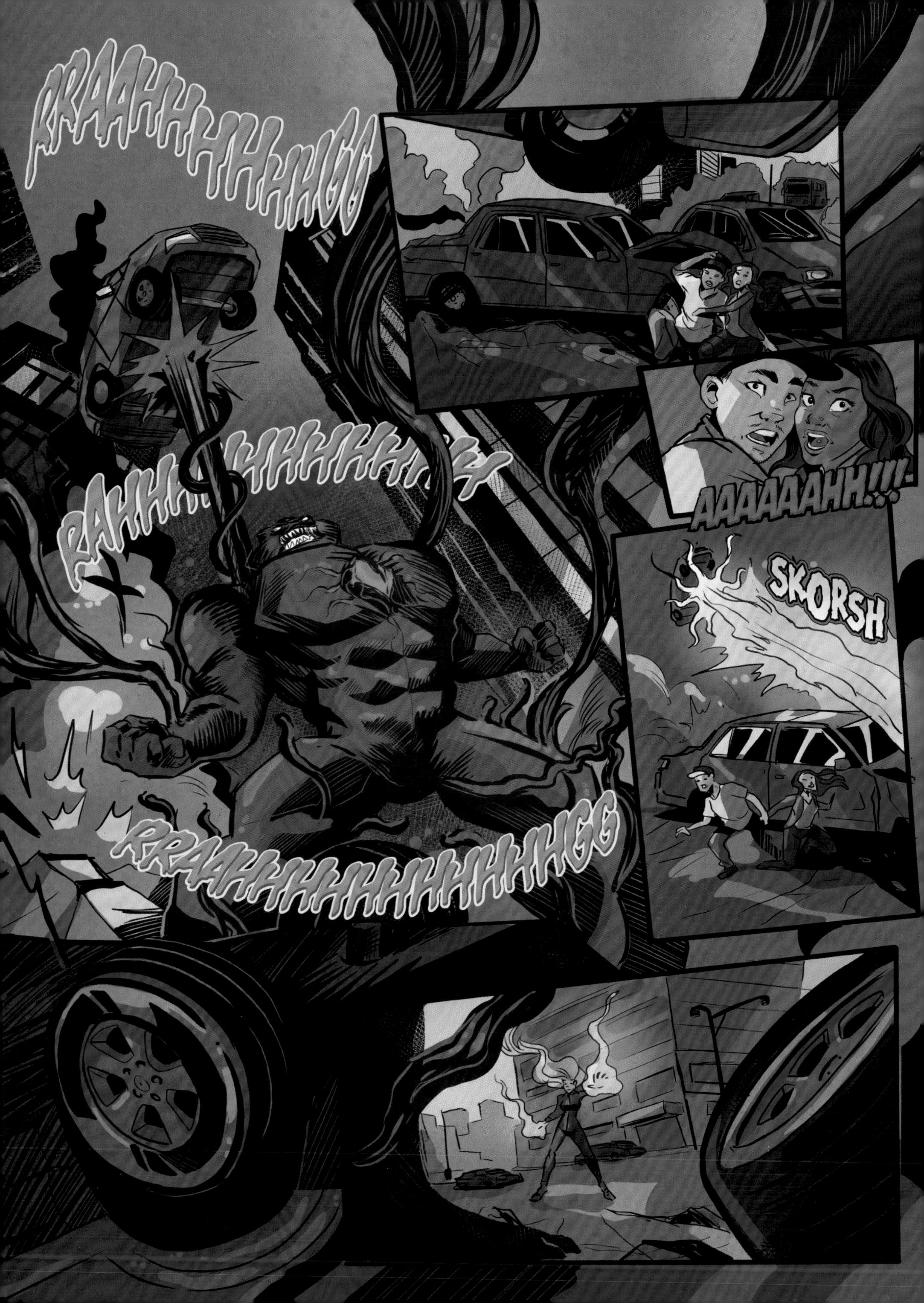
RRAAHHHHHHHGG
RAHHHHHHHHHHHGG
RRAAHHHHHHHHHHHHGG
AAAAAAHH!!!
SKORSH

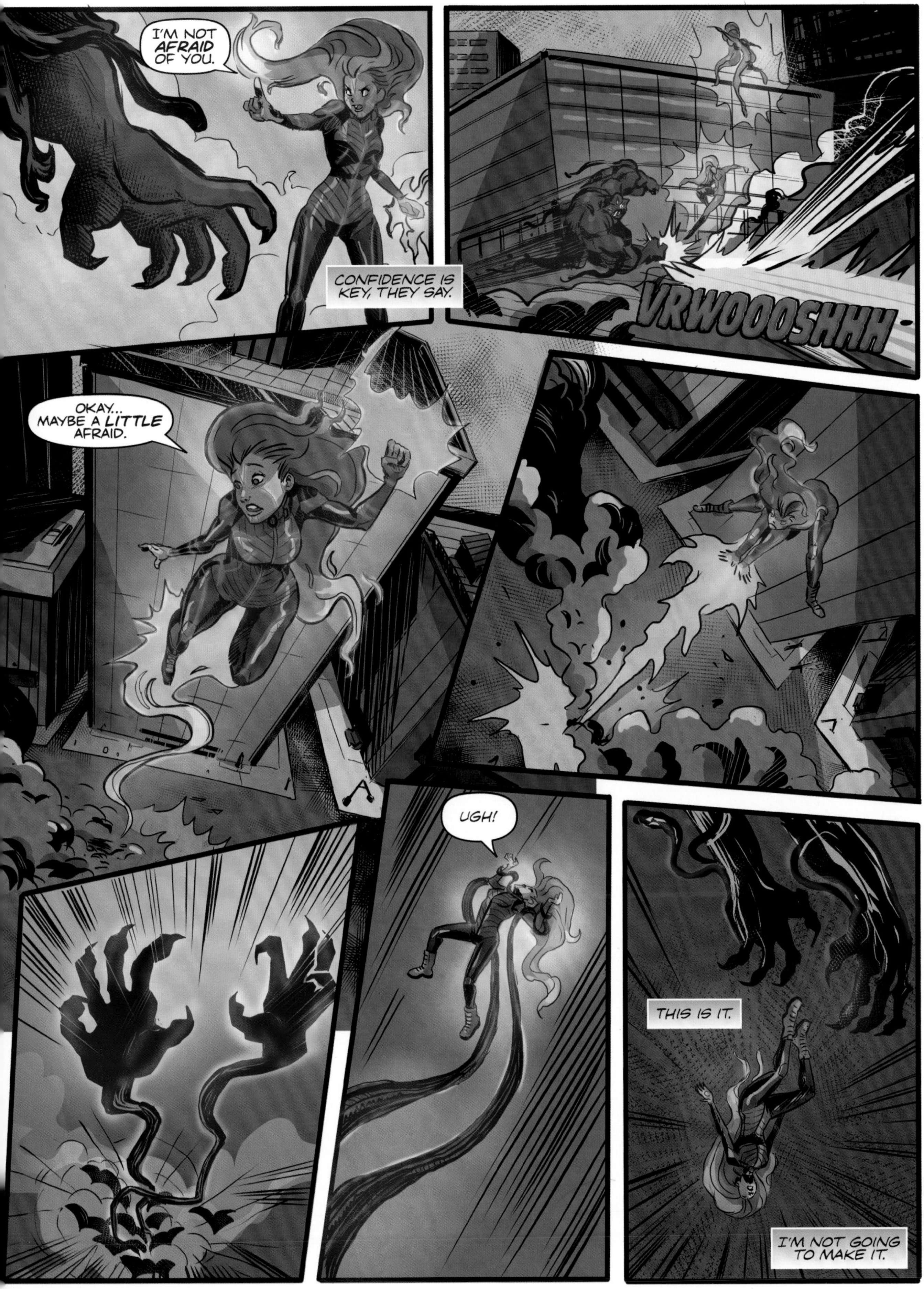
I'M NOT AFRAID OF YOU.
CONFIDENCE IS KEY, THEY SAY.
VRWOOOSHHH
OKAY... MAYBE A LITTLE AFRAID.
UGH!
THIS IS IT.
I'M NOT GOING TO MAKE IT.

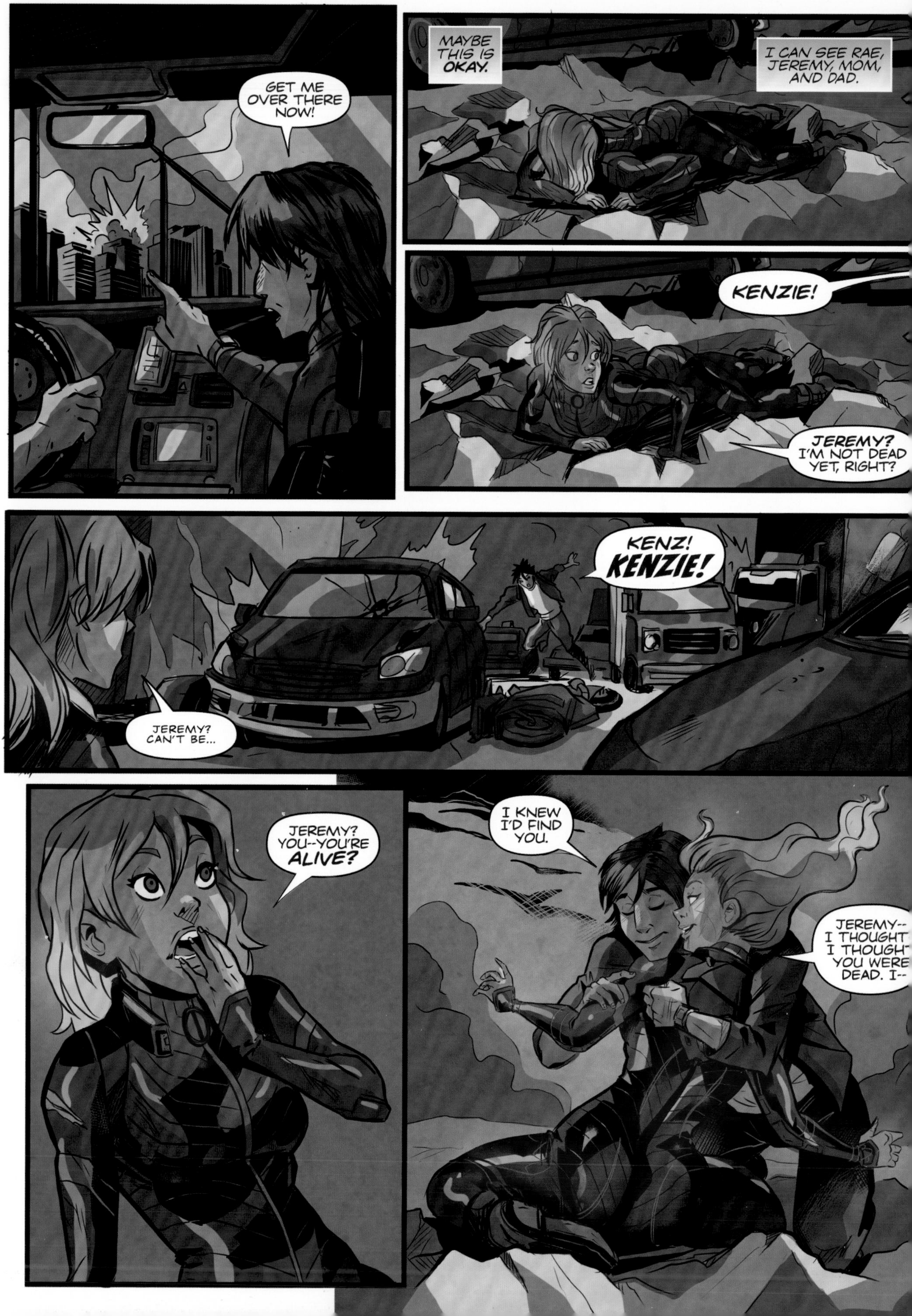
GET ME OVER THERE NOW!
MAYBE THIS IS OKAY.
I CAN SEE RAE, JEREMY, MOM, AND DAD.
KENZIE!
JEREMY? I'M NOT DEAD YET, RIGHT?
KENZ! KENZIE!
JEREMY? CAN'T BE...
JEREMY? YOU--YOU'RE ALIVE?
I KNEW I'D FIND YOU.
JEREMY-- I THOUGHT I THOUGHT YOU WERE DEAD. I--

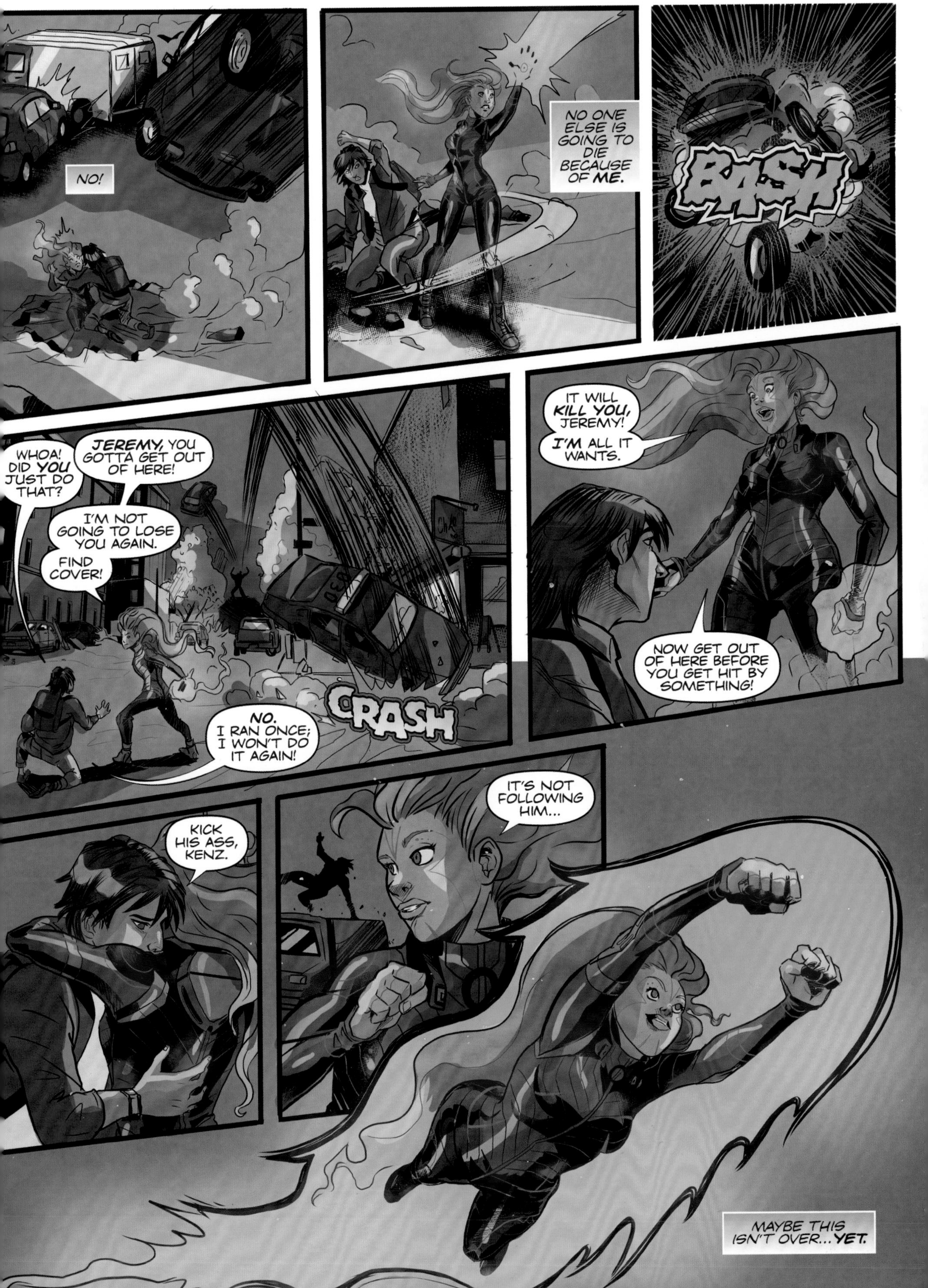
NO!
NO ONE ELSE IS GOING TO DIE BECAUSE OF **ME**.
BASH
WHOA! DID **YOU** JUST DO THAT?
JEREMY, YOU GOTTA GET OUT OF HERE!
I'M NOT GOING TO LOSE YOU AGAIN.
FIND COVER!
CRASH
NO. I RAN ONCE; I WON'T DO IT AGAIN!
IT WILL ***KILL YOU,*** JEREMY!
I'M ALL IT WANTS.
NOW GET OUT OF HERE BEFORE YOU GET HIT BY SOMETHING!
KICK HIS ASS, KENZ.
IT'S NOT FOLLOWING HIM...
MAYBE THIS ISN'T OVER... ***YET.***

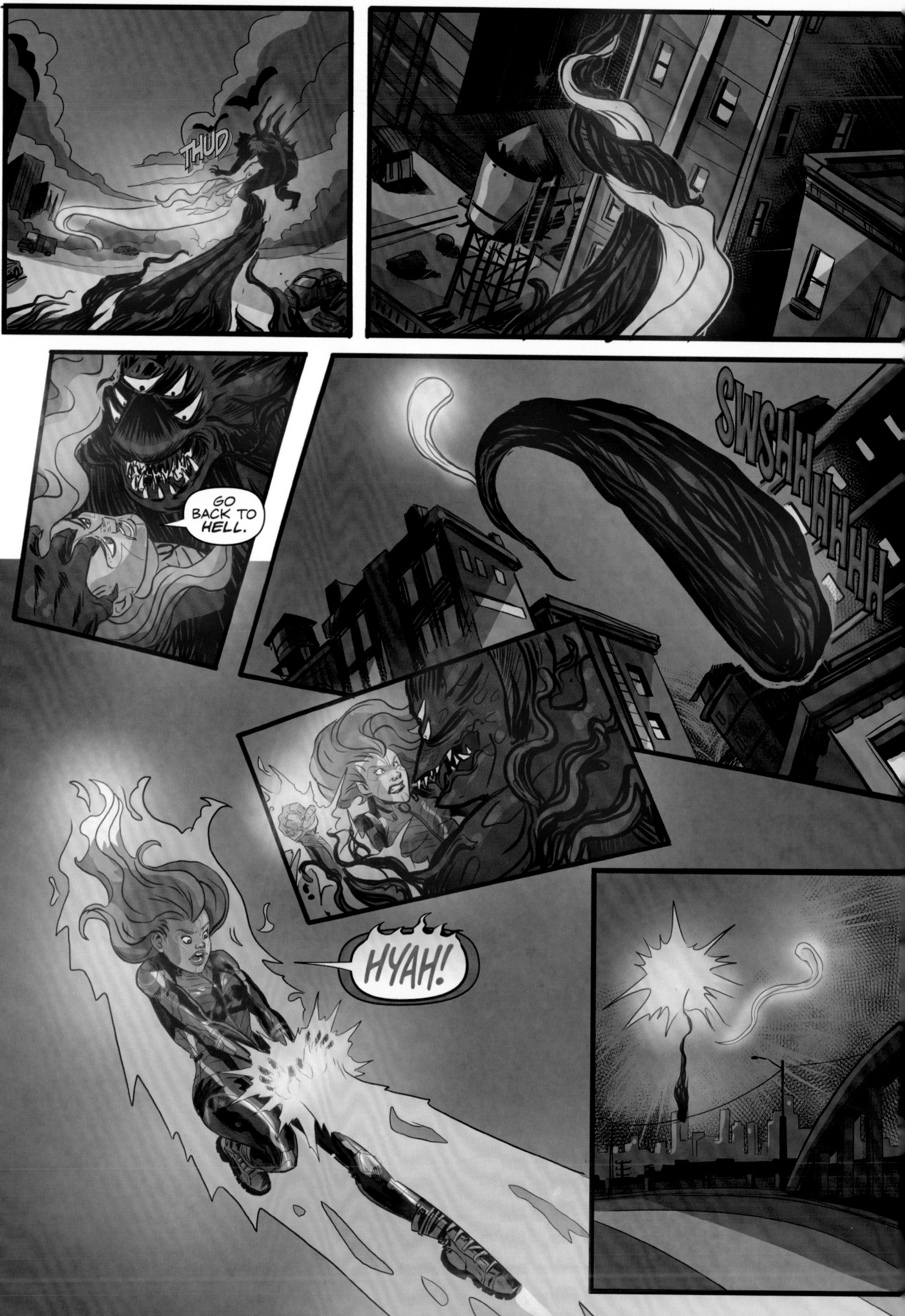
THUD
GO BACK TO HELL.
SWSHHHHHHH
HYAH!

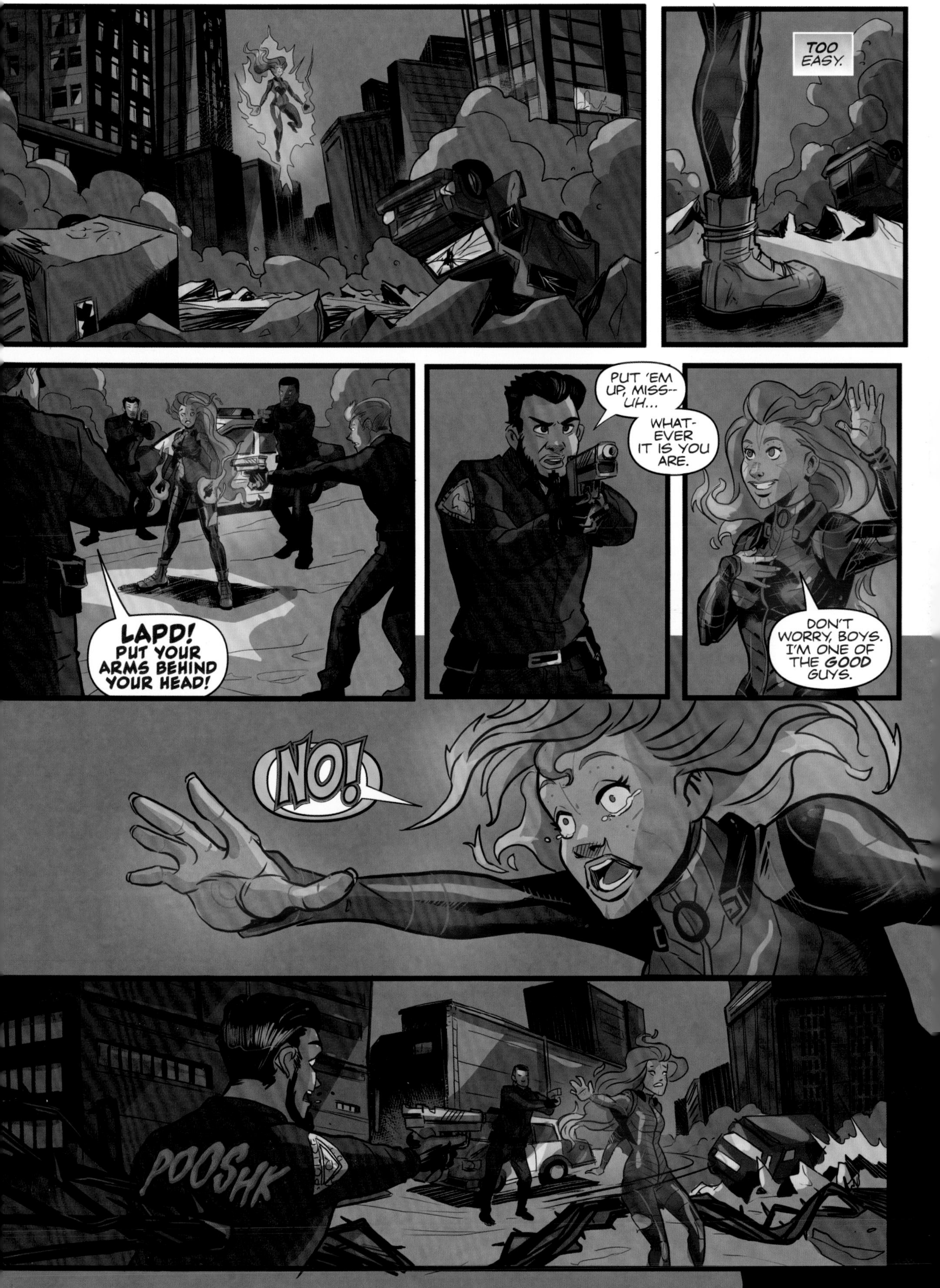
TOO EASY.
LAPD! PUT YOUR ARMS BEHIND YOUR HEAD!
PUT 'EM UP, MISS-- UH...
WHAT-EVER IT IS YOU ARE.
DON'T WORRY, BOYS. I'M ONE OF THE GOOD GUYS.
NO!
POOSHK

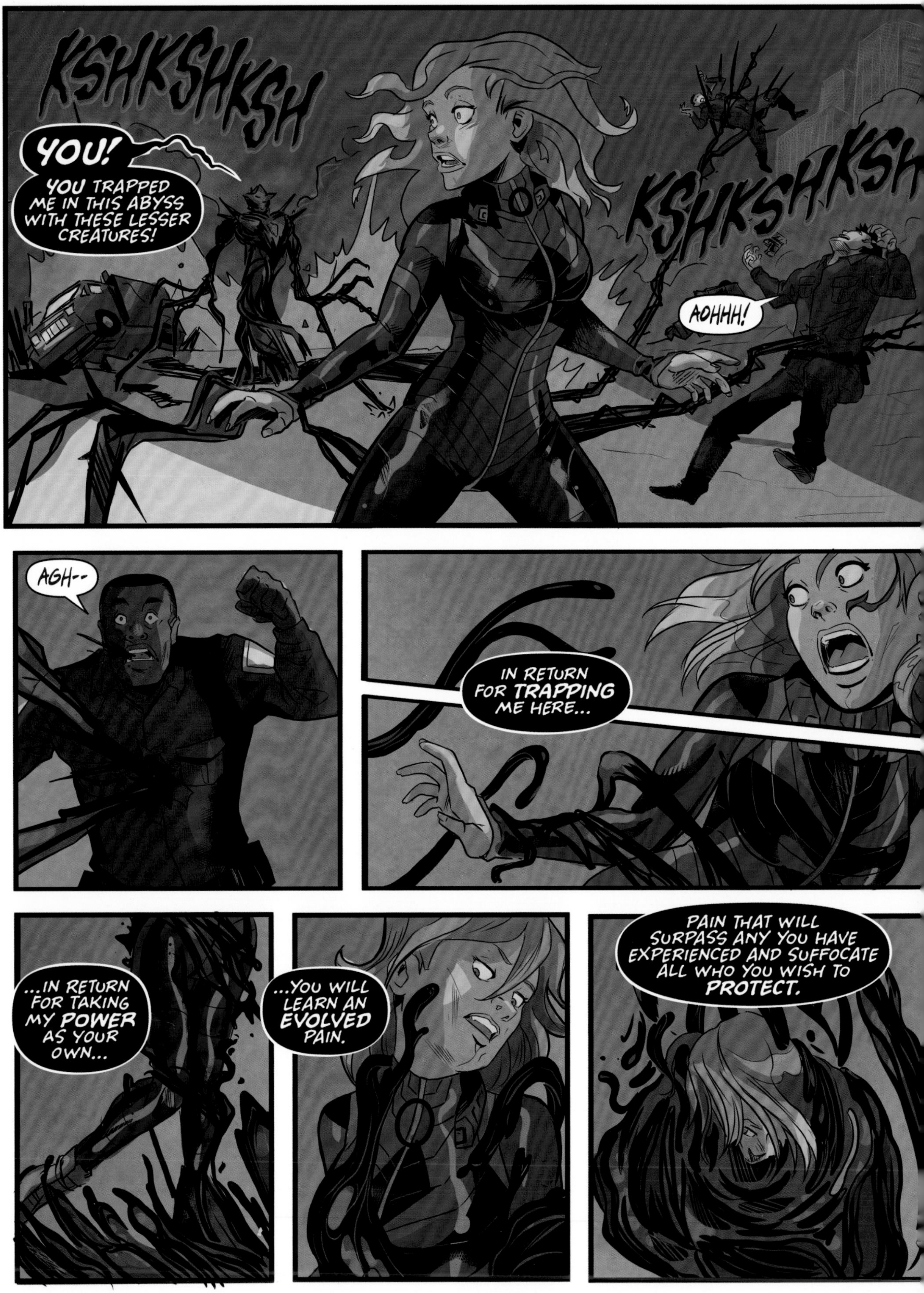
KSHKSHKSH
YOU!
YOU TRAPPED ME IN THIS ABYSS WITH THESE LESSER CREATURES!
KSHKSHKSH
AOHHH!
AGH--
IN RETURN FOR TRAPPING ME HERE...
...IN RETURN FOR TAKING MY POWER AS YOUR OWN...
...YOU WILL LEARN AN EVOLVED PAIN.
PAIN THAT WILL SURPASS ANY YOU HAVE EXPERIENCED AND SUFFOCATE ALL WHO YOU WISH TO PROTECT.

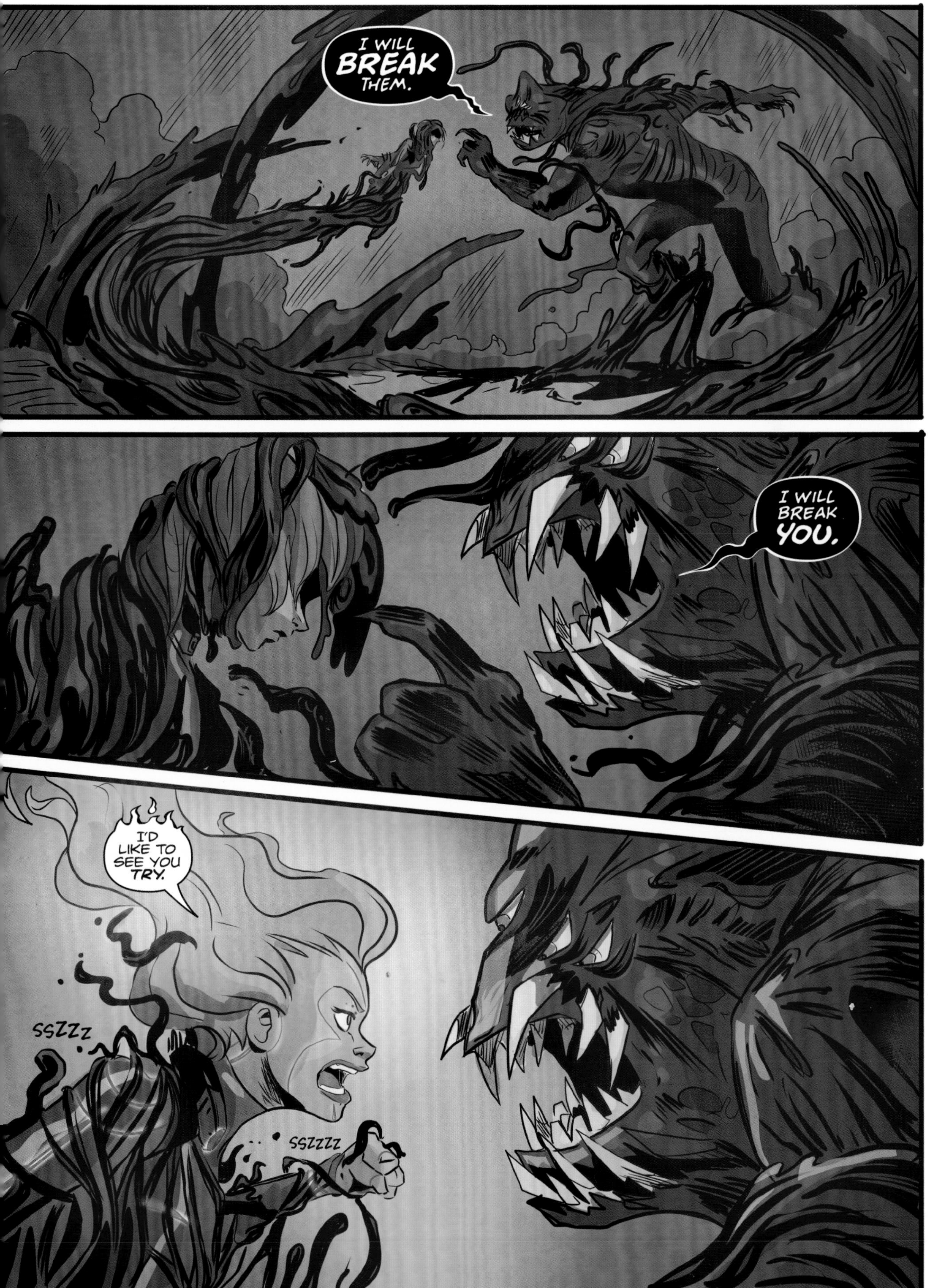
I WILL BREAK THEM.
I WILL BREAK YOU.
I'D LIKE TO SEE YOU TRY.
SSZZZ
SSZZZZ

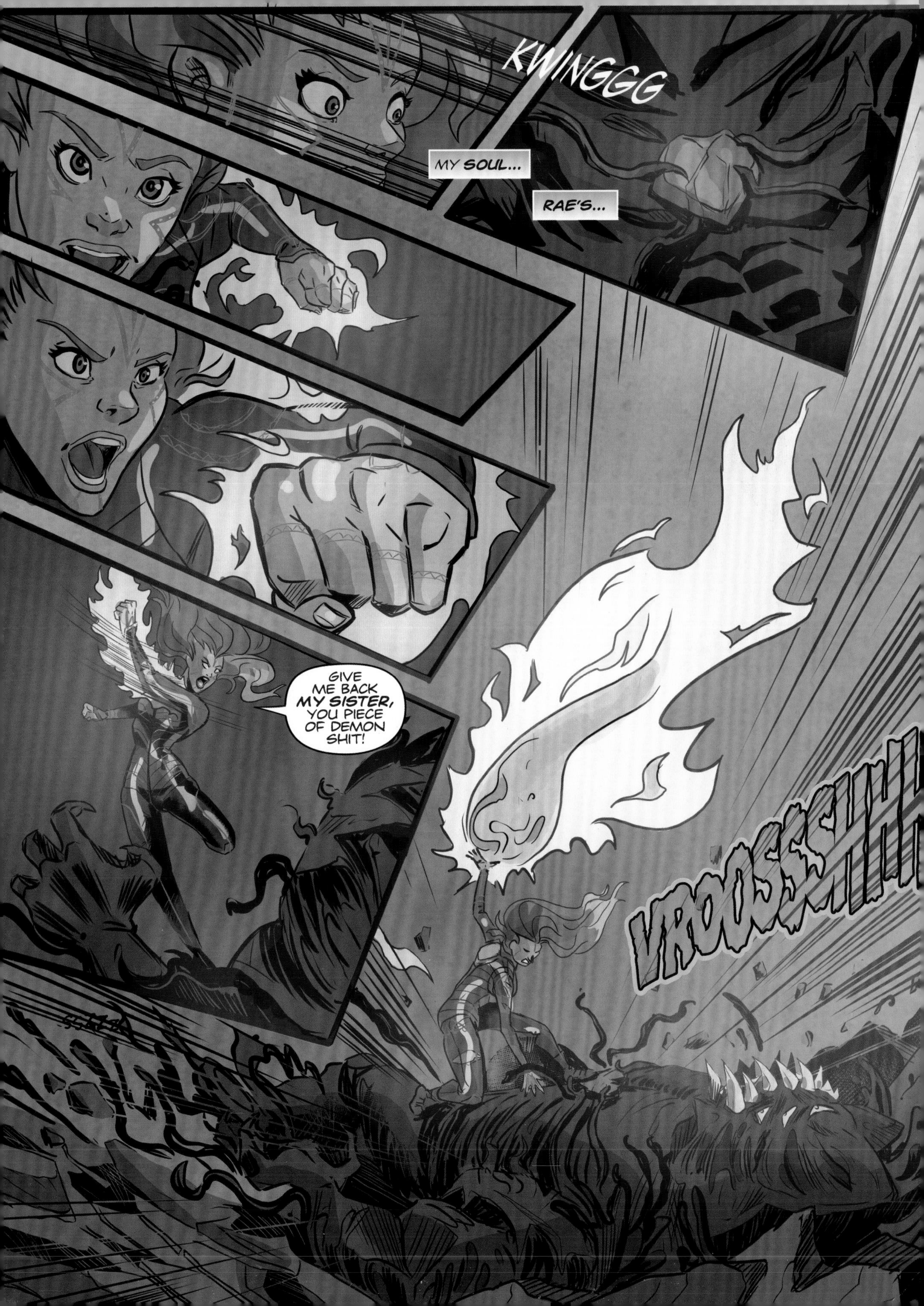
KWINGGG
MY SOUL...
RAE'S...
GIVE ME BACK MY SISTER, YOU PIECE OF DEMON SHIT!
VROOSSSHHH

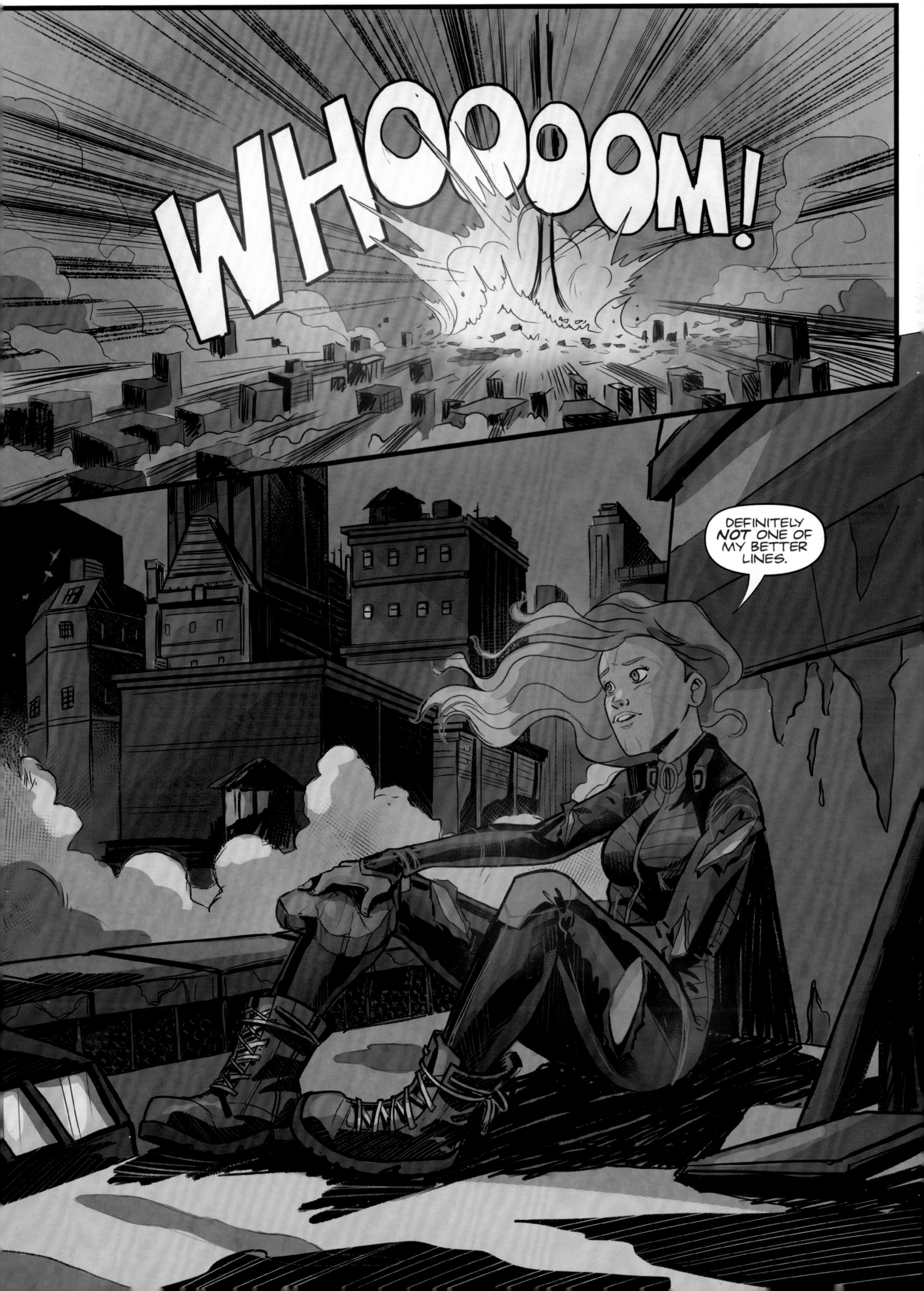
WHOOOOOM!
DEFINITELY NOT ONE OF MY BETTER LINES.

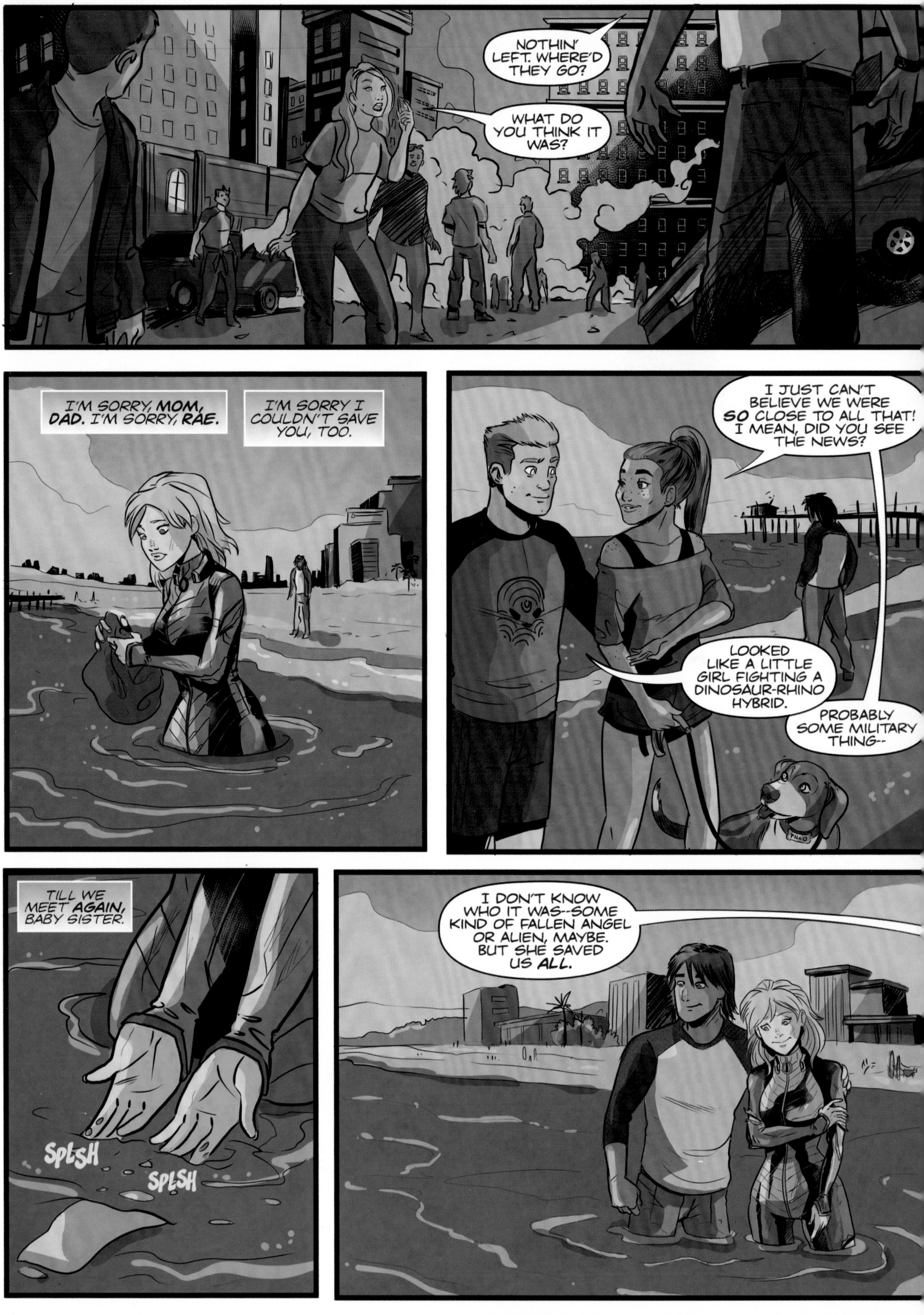
NOTHIN' LEFT. WHERE'D THEY GO?
WHAT DO YOU THINK IT WAS?
I'M SORRY, MOM, DAD. I'M SORRY, RAE.
I'M SORRY I COULDN'T SAVE YOU, TOO.
I JUST CAN'T BELIEVE WE WERE SO CLOSE TO ALL THAT! I MEAN, DID YOU SEE THE NEWS?
LOOKED LIKE A LITTLE GIRL FIGHTING A DINOSAUR-RHINO HYBRID.
PROBABLY SOME MILITARY THING--
TILL WE MEET AGAIN, BABY SISTER.
SPLSH
SPLSH
I DON'T KNOW WHO IT WAS--SOME KIND OF FALLEN ANGEL OR ALIEN, MAYBE. BUT SHE SAVED US ALL.

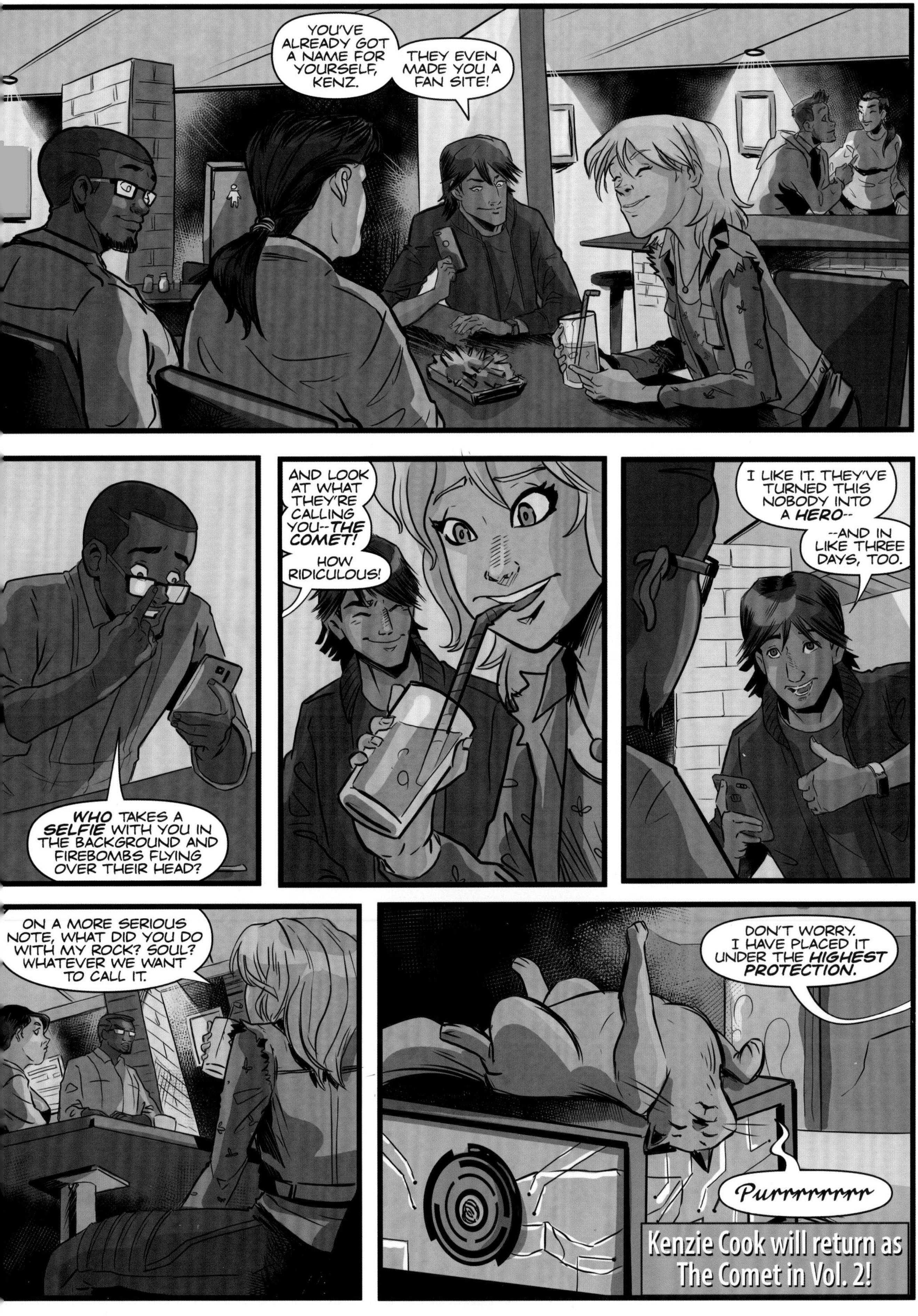

YOU'VE ALREADY GOT A NAME FOR YOURSELF, KENZ.
THEY EVEN MADE YOU A FAN SITE!
WHO TAKES A SELFIE WITH YOU IN THE BACKGROUND AND FIREBOMBS FLYING OVER THEIR HEAD?
AND LOOK AT WHAT THEY'RE CALLING YOU--THE COMET!
HOW RIDICULOUS!
I LIKE IT. THEY'VE TURNED THIS NOBODY INTO A HERO--
--AND IN LIKE THREE DAYS, TOO.
ON A MORE SERIOUS NOTE, WHAT DID YOU DO WITH MY ROCK? SOUL? WHATEVER WE WANT TO CALL IT.
DON'T WORRY. I HAVE PLACED IT UNDER THE HIGHEST PROTECTION.
Purrrrrrrrr
Kenzie Cook will return as The Comet in Vol. 2!

An Imprint of Insight Editions
PO Box 3088
San Rafael, CA 94912
www.insightcomics.com

Find us on Facebook:
www.facebook.com/InsightEditionsComics

Follow us on Twitter:
@InsightComics

Follow us on Instagram:
Insight_Comics

Library of Congress Cataloging-in-Publication Data available.

ISBN: 978-1-68383-170-9

Publisher: Raoul Goff
Associate Publisher: Vanessa Lopez
Executive Editor: Mark Irwin
Assistant Editor: Holly Fisher
Editorial Assistant: Jeric Llanes
Senior Production Editor: Elaine Ou
Design Support: Amy DeGrote
Production Manager: Greg Steffen

ROOTS of PEACE REPLANTED PAPER

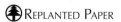

Insight Editions, in association with Roots of Peace, will plant two trees for each tree used in the manufacturing of this book. Roots of Peace is an internationally renowned humanitarian organization dedicated to eradicating land mines worldwide and converting war-torn lands into productive farms and wildlife habitats. Roots of Peace will plant two million fruit and nut trees in Afghanistan and provide farmers there with the skills and support necessary for sustainable land use.

Manufactured in China by Insight Editions

10 9 8 7 6 5 4 3 2 1